Fall colors at Black Mesa State Park (Hikes 1 and 2)

HIKING OKLAHOMA

A GUIDE TO THE STATE'S GREATEST HIKING ADVENTURES

Jamie Fleck

FALCON GUIDES

GUILFORD, CONNECTICUT

*To all the Oklahomans who continue to preserve and hold close
to their heart the natural beauty of their incredible state. May
this book help you continue to be proud of Oklahoma.*

FALCONGUIDES®

An imprint of Globe Pequot, the trade division of The Rowman & Littlefield Publishing Group, Inc.
4501 Forbes Blvd., Ste. 200
Lanham, MD 20706
Falcon.com

Falcon and FalconGuides are registered trademarks and Make Adventure Your Story is a trademark of The Rowman & Littlefield Publishing Group, Inc.

Distributed by NATIONAL BOOK NETWORK

Copyright © 2021 The Rowman & Littlefield Publishing Group, Inc.

All photos © Jamie Fleck

Maps by The Rowman & Littlefield Publishing Group, Inc.

British Library Cataloguing in Publication Information available

Library of Congress Cataloging-in-Publication Data

Names: Fleck, Jamie, 1984– author.
Title: Hiking Oklahoma : a guide to the state's greatest hiking adventures / Jamie Fleck.
Description: Guilford, Connecticut : FalconGuides, 2021. | Includes index. | Summary: "Includes photography, vital hike specs, trailhead GPS coordinates, turn-by-turn directions, and informative maps to 48 of Oklahoma's most scenic day hikes. Features trails in Red Carpet Country (northwest Oklahoma), Great Plains Country (southwest Oklahoma) Frontier Country (central Oklahoma), Chickasaw Country (south central Oklahoma), Green Country (northeast Oklahoma), and Choctaw Country (southeast Oklahoma)"— Provided by publisher.
Identifiers: LCCN 2021009758 (print) | LCCN 2021009759 (ebook) | ISBN 9781493056583 (paperback) | ISBN 9781493056590 (epub)
Subjects: LCSH: Hiking—Oklahoma—Guidebooks. | Trails—Oklahoma—Guidebooks. | Oklahoma—Guidebooks.
Classification: LCC GV199.42.O5 F54 2021 (print) | LCC GV199.42.O5 (ebook) | DDC 796.5109766—dc23
LC record available at https://lccn.loc.gov/2021009758
LC ebook record available at https://lccn.loc.gov/2021009759

CONTENTS

Green Country (Northeast Oklahoma)

Choctaw Country (Southeast Oklahoma)

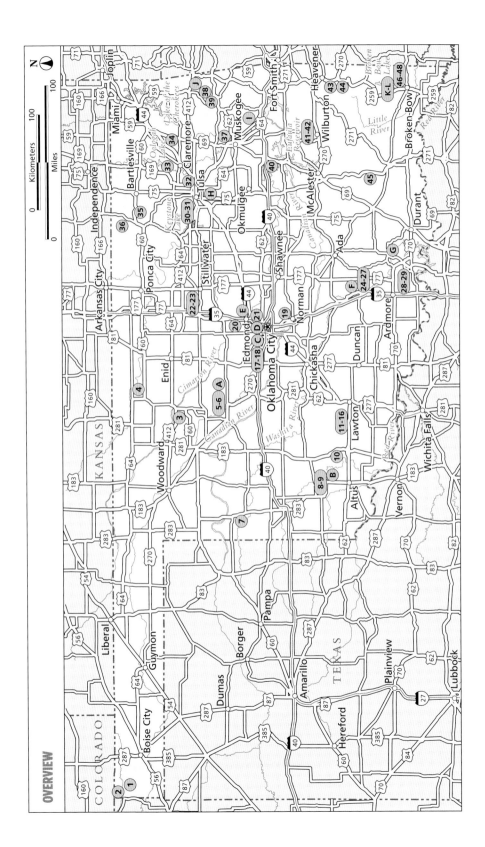

OVERVIEW

ACKNOWLEDGMENTS

The words "thank you" do not seem adequate to express my appreciation for everyone who helped make this book possible. I hope for all those who helped me that including you as a part of these acknowledgments will add a little more emphasis on how truly grateful I am.

First of all, to the people at Globe Pequot. Katie O'Dell—thank you for going through all the hoops with me on this and believing in me. I am honored that you and Globe Pequot entrusted me with such a special project for a state that has been wanting something like this for a long time. Meredith Dias and Paulette Baker—I am grateful to you both for your invaluable time, effort, and expertise to make this book even better than it could be. I thank all of you for helping this book come to life.

A huge thank you to the following park managers, rangers, biologists, naturalists, and administrators: Curt Allen, JaNae Barnard, Sandie Blay, Jim Bonnarens, Brandon Boydstun, Brandon Bundy, Julie Cameron, Rick Cantu, Cathi Carr, Nick Conner, Scott Copelin, Tom Creider, Craig Dishman, Jeff Edwards, Chad Everett, Scott Fraley, Katie Hawk, Glen Hensley, Sue Hokanson, Brenda Holt, Ryan Howell, Bill Jackson, Shane Kasson, Richard Keithley, Polly Kiker, Aron Maib, Loran Mayes, Adam Miller, Kevin Mohr, Rocky Murdaugh, Roberta Pailes, Ron Parker, Terence Peck, Stacey Reese, Jonathan Rich, Pete Singleton, Quinton Smith, Angelina Stancampiano, Wade Thompson, Jeremy Tubbs, Jill Vanegmond, Jeff Walker, Bob Webster, Chasidy Wilmot, and Larry Wolcott. For those I got to meet personally, I will cherish those times and hope we can meet again. For those I never got to meet but had the privilege of conversing with you by e-mail or phone, thank you for spending the time to help someone you never met.

Last, but most important, so much gratitude for my husband, Koby. This book project has been a wild ride. We have probably never seen so much of Oklahoma as we have from doing this book. We put so many miles on the car and a lot of wear and tear on our hiking boots. Much laughter was had, and our tent has seen all kinds of weather. You and I have hiked hundreds of miles together, making sure we got the information right for my readers. We have so many stories to share after all our adventures on the trails, on ones we had already hiked and ones that were new. Thank you for being my steadfast partner, not only on the trails and on the road but also in life.

MEET YOUR GUIDE

When her parents started taking her and her twin sister on cross-country road trips at just 5 years old, **Jamie Fleck** became an avid traveler. Since then, she has ventured out and experienced the outdoors in forty-five of the fifty United States and twenty-two countries worldwide. From living in Texas, Boston, Los Angeles, and Oklahoma, Jamie has experienced firsthand all that Oklahoma has to offer compared to other regions in the United States. She has hiked, camped, and photographed nearly 90 percent of the state parks, national lands, and regional outdoor areas in Oklahoma.

Jamie leans on her technical and practical skills to be accurate and detailed when traversing the trails and documenting her travels. She also taps into her creative side as a professional freelance photographer and contribution writer. She has leveraged her photography skills for more than a decade, working with numerous outdoor companies and well-recognized brands. Jamie continues to commemorate her devotion to traveling and finding underrated places in the outdoors to create experiences for the public through her photography.

She has called the Tulsa, Oklahoma, area home for almost fifteen years and currently divides her time between Oklahoma and Texas. Jamie resides with her husband and affectionate cat. She continues to hit the trails with her husband. Their cat has yet to muster the courage to go hiking with them.

To follow along on Jamie's adventures, you can find her on Instagram: @morningsbythesea and her website: www.flecksoflove.com.

BEFORE YOU HIT THE TRAIL

Hiking Oklahoma focuses on some of the most scenic day-hike trails in Oklahoma. While not all the scenic trails in Oklahoma were able to make it in this book, you will gain first-hand knowledge of both popular and less-known trails that offer a rewarding view and display the state's natural beauty. The sixty hikes covered in this book vary in difficulty to engage novice as well as experienced hikers. This book is organized by the state's six regions and will guide you through the trails that await you as you explore Oklahoma with a new perspective. Use the Overview Map to locate the hikes nearest you. Detailed information is provided for each of the trails, with chapter sections explained below.

START
This indicates the starting location for the hike.

ELEVATION GAIN
Elevation is generally the most important factor in determining a hike's difficulty. The numbers listed indicate the total amount of elevation gained during the course of the hike. Most often, but not always, the trailhead lies at the low point and the end lies at the highest point. Some of the hikes have several ups and downs along the way, requiring more elevation gain and effort than others. Hikes in urban areas of Oklahoma generally have very minimal elevation changes.

Elevation also affects difficulty. At higher elevations, lower atmospheric pressure creates thin air that requires higher breathing rates and more effort to pull enough oxygen into the lungs. Since most of Oklahoma lies at lower elevations, hikers will encounter thinner air on only a few of the hikes in this guide. The moderately higher elevations encountered on hikes in western Oklahoma (Black Mesa, Quartz Mountain area, the Wichita Mountains) and in southeast Oklahoma (Ouachita National Forest area and Beavers Bend State Park) will require only a little additional effort.

DISTANCE
The distance specified in each description is listed as a round-trip distance from the trailhead to the end of the route and back. Hike lengths have been estimated as closely as possible using GPS units. The final figure is the author's best estimate.

DIFFICULTY

Assessing the difficulty of a hike is very subjective. The elevation, elevation change, length, trail condition, weather, and physical condition of a hiker all play a role. However, even subjective ratings will give some idea of difficulty. For this guide, elevation gain and variation in path levels were the most significant variables in establishing levels of difficulty. Most of the hikes, except in western Oklahoma and southeast Oklahoma, have only small elevation gains and are rated easy or moderate. Most of the difficult hikes are located in western Oklahoma and southeast Oklahoma. Within each category there are many degrees of difficulty. Poor trails, excessive heat with no shade, paths that involve rock scrambling, and other factors may result in a more difficult designation than would otherwise seem to be the case from simply the elevation change and trail length. Carrying a heavy backpack can make even an "easy" day hike more strenuous.

HIKING TIME

The hiking time is a rough estimate of the time within which the average hiker will be able to complete the hike. Very fit, fast-moving hikers will be able to complete it in less time. Slower-moving hikers or those preoccupied with activities such as photography may take longer. To come up with this information, an estimation was made that most people hike at 2 to 3 miles per hour. For longer hikes with more elevation changes, estimates are closer to 2 miles per hour. For short, flat hikes, 3 miles per hour can be easily attained. Other factors such as a rough trail or particularly big elevation changes were also taken into account.

SEASONS/SCHEDULE

This section specifies designated hours and days of the year that a park or trail area is open. Generally, most areas are open for day use, or sunrise to sunset. Some, such as private and national lands, are closed on holidays.

Most trails in Oklahoma have something to offer year-round, and the scenery is beautiful no matter what the season. Hikes that have more-specific seasonal experiences, such as wildlife arrivals, foliage, or blooming fauna, are noted with the ideal season to visit. Summers are humid in Oklahoma, so with the heat index, trails with little to no shade should be traveled with caution. Generally, the

Autumn in all its glory at the Lower Mountain Fork River (Hike 47)

hottest times of the year in Oklahoma are July through September. Winters are generally mild in November and December, but may get icy January through March. Occasional light snow does not linger for more than a couple of days on the ground, so snow-packed trails are not usually a concern. Springtime is rainy, and tornado season spans April and May. However, the wildflower viewing is spectacular in spring when the weather is decent. Autumn is the optimal season, particularly in areas such as eastern Oklahoma and the Talimena Scenic Byway, where the fall foliage is on full display. Be prepared, and always check the weather forecast.

FEES AND PERMITS

At time of publication, twenty-four of the Oklahoma state parks require a parking pass for day-use visitors. This number is subject to change. State parks included in this guide that require this fee will have "Parking pass for day-use visitors" noted in this section. Visitors who have paid for camping sites, select concession areas (identified and approved by state park management), or golf course usage are generally exempt from having to pay for the parking pass. Parking pass discounts are available for State of Oklahoma and Oklahoma Tribe license plate owners, honorably discharged veterans who are Oklahoma residents, certified disabled persons under state/federal law and their spouses, and persons 62+ years of age along with their spouses. Parking passes (daily, three-day, weekly, and annual) are available via the Premium Parking mobile app, online at www.travelok.com, and via parking pay machines at applicable state parks.

A majority of privately owned properties and properties owned by a local municipality also require a day-use fee. Generally, all National Park Service areas and state parks require a fee for camping sites.

TRAIL CONTACT

The trail contact lists the name, address, website, and/or phone number of the managing agency for the lands through which the trail passes. Call, write, or check the website for current information about the hike.

DOG-FRIENDLY

This section describes whether dogs are allowed on the trail. Dogs usually need to be leashed when they are allowed on the trail. Please be respectful and pick up after your dog. Some protected areas in Oklahoma prohibit all animals, not just dogs. These areas will be specified as "no animals permitted."

TRAIL SURFACE

The trail surface describes the material that composes the trail. Most often it is simply a dirt path consisting of the native materials that were there when the trail was built, such as tree roots and rocks. On occasion, gravel is added or the trail may be paved. In a few instances the hike follows a dirt road or even a paved road. Be cautious when crossing vehicular roads.

Pronghorn roaming in the Black Mesa Valley (Hikes 1 and 2)

LAND STATUS

The land status simply tells which agency, usually federal or state, manages the land in which the trail lies. In this guide Oklahoma State Parks, Oklahoma Department of Wildlife Conservation, US Fish and Wildlife Service, USDA Forest Service, and National Park Service are the most common land managers.

NEAREST TOWN

The nearest town is the closest city or town to the hike's trailhead that has at least minimal visitor services. The listed town will usually have gas, food, and limited lodging available. Please note that in smaller towns, the hours these services are available may be limited.

OTHER TRAIL USERS

This describes other users you might encounter on the hike. Mountain bikers, cyclists, rappelers, anglers, and hunters are the most common.

MAPS

The maps provided in this guide are as accurate and current as possible. When used in conjunction with the hike description and the additional maps listed for each hike, you should have little difficulty staying on track.

When possible, at least two types of maps are listed for each hike. Most of the state parks have park and trail system maps that are free to the public on the state park website, state park mobile app, and/or at the park offices. The National Forest Service maps do include trails, but the maps are usually broad in nature and do not include much detail. They are still very useful for locating trailheads, campgrounds, and roads. Most of the National Park Service and National Wildlife Refuge areas have trail maps or detailed brochures available online and at the parks.

United States Geological Survey (USGS) topographic quadrangles are usually the most detailed and accurate maps available when it comes to natural features. If you learn how to use them, they help you visualize mountains, canyons, lakes, rivers, creeks, roads, and many other topographical features. Most of the more well-known hikes in this guide do not require a topo map; however USGS quads are particularly handy for lesser-used trails and when hiking off-trail. USGS quadrangles for less-populated parts of Oklahoma can be out-of-date and may not show newer roads and trails. However, they are still helpful for their topographic information. USGS quadrangle maps are available at outdoor stores or online directly from USGS. To order USGS maps for a specific trail, refer to the exact map name as listed in the hike description.

GPS (Global Positioning System) units, particularly those with installed maps, can be extremely useful for finding trailheads and off-trail routes when used with paper maps. For backcountry hikers and campers, researching the area beforehand and bringing a paper map and compass with you are a must. GPS units are not reliable in areas with no cell phone reception, and batteries for devices can bite the dust at the least-opportune moment.

FINDING THE TRAILHEAD

This section provides detailed directions to the trailhead. With an up-to-date state highway map or GPS unit, you can easily pinpoint the starting point from the directions. In general, the nearest town or largest intersection is used as the starting point. State highways use the abbreviation "OK" in this guide. There are also rural roads—paved or gravel—that lead to some of the hiking destinations. These types of roads are denoted by the first letter of the cardinal direction followed by a series of numbers, e.g., E9560 Road. Some counties in Oklahoma recently updated to the E911 system, so rural road names and signs have been changed. Some of these updates are not yet reflected on internet-based map services.

Distances were usually measured using Google maps from the trailhead GPS coordinates. GPS systems on your cell phone may not be reliable or accurate, especially in remote areas with little to no cell service. Do not rely solely on online map applications.

All the hikes featured in this guide have trailheads that can be reached by a regular passenger vehicle. Inclement weather, wet and icy road conditions, and the infrequent tornado can temporarily make some roads impassable. Check road conditions with park staff prior to venturing into remote areas or unimproved dirt roads. Always have basic emergency equipment—extra food and water, additional clothing, and other items—on hand for survival in the rare circumstance your vehicle becomes incapacitated. Fill your gas tank, and make sure your vehicle is current on required maintenance before heading out on the road.

Theft and vandalism can happen to vehicles parked at the trailheads. Ask park staff and management of any incidences you need to be aware of. Either pack your valuables in the trunk out of sight or, best, do not leave valuables in the car at all.

THE HIKE

All the hikes selected for this guide can be done easily by people in good physical condition. A little scrambling may be necessary for a few of the hikes, but none require any rock-climbing skills. A few of the hikes, as noted in their descriptions, travel across roads or are on very faint trails. You should have an experienced hiker, along with a compass, USGS quad, and GPS unit, with you before attempting any of those hikes.

The trails are often marked with ties, blazes, plastic or metal tree markings, or rock cairns. Most of the time the paths are obvious and easy to follow, but the marks help when the trails are not as popular or the paths are hard to discern. Cairns are piles of rock built along the route. Tree blazes are painted on trees, usually at shoulder or head height. Blazes can be especially useful when a forest trail is obscured by snow. Be sure not to add your own blazes or cairns, which could confuse other hikers. Let the official trail workers make the markings. Sometimes, especially in wooded areas, small plastic or metal markers are nailed to trees to indicate the route.

Checkered white butterfly blending in the Osage Hills (Hike 35)

Possible backcountry campsites are often suggested in the descriptions. Many primitive campsites are generally available. In the national forests, there are usually few restrictions in selecting a campsite, provided that it is well away from the trail or any water source. Most state and national parks require that certain backcountry campsites be used. The state parks charge a small fee; the national parks sometimes do.

After reading the descriptions, select the trail that appeals the most to you. Take heed of your physical limitations and the supplies you have on hand. Do not overextend yourself to complete any of the hikes. You are hiking because you want to enjoy nature and have a good time. You don't need to prove anything by finishing a hike!

MILES AND DIRECTIONS

To help you stay on course, a detailed route finder sets forth mileages between significant landmarks along the trail.

A path through the woodlands (Hike 43)

INTRODUCTION

Oklahoma tends to astonish both locals and visitors with its natural beauty. Often mistaken as being completely flat due to its inclusion in the Great American Desert region in the 1800s, its topography is quite comprehensive—mountain ranges, rivers, lakes, forests, and prairies for most of the state; deserts in the west. The diversity of flora and fauna is a marvel. The state's native history is also rich, in both its successes and its failures. Long before the Europeans settled in the area and the land runs of the late nineteenth century, indigenous peoples relied on the Oklahoman soil for food, were replenished by the vast rivers, and sought refuge and shelter in the escarpments and woodlands. Except for the American Indians already dwelling there, many other people regarded Oklahoma as unlivable for years. It was also one of the last territories to receive statehood. Both factors possibly worked out in Oklahoma's favor and may have reduced the amount of human damage that could have been done to its environment. Although Oklahoma's natural landscape still has been altered over the centuries by European settlement, lack of funding and protection, and other kinds of human impact, much of the state has been preserved on behalf of efforts made by the Civilian Conservation Corps (CCC) back in the 1930s. Today, state and local governments, recreational organizations, conservancy groups, and earth-loving volunteers make up the backbone of keeping Oklahoma's treasured ecology and biodiversity intact.

With its simple rectangular shape and a panhandle adjoined to the west, Oklahoma can easily be sectioned into east, west, and central. Eastern Oklahoma is recognized for its immense greenery, craggy bluffs, winding rivers, and intermingled grassland. Western Oklahoma paints a different picture and invokes the Wild West with its rocky peaks and cactus-dotted plains. It also holds the honor of having the highest point in all the state. Central Oklahoma is nearly a combination of the two—swathed in cross timbers, it holds characteristics of forestry as well as arid landscape. The Oklahoma Department of Tourism and Recreation categorizes Oklahoma into six regions: Red Carpet Country and Great Plains Country to the west, Frontier Country and Chickasaw Country in the heart of the state, and Green Country and Choctaw Country to the east. This book is divided into those sections.

WEATHER AND SEASONS

Oklahoma experiences seasons, which allows hikers to enjoy all kinds of scenery at different times of the year. Springtime usually commences toward the end of April or during the month of May, with a decent amount of precipitation and the infrequent but to be expected tornado. Temperatures are pleasant for the majority of the time. Spring season is short-lived, but the abundance of blooming wildflowers and birthing of American bison the season brings makes up for its fleeting duration. Summers can be long, harsh,

Leaves changing color in the Black Mesa Valley (Hikes 1 and 2)

and humid. Temperatures are usually at their peak—and in triple digits—for the first two weeks of August. However, the heat and humidity can already be strong starting in June and then continue through mid-October. Mosquitoes and ticks, unfortunately, are also major participants during this time of year. Fall is glorious in Oklahoma. The temperatures have waned and are near-perfect. Most of the state is blanketed with deciduous trees, and during the last week of October through mid-November those trees seem ablaze in fiery hues wherever you go. Winters are less concrete. While temps can range from the low 30s to high 50s, once in a while there is a year where severe ice storms pass through. Snowfall (not ice storms!) is uncommon and thus generally well received.

The state lies in the center of the country, with not enough topographical barriers to block any cold weather fronts or disruptive changes in weather patterns. Blustery winds sweep through the state several times a month. (This is a reminder of why Oklahoma was considered the "dust bowl.") Extreme swings in temperature and random storms can pass through at any time. It is common to enjoy sunny, 75°F weather one day and have freezing rain and icy temperatures the next.

FLORA AND FAUNA

Greenery and wildlife are diversified across the state, depending on the geography and climate. Most of eastern and central Oklahoma are awash in hardwood trees and cross timbers. Prairies blend in with the forests and bloom with colorful wildflowers and tall-grasses. In the western part of the state, you will be surprised by a wide range of desert plants and cacti. Invasive species in Oklahoma, such as the resilient eastern redcedar and ever-spreading lespedeza, are generally controlled by managed burns or grazing.

White-tailed deer, nine-banded armadillos, raccoons, wild turkeys, turtles, butterflies, sparrows, and hawks can be seen frequently all over Oklahoma where lush forests dominate and water sources are more accessible. To the west, owls, prairie dogs, elk, eastern collared lizards, and bats roam the dry plains, caves, and jagged mountains. American bison, a protected animal in this state, can be found on national lands and within nature conservancies.

NATIVE LANDS

Oklahoma, according to historical records, has had people dwelling on its lands for more than 30,000 years. Its name derives from the Choctaw language, *okla*, meaning "people," and *humma*, meaning "red." American Indians had been calling this beautiful state home long before the Indian Removal Act of 1830 was passed and the state was branded as "Indian Territory." Many American Indian tribes were forced to relocate to Oklahoma as a result of the legislation and were coalesced with tribes already living there. There were five individual republics—the Cherokee, Chickasaw, Choctaw, Creek, and Seminole—a majority being peaceful despite the unfair circumstances. Uneasiness culminated with the arrival of the "Boomers" (those who moved during the economic boom). The overwhelming capacity inevitably resulted in the start of the land run of 1889, which brought the "Sooners" (those who arrived in Indian Territory before securing government permission). After the five republics unsuccessfully petitioned the US government for their own lands to be combined into a separate state under the name Sequoyah in 1907, their lands were merged with the rest of the Oklahoma territories—the beginning of Oklahoma as a state.

Today, the preservation of native lands in Oklahoma, as well as the sustainment of American Indian heritage, is vital. Conservation of native lands is not only important for the environment and wildlife these lands protect, but also for the people who live on the land and regard it sacred and for Oklahomans who can learn from these tribes. With continual progress, reverence, and representation, native people and their lands in Oklahoma will flourish.

The following thirty-nine American Indian tribes can be found in these specific regions:

- *Red Carpet Country (Northwest Oklahoma):* Kaw Nation, Otoe-Missouria Tribe, Ponca Tribe of Oklahoma, and the Tonkawa Tribe

- *Great Plains Country (Southwest Oklahoma):* Apache Tribe, Caddo Nation, Comanche Nation, Delaware Nation, Fort Sill Apache Tribe, Kiowa Tribe, and the Wichita and Affiliated Tribes

- *Frontier Country (Central Oklahoma):* Absentee Shawnee Tribe, Alabama-Quassarte Tribal Town, Cheyenne and Arapaho Tribes, Citizen Potawatomi Nation, Iowa Tribe, Kialegee Tribal Town, Kickapoo Tribe of Oklahoma, Sac and Fox Nation, Seminole Nation of Oklahoma, and Thlopthlocco Tribal Nation

- *Chickasaw Country (South Central Oklahoma):* Chickasaw Nation

- *Green Country (Northeast Oklahoma):* Cherokee Nation, Delaware Tribe of Indians, Eastern Shawnee Tribe of Oklahoma, Euchee/Yuchi Tribe of Indians, Miami Tribe of Oklahoma, Modoc Nation, Muscogee/Creek Nation, Osage Nation,

Ottawa Tribe, Pawnee Nation of Oklahoma, Peoria Tribe of Indians of Oklahoma, Quapaw Tribe of Oklahoma, Seneca-Cayuga Nation, Shawnee Tribe, United Keetoowah Band of Cherokee Indians, and Wyandotte Nation

- *Choctaw Country (Southeast Oklahoma):* Choctaw Nation of Oklahoma

LAND OWNERSHIP

State Parks

State park management falls under the Oklahoma Department of Tourism and Recreation. Trails within state parks are the most popular, and thus the most crowded. Most trails in state parks are primitive. Not all trails are clearly marked, so be sure to refer to the state park map (available online at www.travelok.com or within the OK State Parks mobile app.)

Most state parks offer a decent number of amenities, such as campsites, restrooms, and an information station. Some state parks have lodging and dining on-site. Others cater to families as well, offering additional recreational activities such as swimming pools and miniature golf. State parks with lakes or another water source that allow fishing usually have designated fishing piers/docks and possibly a bait shop.

At time of publication, twenty-four of Oklahoma's state parks require a parking pass for day-use activities. The parking pass can be purchased at pay machines located in participating parks, online at www.travelok.com, or through the Premium Parking mobile app. If you prefer to obtain the parking pass through the Premium Parking mobile app, you will need to know the location number of the specific park. The Premium Parking location number for each park usually starts with a "P" and then four numbers. Those who enjoy camping at the state parks do not need a parking pass for the days your campsite has been reserved for. Discounts are available for in-state residents, senior citizens, and veterans. State parks that do not require a parking pass have free entrance.

Municipal Parks

Rules and regulations for parks owned and managed by local cities vary. Check with the local department of parks and recreation before you hit the trail. Most municipal parks have well-maintained trails, including ones with paved surfaces and/or that are ADA-compliant. While trails within metro areas may not have as much greenery as those out in the wilderness, they are usually created because they offer something special in terms of a scenic point, type of greenery/wildlife, adventure, or convenience.

National Parks, National Forest Service, and National Wildlife Refuges

National Park and National Forest Service areas are by far the most protected and therefore have the most rules and regulations. What might be acceptable in a state park may not be acceptable on national land. Visit www.nps.org prior to your trip to have a good understanding of any restrictions. National Wildlife Refuges are managed by the US Fish and Wildlife Service and are sanctuaries for endangered wildlife and fragile ecosystems. Please be respectful and educated of what these national places are protecting. Stay on designated trails, and help maintain the primitiveness of these extraordinary areas.

Private Land and Nature Conservancies

Privately owned land and nature conservancies have their own set of rules and regulations. Land under private ownership could be personal property or land granted through a trust. If there is no designated public entrance, you must obtain permission from any owners before traversing private land. Nature conservancies are open to the public and are managed by private, nonprofit organizations. As they also provide refuge to certain threatened wildlife and environments, they tend to have strict rules when it comes to human impact. Pets are generally not permitted.

PRECAUTIONS

Hunting

Hunting is considered both a recreational sport and a necessary form of wildlife management in the state of Oklahoma. Most lands managed by the Oklahoma Department of Wildlife Conservation (ODWC) permit hunting as long as you have an up-to-date official hunting license. Hunting is also permitted in some areas of the Ouachita National Forest and state parks, while controlled hunting can

American bison grazing at the Chickasaw National Recreation Area (Hike 25)

be conducted in the Wichita Mountains Wildlife Refuge. Open season for hunting in Oklahoma usually occurs from the beginning of October through the middle of January the following year. Try to avoid areas that are open to hunters during the hunting season. If you end up on a trail with hunters, make sure to wear bright clothing. Most hunters wear fluorescent orange as a precaution; that could be a good color for you to wear as well. For official hunting season dates, regulations, and areas that allow hunting, refer to the ODWC's website at www.wildlifedepartment.com. Individual park's and land management's official websites and social media may also include updates on hunting, especially controlled hunts.

Poisonous Plants

The head trio of poisonous plants—the eastern poison ivy, Atlantic poison oak, and poison sumac—can all be found in Oklahoma. Eastern poison ivy is the most prevalent, occurring throughout Oklahoma, while Atlantic poison oak and poison sumac can be found in eastern Oklahoma and southeast Oklahoma, respectively. Study visuals of these plants before hitting the trail. Nonpoisonous doppelgangers of eastern poison ivy, such as Virginia creeper and boxelder, can sometimes cause panic. Your best bet to avoid brushing up against any of these plants is just to stay on the trails. If you come into contact with any poisonous plants, quickly wash all affected areas as well as clothing with lots of warm water and soap. Reactions can take up to 72 hours to manifest, so do not assume that there was no contact. Calamine and oatmeal-based lotions, corticosteroid creams, and oral antihistamines can all help soothe minor reactions. If your reaction is abnormal or severe, make sure to receive medical assistance from a doctor as soon as possible.

Insects
Disease-bearing mosquitoes and ticks are ubiquitous during Oklahoma summers, when the humid climate is especially welcoming. Insect repellent, long-sleeved shirts, and long pants are your friends and saviors while on the trail. If you stick to the path, you will avoid walking into unmaintained brush or grassy areas—favorite dwelling places for ticks. If you do happen to be on a trail that is a playground for ticks, make sure to remove any ticks with tweezers as soon as possible. Ticks can be very tiny and difficult to notice, so look carefully. Then wash yourself off thoroughly with soap and water. Occasionally, bees, wasps, and hornets will follow along with you. Do not swat at them. If you do, they will likely sting you as part of their defense mechanism. Wear light-colored clothing, go fragrance-free, and maintain your cool.

Snakes
While fear of snakes is often understandable, learning about them may help you realize their importance to the ecosystem and how to avoid getting bitten. In general, snakes avoid people. It is when they are provoked, feel unsafe, or get mishandled that they attack. Snakes do not have eardrums and therefore "hear" vibrations in the ground. Most of the time, they know to stay back from a designated trail for their own safety, especially when they hear the pounding of hiking boots approaching. Again, the importance of staying on the trail—if you stick to the designated path, you will lower your chances of encountering and getting bitten by a snake. If you find a snake in your path, do not panic. Do not try to touch or handle it either. This will give the snake a reason to attack. Turn around on the trail and head back.

The most common venomous snakes in Oklahoma are the varietal rattlesnake, cottonmouth, and copperhead. If you do get bitten by a snake, whether venomous or not, seek immediate medical help. Try to cleanse the area around the bite as best as you can, then cover it lightly with sterile wrappings. Keep the area with the bite still and below your heart until medical attention arrives.

Inclement Weather
Oklahoma weather can be fickle. Carrying a lightweight, waterproof jacket or poncho will help during a passing rainstorm or thunderstorm. Flash floods are infrequent but do happen. Stay on higher ground and away from water sources. Whenever you see lightning strike, head to lower ground in less-exposed areas. Check the hourly weather report before embarking on any trail. Plan responsibly to make sure you complete a trail before bad weather hits, or postpone the hike to a day with more favorable weather.

When hiking in Oklahoma, it is highly likely that you will come across a creek bed or two. Most streams and creeks in Oklahoma are seasonal and therefore filled with water only after heavy precipitation. In a scenario where you need to wade through a flowing stream, always look ahead and determine whether you feel safe going across. If you feel any unsettledness, simply turn around and head back. It is not worth crossing when you are unsure, especially with a swollen crossing, as strong currents may exist. Also, rocks in the streambed can be dangerously slippery. They are not always reliable ways to get across. If the water level is low, waterproof hiking boots or sandals are not only supportive

A warm, sunny day at Cedar Lake in the middle of autumn (Hike 43)

but also provide comfort for the rest of the trail. There is no reason to hike in soggy socks and wet shoes if you can avoid it with the proper footwear.

Equipment

The right hiking shoes will probably be one of the best investments you make for your trailblazing adventures. Find a pair of hiking shoes that are durable, waterproof, have great traction, maintain ankle and sole support, have toe guards, and are comfortable. These characteristics will help make your time on the trails enjoyable as well as safer.

Wear layers of clothing to be warm during the cold mornings and evenings during the summer. Clothes made of materials that wick away perspiration but do not absorb full moisture are better to wear in summer. Hats and sunscreen will go a long way in preventing sunburn and heatstroke, no matter the season. Because wool insulates heat, clothing made of wool are better in the colder months. Bring gloves with touch-screen fingers for handling devices and extra socks to keep you warm in the fall and winter. The types and amounts of items you bring to wear can, depending on the season, prevent you from falling victim to heat exhaustion or hypothermia.

Daypacks are useful even if you are not backpacking. They can store your water supply, meals and snacks, extra clothing, rain jacket, camera, and valuables. Bring a lightweight yet durable daypack that sits comfortably on your shoulders and back. On a long trail, the way a daypack falls on your body can make a huge difference.

Other items that would be helpful on the trail, just in case, include trekking poles, a paper map, a compass, a packable first-aid kit, food and water, additional clothing, insect repellent, sunscreen, waterproof matches, a rechargeable battery pack, and a fully charged cell phone. For longer hikes in the wilderness, a backpacking tent and blanket may be necessary.

Water

Possibly one of the most dangerous things you can do on a trail is not bring enough water. Dehydration in summer can accelerate heat exhaustion; dehydration in winter can accelerate hypothermia. Although high altitudes are not a likely scenario in Oklahoma, it is still a good idea to drink ample amounts of water and electrolytes when hitting trails at higher elevations. Uncontaminated or safe water sources are rare along the trails, so make sure to bring an adequate amount of water in reusable water bottles. The rule of thumb is 0.5 liter of water for every hour you are on the trail—1 liter of water for every hour you are on a difficult trail or a trail with no shade in the summer. If you must resort to drinking from a natural water source, make sure to bring proper water filtration or treatment.

Should a hiker suffer from heat exhaustion, place the person in the shade and provide them with frequent drinks of electrolyte-based liquids and intermittent snacks. For a hiker suffering from hypothermia, extra dry clothes and warm fluids can help keep them warm and awake until medical care is available.

WILDERNESS ETHICS

It is plain and simple. To prolong the life of this extraordinary world we live in, we must be good stewards of the natural beauty it holds. Most of the time this just requires that we act with mindfulness and in consideration of the long-term effects of our actions. Below are guidelines that we, as stewards of the outdoors, should adhere to so that we and future generations can continue to enjoy the trails we hike on and be in awe of the scenery that encompasses us. Most of the principles are expedient and help reduce whatever harmful impact we might make on the environment.

Leave No Trace

This phrase is pretty self-explanatory. It means to leave an area with no trace that you were even there. For example:

- Keep group sizes small whether hiking or camping. Try to avoid peak times to lessen the impact crowds make.

- Bring equipment that is small, lightweight, and blends in with the natural landscape.

- Be sufficiently prepared for your hike so that additional people and resources do not have to be used to rescue you.

- Whatever you bring with you, you must bring back out.

For more on Leave No Trace principles, visit www.LNT.org.

Camping

Leave No Trace principles do not apply only to hiking; they apply to camping as well. Campfires can leave permanent blemishes, and waste not properly disposed of can cause major contamination in water sources. Here are some of the guidelines to adhere to when camping:

- If there are designated camping sites, try to use those first before creating a new site.

- Set up your camp at least 200 feet from any water sources.

- Place your campsite out of view to lessen visual impact.

- Try to use a packable stove instead of having a campfire. If you create a campfire, build one within a designated fire ring. Use only downed, dead wood nearby or locally purchased wood. Make sure to fully put out fires once you are done.

- Do any bathing or dishwashing away from water sources. Try not to use soap; even biodegradable soap can cause contamination.

- Holes for human waste must be dug at least 200 feet from any water sources and fully covered with surrounding natural materials.

Camping at Black Mesa State Park (Hikes 1 and 2)

Staying on Designated Trails

Venturing off the official trail, taking undesignated trails, and making shortcuts on switchbacks can cause many years' worth and sometimes irreversible damage to the ecosystem and geology surrounding the trail. Trail routes are created for a reason. The specified route is to keep people away from fragile wildlife, fauna, or formations. If the route was not made to lead somewhere, do not try to create a new route to get there.

Animals

Some trails allow dogs, and some do not. Verify whether a trail is dog-friendly before bringing your dog, and check for any service animal exceptions. All dogs must be leashed to prevent accidents, hounding of wildlife, and/or damage to the environment. Please remember to either bury your dog's waste or pack it out with you from the trail.

For those bringing your horse to an equestrian trail, please follow the Leave No Trace principles and take into consideration the accommodations your horse will need.

Respecting Others

Unless you are on a backcountry trail, it is likely you will not be alone. Day-hiking trails are some of the friendliest spots to meet people and learn new things. If the out and back trail you are on is narrow, make sure to leave room for people headed your way. For multiuse trails, other trail users may include cyclists, mountain bikers, and equestrians. While those on a bike should yield to hikers—and usually make some indication that they are coming near you—do not assume that they will yield; be courteous. Stay off to the side of the trail when nearing equestrians so that horses have sufficient room to pass. Respect others and nature, make new friends, and have a blast on the trails!

MAP LEGEND

Interstate Highway	Airfield
US Highway	Boat Launch
State Highway	Bridge
County/Local Road	Building/Point of Interest
Unpaved Road	Campground
Railroad	City/Town
Featured Trail	Dam
Trail	Gate
Small River/Creek	Mountain/Peak
Body of Water	Parking
Marsh	Picnic Area
Spring	Restrooms
Waterfall	Scenic View/Overlook
National Forest	Tower
National Historic Site/Wilderness/Refuge/Recreation Area/Grassland	Trailhead
State/Local Park	Visitor/Information Center
Preserve/Reserve/Wildlife Management Area/Nature Center/Natural Recreation Area	

RED CARPET COUNTRY (NORTHWEST OKLAHOMA)

NORTHWEST OKLAHOMA is vastly different from the rest of Oklahoma, mainly in climate, landscape, wildlife, and vegetation. It consists of deserts resembling those of neighboring New Mexico, towering buttes such as Cathedral Mesa, and floodplain areas that provide sanctuary to all kinds of wildlife. Black Mesa, the highest point in Oklahoma, also lies in this region. The desolate beauty of this region evokes the spirit of the Wild West with its bounty of prickly pear– and yucca-festooned bluffs, piñon pine and juniper woodlands, and windswept mixed-grass prairies. It is possible to encounter owls, bats, migratory cranes, and wild turkeys in this area.

The buttes of the Black Mesa Nature Preserve (Hikes 1 and 2)

1 VISTA TRAIL (COMBINED WITH BIRD HAVEN TRAIL)

BLACK MESA STATE PARK

Although the Black Mesa area is primarily known as home to the tallest point in Oklahoma, it is also distinctive for its topography, geology, and climate. Like states neighboring the area, the terrain is arid desert and the air is dry. On this route hikers can experience rare wildlife and flora not found anywhere else in the state.

Start: Vista Trailhead, west of the Black Mesa State Park Office
Elevation gain: 4,308 to 4,379 feet
Distance: 1.97 miles out and back with an additional spur
Difficulty: Easy to moderate due to uneven terrain
Hiking time: 1–1.5 hours
Seasons/schedule: Open year-round, sunrise to sunset
Fees and permits: None (subject to change)
Trail contacts: Black Mesa State Park & Nature Preserve, CR 325, Kenton 73946; (580) 426-2222
Dog-friendly: Leashed dogs permitted
Trail surface: Dirt and rocky path

Land status: Oklahoma State Parks
Nearest town: Kenton to the northwest, Boise City to the southeast
Other trail users: None
Maps: USGS Kenton SW; Black Mesa State Park and Nature Preserve map (available online at www.travelok.com/state-parks and via the Oklahoma State Parks mobile app)
Special considerations: There is no shade on this hike during summer.
  Rattlesnakes may be present on this trail.
  Yellow rectangular metal signs with the word "Trail" serve as trail markers.

FINDING THE TRAILHEAD

From the US 412/US 385 and US 287 junction, head west on OK 325 W/Main Street through Boise City for a little over 20 miles. You will reach a fork on OK 325 with signage indicating to turn left (west) for Black Mesa State Park. This rural road has no designated name. Continue west for 4.5 miles and turn right (north) on N0080 Road. After 1.2 miles turn left (west) on E0120 Road and continue for 0.4 mile. Turn right (north) at the dead end and go across the small bridge. In about 0.2 mile you will see the park office to your left (west); the Vista Trailhead is right behind it. GPS: N36° 50.2507′ W102° 52.996′

THE HIKE

With astounding views all along the trail, the Vista Trail is best ventured on during sunrise or sunset. At dawn you may encounter a flock of wild turkeys and feel the cool breeze enveloping you as you traverse the desert rocks. At sundown you can witness the pastel hues of the panhandle sky hovering above striking wildflowers and cacti—perhaps even get a glimpse of a burrowing owl hiding among the campground trees below you.

Sunset view from the Bird Haven Trail

The Vista Trail begins behind the park office (west). You will ascend the rocky path for about 140 feet in elevation until you reach the 0.25-mile mark. The trail heads north during this ascent to reach an overlook on your right (east) at 0.04 mile. There will be a bench at the 0.16-mile mark if you wish to continue enjoying the view of the campgrounds and Lake Carl Etling. After the bench, bear left (west) across the slabs of rock. The trail starts to head northwest and descend at 0.27 mile and continues to descend for about 50 feet in elevation until the Bird Haven Trail connection. Before reaching the Bird Haven Trail, there will be a side trail to your right (east) and a barbed-wire fence to your left. The trail winds north before you bear right (east) down a mowed-grass path to reach the Bird Haven Trail at 0.37 mile.

When you reach the connection, bear right (southeast) to head down the Bird Haven Trail. The trail eventually winds east, where you will be greeted with a beautiful mixture of wildflowers along with informational signage. At the 0.52-mile mark, you reach the end (also the entrance) of the Bird Haven Trail. A petrified log exhibit will be to your left (north). Turn around to head back to the Vista Trail. The view is especially spectacular heading back to the Vista Trail during sunset. You will encounter the Vista Trail connection that you were once at when the mileage reads 0.67 mile. Continue straight (north) to complete the Vista Trail.

At 0.7 mile bear right (east). You will start a steady ascent of 40 feet in elevation until 0.87 mile. The path winds north at 0.83 mile, and views of Lake Carl Etling become visible again to your right (east). After enjoying the view, head away from the ridge by continuing northwest on the trail. The trail starts winding west at 1.04 miles and then heads north at 1.07 miles. You will descend some rocks for about 20 feet in elevation before the path levels out at 1.09 miles. The Vista Trail ends before the auto road at 1.13 miles. Turn around and head back the way you came without going on the Bird Haven Trail at the 1.58-mile mark. Bear left (west) to head back to the Vista Trailhead.

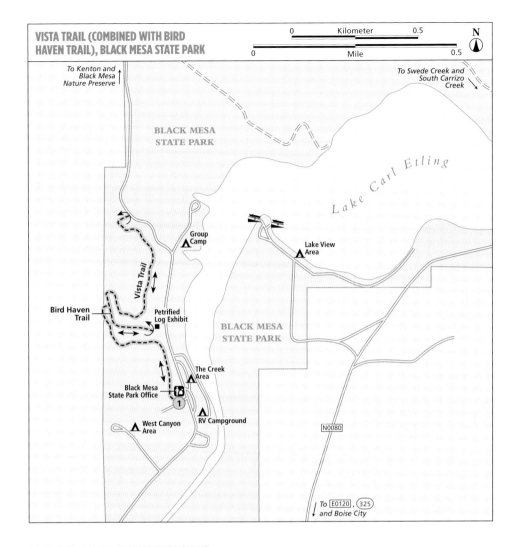

VISTA TRAIL (COMBINED WITH BIRD HAVEN TRAIL), BLACK MESA STATE PARK

MILES AND DIRECTIONS

0.0 Start at the Vista Trailhead, behind (west of) the park office.

0.04 Reach an overlook to your right (east).

0.16 Reach a bench straight ahead to the north. Bear left (west). Views of the campgrounds and Lake Carl Etling end.

0.32 Bypass the side trail to your right (east).

0.36 Bear right (east) down the mowed-grass path to connect with the Bird Haven Trail.

0.37 Bear right (southeast) to go down the Bird Haven Trail.

0.43 A bench to your right (north) has wildflower informational signage.

0.52 Reach the end/entrance of the Bird Haven Trail. A petrified log exhibit will be to your left (north). Turn around to head back to the Vista Trail.

0.67 Reach the Vista Trail connection. Continue straight (north), back on the Vista Trail.

Top left: Wildflowers on the Bird Haven Trail
Top right: Cacti at sunset
Bottom: Wild turkeys along the Vista Trail

0.83 Views of Lake Carl Etling appear to your right (east).

1.13 Reach the paved road and the end of the Vista Trail. Turn around and head back the way you came, bypassing the Bird Haven Trail.

1.58 Reach the Bird Haven Trail connection. Bear left (west) to head back to the Vista Trailhead.

1.97 Arrive back at the trailhead.

2 BLACK MESA SUMMIT TRAIL

BLACK MESA NATURE PRESERVE

On the Black Mesa Summit Trail, you will reach the highest point in Oklahoma and have the opportunity to see New Mexico and Colorado. You will also be surrounded by several monumental rock formations as you traverse the vast and awe-inspiring Black Mesa Valley.

Start: Black Mesa Summit Trailhead, west of the Black Mesa Nature Preserve parking lot
Elevation gain: 4,315 to 4,977 feet
Distance: 8.48 miles out and back
Difficulty: Moderate due to uneven terrain and steep changes in elevation
Hiking time: At least 4 hours
Seasons/schedule: Open year-round, sunrise to sunset; best during spring and fall due to lack of shade in summer
Fees and permits: None (subject to change)
Trail contacts: Black Mesa State Park & Nature Preserve, CR 325, Kenton 73946; (580) 426-2222
Dog-friendly: Leashed dogs permitted
Trail surface: Dirt and rocky path
Land status: Oklahoma State Parks
Nearest town: Kenton to the south, Boise City to the southeast

Other trail users: None; equestrians and motorized vehicles prohibited
Maps: USGS Kenton; Black Mesa State Park and Nature Preserve map (available online at www.travelok.com/state-parks and via the Oklahoma State Parks mobile app)
Special considerations: The main trail is located in the Black Mesa Nature Preserve, 25 miles north of Black Mesa State Park. The Black Mesa Nature Preserve is managed by Black Mesa State Park and is a protected area; camping is prohibited.

Pack enough water, especially during the summer months. With no shade on this trail and the considerable distance, the heat can be intense.

Green metal arrows serve as trail markers.

FINDING THE TRAILHEAD

From the US 412/US 385 and US 287 junction, head west on OK 325 W/Main Street through Boise City for 35.2 miles. (During this segment, OK 325 will head north and then back west.) You then make a right (north). After traveling 4.9 miles you will see the parking lot and trailhead to your left (west). GPS: N36° 57.430' W102° 57.433'

THE HIKE

With no shortage of prickly pear, fluff grass, bluestem short grass, and plains yucca, the terrain of Black Mesa is like none other in Oklahoma. Occasionally, a pinyon jay will flutter around as you navigate the summit, and you may encounter some mule deer in the valley around dusk. The Black Mesa area is one of the darkest places in Oklahoma, making it an optimal place for stargazing. Each year, people from all over the world attend the Okie-Tex Star Party event to observe the astronomical extravaganza.

View of Black Mesa from its summit

The Black Mesa Summit Trail leads to the highest point in Oklahoma. It heads west for the majority of the route. Starting off at 4,432 feet in elevation, it is an easy hike and remains relatively flat until close to the 2.6-mile mark. At 0.15 mile, you reach a bend where the trail heads northwest; it will eventually go back to heading west again. The trail surface starts to get rocky at 0.62 mile and will change between heading north and south a couple times before the 1.0-mile mark. The trail resumes heading west at 1.16 miles, where you will see a bench with "Mile 1" carved into it. (Trail mileage in this guide is based on hiking the trail with an independent GPS program, and readings may be different. However, markers physically stationed are useful benchmarks as well.) After 1.5 miles, the trail heads southwest before you reach a fork at 2.0 miles. Bear left (west) at the fork (the right side is an unofficial trail). The trail heads back south just before you reach the "Mile 2" bench at 2.18 miles.

Highest point obelisk

At 2.61 miles you begin a rocky ascent, with the starting elevation estimated at 4,545 feet. Cross over a seasonal creek bed at 2.65 miles. A couple of switchbacks veering between north and south occur after 2.78 miles until the 3.07-mile mark. During this segment, take the time to survey the epic view that lies below you—it will truly take your breath away. Shrub-covered buttes, multihued mesas, and roaming livestock outline the valley. You will reach the "Mile 3" bench at 2.97 miles. At 3.15 miles the trail plateaus at 4,919 feet in elevation as you reach the summit of Black Mesa. Continue in a southwesterly

Dinosaur tracks

WHERE DINOSAURS ONCE ROAMED

Cimarron County, where Black Mesa State Park and the Nature Preserve are located, is the only region in Oklahoma that contains rock formations from the Jurassic period. The Morrison Formation, which is from the Upper Jurassic period, lies in this area of the Oklahoma panhandle and is rich in dinosaur fossils. More than 6,000 dinosaur bones were discovered from the Morrison Formation by the late and revered paleontologist Dr. John Willis Stovall. East of OK 325, near the Black Mesa Summit Trailhead, visitors have the rare opportunity to see preserved dinosaur tracks made by a three-toed dinosaur.

BLACK MESA SUMMIT TRAIL, BLACK MESA NATURE PRESERVE

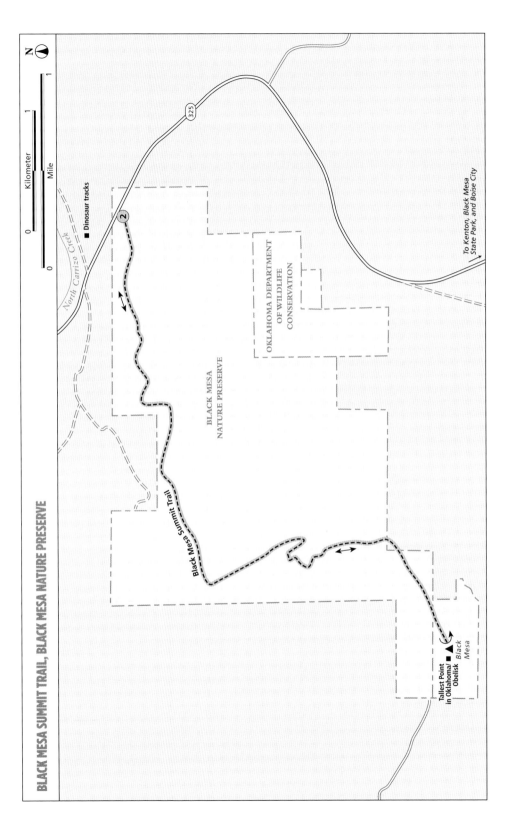

N

Kilometer
0   1

Mile
0   1

■ Dinosaur tracks

North Carrizo Creek

325

2

BLACK MESA
NATURE PRESERVE

OKLAHOMA DEPARTMENT
OF WILDLIFE
CONSERVATION

Black Mesa Summit Trail

Tallest Point
in Oklahoma/
Obelisk ■ ▲
Black
Mesa

To Kenton, Black Mesa
State Park, and Boise City

Three Sisters formation at night

direction until you reach the obelisk at 4.24 miles. Take note of the unique desert plant life sprinkled across the mesa, as well as the igneous rocks that give Black Mesa its name. The obelisk designates the highest point in the state at 4,972.97 feet in elevation. After commemorating your achievement, turn around and return to the trailhead.

MILES AND DIRECTIONS

- **0.0** Start at the Black Mesa Summit Trailhead.
- **0.62** The trail starts to get rocky.
- **1.16** Reach the "Mile 1" bench.
- **2.0** Reach a fork. Take the left (west) side of the fork.
- **2.18** Reach the "Mile 2" bench.
- **2.61** Start a rocky ascent from 4,545 feet in elevation.
- **2.65** Cross over the seasonal creek bed.
- **2.78** Traverse a couple switchbacks that veer north and then south.
- **2.97** Reach the "Mile 3" bench.
- **3.15** Reach a plateau. You will be at about 4,919 feet in elevation at this point.
- **4.24** Reach the "highest point in Oklahoma" obelisk at 4,973 feet in elevation. Turn around and return to the trailhead.
- **8.48** Arrive back at the trailhead.

3 CATHEDRAL MOUNTAIN TRAIL

GLOSS MOUNTAIN STATE PARK

Reminiscent of desert landscapes of the Southwest, the red-hued mesas of Gloss Mountain State Park enrapture visitors with their shimmering selenite layers. The Cathedral Mountain Trail offers stunning panoramic views of Gloss Mountain State Park's finest—Lone Peak, The Sphinx, and Lookout Mountain.

Start: Cathedral Mountain Trailhead, north of the Gloss Mountain State Park parking lot
Elevation gain: 1,394 to 1,553 feet
Distance: 1.55-mile lollipop
Difficulty: Moderate due to steep stairs and narrow paths along the cliffsides
Hiking time: 1.5–2 hours
Seasons/schedule: Open year-round, sunrise to sunset
Fees and permits: None (subject to change)
Trail contacts: Major County Economic Development Corporation in Fairview; (580) 227-2512 (no one physically stationed at the park)
Dog-friendly: Leashed dogs permitted
Trail surface: Dirt and rocky path

Land status: Oklahoma State Parks in partnership with the Gloss Mountain Conservancy
Nearest town: Fairview
Other trail users: None
Maps: USGS Glass Mountains; Gloss Mountain State Park map (www.ok majordev.org/gloss-mountain-state -park.html)
Special considerations: Gloss Mountain State Park is a gated park. Please ensure that you leave adequate time to return to the parking lot before sunset, when the entrance/exit is locked.
 The stairs leading to the top of Cathedral Mountain are rusted; exercise caution when using them.
 Rattlesnakes may be present on this trail from spring to the beginning of fall.

FINDING THE TRAILHEAD

From the US 60 and OK 58 junction in Fairview, head north on US 60 E for 6 miles. Turn left on US 412 W and travel another 5.5 miles. You will see the Gloss Mountain State Park sign and road to the parking lot on your right (north). GPS: N36° 21.797' W98° 34.811'

THE HIKE

As you head out to western Oklahoma, you will encounter the antithesis of what outsiders envision Oklahoma's landscape to be. The Gloss Mountains are mesas and buttes composed of red sandstone, shale, and gypsum rings over millions of years. The gypsum layers contain selenite crystals, the source of the reflective-glass effect that makes the Gloss Mountain area a distinctive place to explore.

 The Cathedral Mountain Trail begins north of the parking lot. You will cross over a couple footbridges before ascending the metal staircase. The ascent is a gain of 120 feet in elevation, and the 150 stairs are rusted—use caution. There are a couple benches and a picnic table up the stair route. From there you can take a break or just enjoy the view.

Vista from top of
Cathedral Mountain

The stairs end at the 0.12-mile mark. You will have to cross a large slab of rock before scrambling to the top of Cathedral Mountain.

Once you have reached the top of Cathedral Mountain, look ahead to the north for the metal disc-shaped markers planted in the ground. Bear left of those markers to continue on the trail. There are several paths to vistas on your left (west). After crossing through a cluster of cedar trees and their unearthed roots, come to a bench to your left (west) at 0.18 mile. At 0.21 mile there will be a couple of trail markers and a vista to your left (west).

Reach a hill 0.25 mile into the trail; head left (west) of the hill. After 0.33 mile, the path widens and there are several paths to vistas and diversions. Continue straight (north) toward the Lone Peak overlook. Stay left at the fork at 0.44 mile. Shortly after, views of Lone Peak become visible to your right (northeast). Continue to the overlook of Lone Peak, which you reach at 0.59 mile. Although there is a fence guarding the overlook for safety reasons, you can still see Lone Peak to the left (west).

Bear right (east) toward the metal trail marker and head toward the east side of Cathedral Mountain. The path narrows along the rim for a majority of the remaining

Bald Knob and Lookout Mountain

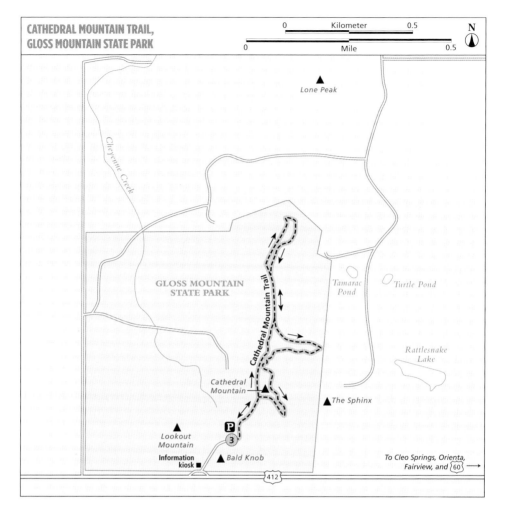

Kilometer

Mile

N

Lone Peak

Cheyenne Creek

GLOSS MOUNTAIN STATE PARK

Cathedral Mountain Trail

Tamarac Pond

Turtle Pond

Rattlesnake Lake

Cathedral Mountain

The Sphinx

Lookout Mountain

P

3

Information kiosk

Bald Knob

To Cleo Springs, Orienta, Fairview, and 60

412

trail, so exercise caution. At 0.67 mile, the path becomes rocky for a short period before returning to a dirt surface. Several points in the trail merge with the opposite part of the loop you were previously on, heading north. At any of these points, stay on the east side of Cathedral Mountain. The same goes for when you reach the hill that you encountered earlier (at the 0.25-mile mark). Stay on the left (east) side of the hill and continue straight.

Reach a fork in the trail at 0.93 mile. Heading left (east) will lead you to another overlook. From this overlook, among all the oil and gas wells, you will get glimpses of Rattlesnake Lake, Tamarac Pond, and Turtle Pond. Close to the 1.0-mile mark, the path returns to a rocky surface. Once you loop around the overlook, the trail winds north before reconnecting with the path you were on before you started the loop. Continue straight (west), away from the cliffside. After a diversion to your right (north), the path returns to a dirt surface at 1.12 miles. A trail marker greets you to your right (west) at 1.16 miles. Here again you will see the trail meeting the original path you were on headed toward the Lone Peak Overlook. Head straight (southwest) toward the cluster of cedar trees.

Bearing left (east) at the fork at 1.19 miles will lead you to an overlook of The Sphinx formation. The path begins to narrow and wind south before you reach the overlook at 1.33 miles. The trail then winds west, returning you to the metal stairs. Facing south, you have panoramic views of Lookout Mountain and Bald Knob. Head back to the parking lot.

MILES AND DIRECTIONS

0.0 Start at the trailhead, north of the parking lot.

0.06 Climb up the stairs.

0.12 Stairs end. Scramble up the rocks to the top of the mesa.

0.13 Bear left (west) to continue on the trail. Follow the metal disc-shaped markers.

0.25 Reach the fork at the hill. Bear left (west) of the hill.

0.44 Reach another fork. Stay on the left side of the fork.

0.59 Reach the overlook of Lone Peak to the left (west) of the fence. Bear right (east) toward the trail marker and the east side of Cathedral Mountain.

0.69 Reach a fork. Continue straight along the east side of Cathedral Mountain.

0.9 Reach the same hill you encountered earlier at the 0.25-mile mark. Bear left (east) of the hill and continue straight.

0.93 Reach a fork in the path. Bear left (east).

0.95 Come to an overlook on your left (north).

0.99 Reach another overlook to your left (north).

1.03 Continue straight to the easternmost point of the mesa.

1.06 The path heads right (north) and reconnects with the original path. Continue straight (west).

1.07 Bypass the path diversion to your right (north).

1.12 The path becomes a red dirt surface. Stay away from the edge of the cliff.

1.19 Reach a fork. Bear left (east). Do not go back on the original path.

1.24 Reach another fork. Continue straight (south).

1.33 Reach the overlook of The Sphinx formation.

1.42 Reach the stairs from the 0.12-mile mark. Enjoy the views of Lookout Mountain before heading down. Head back the way you came.

1.55 Arrive back at the trailhead.

4 EAGLE ROOST NATURE TRAIL (COMBINED WITH HOOT OWL TRAIL)

SALT PLAINS NATIONAL WILDLIFE REFUGE

Home to the endangered whooping crane, the iconic bald eagle, the magnificent sandhill crane, and thousands of other migratory birds, the Salt Plains National Wildlife Refuge is a wondrous place to see such species up close. The Eagle Roost Nature Trail leads you to the bay and wooded areas where these creatures venture for food during winter.

Start: Eagle Roost Nature Trailhead, across from Bonham Pond
Elevation gain: 1,052 to 1,135 feet
Distance: 2.04-mile lollipop with an additional lollipop for wildlife viewing
Difficulty: Easy
Hiking time: About 1 hour
Seasons/schedule: Open year-round, sunrise to sunset; end of winter, spring, and fall are the best times for wildlife viewing
Fees and permits: None
Trail contacts: Salt Plains National Wildlife Refuge Headquarters, 71189 Harper Rd., Jet 73749; (580) 626-4794

Dog-friendly: Leashed dogs permitted
Trail surface: Dirt and gravel path
Land status: US Fish and Wildlife Service
Nearest town: Jet
Other trail users: No cyclists allowed
Maps to consult: USGS Manchester SW; Salt Plains National Wildlife Refuge maps (available online at www.fws.gov/refuge/Salt_Plains/map.html)
Special considerations: This trail guide includes an additional scenic route, the Hoot Owl Trail—an approximately 0.5-mile lollipop trail that ends up back on the Eagle Roost Nature Trail.

FINDING THE TRAILHEAD

From the US 64 intersection in Jet, travel on OK 38 N for 12.8 miles. Turn left (west) on Harper Road (formerly E0160 Road) toward the Salt Plains National Wildlife Refuge Visitor Center. About 0.2 mile from the visitor center you will reach the Eagle Roost Nature Trailhead, across from Bonham Pond. GPS: N36° 47.135′ W98° 10.930′

THE HIKE

Nestled in the wide expanse of northwestern Oklahoma is a serene retreat for a multitude of wildlife. Each year, hundreds of thousands of birds seek out the Salt Plains National Wildlife Refuge during the winter months to feed on the shores of Sand Creek Bay and on crops planted by the refuge. Coyotes, white-tailed deer, raccoons, armadillos, and

Eagle Roost Pond

many other mammals find shelter among the diverse timber. Not only is the Salt Plains National Wildlife Refuge the largest saline flat in the central lowlands of North America, but it is also a sanctuary for one of the tallest birds in North America, the endangered whooping crane. Whooping cranes can be sighted during the fall, as well as monarch butterflies and sandhill cranes. The Eagle Roost Nature Trail takes you through the various wildlife habitats located in the woods, prairies, marshes, and waterfronts of the salt plains.

The trailhead for the Eagle Roost Nature Trail begins at a footbridge across from Bonham Pond. About 225 feet from the trailhead, you will encounter a fork in the trail. A brown nature trail sign directs you to the left (west), where the path surface changes from dirt to gravel. There is another fork in the path at 0.1 mile. While you may continue straight on the Eagle Roost Nature Trail, it is highly recommended to add an extra 0.5 mile to your hike by heading left (south) and including the Hoot Owl Trail, which this description does. The Hoot Owl Trail is a quick and scenic lollipop that will reward you with sights and sounds of various colorful and chirpy birds. In the finale of winter,

SELENITE CRYSTAL DIGGING

In the southwest portion of the Salt Plains National Wildlife Refuge is an area, designated annually, where you can dig for selenite crystals that form within 2 feet of the salt plains' surface. Millions of years ago, seawater that got separated from the ocean settled in this area and evaporated. Soil from the eventual erosion of neighboring mountains then layered on top of the salt from the evaporated seawater. Selenite crystals, with hourglass inclusions, are created when gypsum and saline sourced from groundwater combine within the soil. Unique in its environment and photo-worthy for its white and salty surface, the salt plains selenite digging area is open to the public April 1 to October 15 each year.

Raccoon sighting

you might come across a raccoon cozying up in the branches or an armadillo or two scampering among the dormant greenery.

The Hoot Owl Trail is meant to be completed in a clockwise direction. A bridge in disrepair on the northern part of the lollipop is no longer part of the main trail, and portions of the northern part of the lollipop can become flooded after a decent rainfall. Look ahead for the gravel surfaces of the trail to know where to connect.

Once you return to the dirt surface of the Eagle Roost Nature Trail, bear left (west). There will be a creek to your right (north) then a marsh to your left (south) shortly after. You come to an observation deck that overlooks Sand Creek Bay at 0.95 mile. In a regular winter, when temperatures remain frigid for quite some time, there are usually hundreds of eagles at the refuge. You may even see some catching fish from the frozen bay. If milo has been planted in abundance on farms surrounding the refuge, this will draw a greater number of crane species to the refuge. Certain factors can affect the number of birds migrating to the refuge, including a mild winter or changes in agriculture, such as a shortage of milo crops.

Once you have finished checking out the sights and looking for migratory birds, continue north on the trail. Eagle Roost Pond will be to your right (east) at 1.1 miles and then Puterbaugh Marsh, close to the 1.4-mile mark. There is a fork at Puterbaugh Marsh; bear right (east) to stay on the trail. Another brown nature trail sign indicates which direction to turn.

After about 0.2 mile of heading east, reach another fork and a third brown nature trail sign. Head in the direction noted by the sign, to your right (south); from here the trail surface returns to gravel. After crossing over a small seasonal creek bed and heading back into a wooded area, you reach the very first intersection you encountered from the trailhead. Continue straight (east) on the gravel path. You will see the trailhead and footbridge ahead of you.

MILES AND DIRECTIONS

0.0   Start at the trailhead and cross over the footbridge.

0.04 Reach a fork. Bear left (west).

0.1   Reach another fork. Bear left (south) to start on the Hoot Owl Trail.

0.17 Reach the Hoot Owl Trail. Bear left (east) to start the loop.

EAGLE ROOST NATURE TRAIL (COMBINED WITH HOOT OWL TRAIL), SALT PLAINS NATIONAL WILDLIFE REFUGE

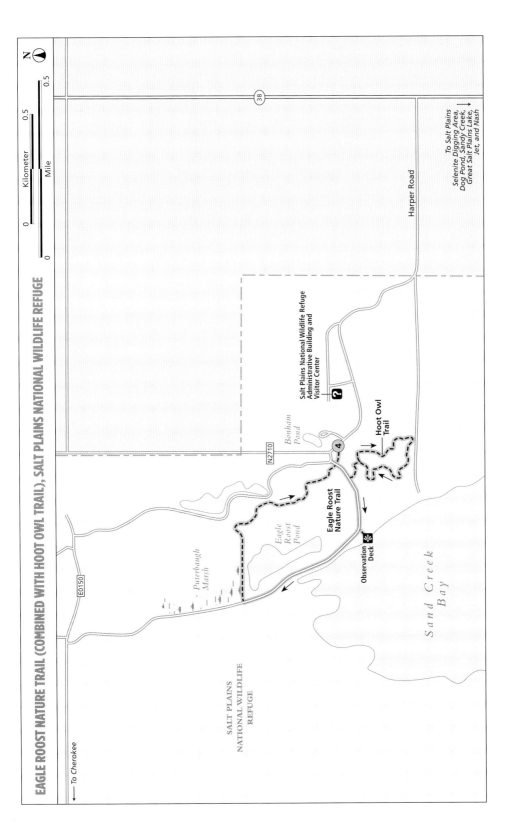

Puterbaugh Marsh

0.2 Come to a bridge, now in disrepair. Continue on the designated trail.

0.73 Complete the Hoot Owl Trail. Turn left (north) to head back to the Eagle Roost Nature Trail.

0.8 Reach the Eagle Roost Nature Trail. Bear left (west).

0.95 Reach the observation deck for Sand Creek Bay.

1.1 Reach Eagle Roost Pond.

1.39 Come to a fork at Puterbaugh Marsh. Bear right (east).

1.6 Reach another fork. Bear right (south).

2.0 Come to an intersection; continue straight (east), back to the trailhead.

2.04 Arrive back at the trailhead.

5 TRAIL TO INSPIRATION POINT (VIA LODGE TRAILHEAD)

ROMAN NOSE STATE PARK

With sweeping views of painting-worthy Bitter Creek Canyon and the glassy surface of Lake Watonga, it is no surprise that so many visitors consider Inspiration Point a favorite feature of Roman Nose State Park.

Start: Lodge Trailhead, south of the Roman Nose State Park Office and Lodge
Elevation gain: 1,365 to 1,486 feet
Distance: 5.32 miles out and back with an additional lollipop to a vista
Difficulty: Easy to moderate due to uneven trail surfaces
Hiking time: 2–3 hours
Seasons/schedule: Open year-round, sunrise to sunset
Fees and permits: None (subject to change)
Trail contacts: Roman Nose State Park Office & Lodge, 3236 S. Hwy. 8A, Watonga 73772; (580) 623-7281
Dog-friendly: Leashed dogs permitted

Trail surface: Dirt and rocky path
Land status: Oklahoma State Parks
Nearest town: Watonga
Other trail users: Mountain bikers, equestrians
Maps: USGS Watonga Lake; Roman Nose State Park map (available online at www.travelok.com/state-parks and via the Oklahoma State Parks mobile app)
Special considerations: Rattlesnakes may be present on this trail from spring to the beginning of the fall season.
   Inspiration Point can also be accessed via the Two Lakes Trailhead.

FINDING THE TRAILHEAD

Heading west on I-40 from downtown Oklahoma City, exit onto US 281 Spur W/US 66 (exit 108) a little after 43 miles. After 4.2 miles US 281 Spur W becomes US 281 N. After 21 miles US 281 N becomes OK 8 N/S Clarence Nash Boulevard. Turn left (north) onto OK 8A N after traveling on OK 8 N for 4.3 miles. After 2.6 miles turn right (northeast) onto P20 Road and continue for 0.4 mile toward the Roman Nose State Park Lodge. The Lodge Trailhead is to the right (east) of the parking lot and south of the lodge. Parking is available in the lodge parking lot. GPS: N35° 56.159' W98° 25.471'

THE HIKE

Inspiration Point showcases the layers of rock formed over millions of years that make the Bitter Creek area so magnificent. Aerial views of Lake Watonga are also visible from this vantage point. Inspiration Point used to be accessible via the Lake Loop Trail from the Cedar Cove area. However, with repairs being made to the dam over Lake Watonga, the Lake Loop Trail is no longer a viable route at the time of publication. This guide instead takes you from the Lodge Trailhead, with a detour to a vista on the Two Lakes Loop

Trail, through the Upper Canyon Spur Trail, up the Lakeshore Loop Trail, and then onto the Mesa Loop Trail to Inspiration Point.

The Lodge Trailhead begins southeast of the Roman Nose State Park Lodge. You immediately head east across a footbridge. After 100 feet you head north down some stairs and enter a wooded area. A side trail will be to your left (west) shortly after. Continue straight (north) to another set of stairs. At 0.05 mile, cross another, much longer footbridge. There is a side trail to your right (east) after the footbridge. Continue straight (north) up the stairs, reaching the Two Lakes Loop connection at 0.1 mile. Bear right (south), and be aware of several unearthed tree roots. A switchback heading north includes a rocky ascent at 0.15 mile.

At the junction at 0.17 mile, bear left (north) to follow a lollipop to a vista. (You can bear right and head south to the Lower and Upper Canyon Spur Trails and Inspiration Point if you want to shorten the hike.) There is a side trail to your left (west) after passing the informational signage at 0.2 mile. The entrance to the lollipop route to the vista is short of the 0.25-mile mark. Continue straight (north), and do the loop portion of the lollipop in a clockwise direction. The vista of Lake Watonga is at 0.34 mile. The loop completes at 0.43 mile. Head back south to the junction you encountered previously at the 0.17-mile mark, which will now clock in at 0.51 mile. Continue straight (south) to head toward the Lower and Upper Canyon Spur Trails.

The trail splits a little after 0.56 mile. Head left (east). The right side (southeast) is an overgrown side trail that eventually merges with the main trail at 0.63 mile. Straight ahead (east) is the Lower Canyon Spur Trail; to your left (north) is the Upper Canyon Spur Trail. Although the Lower Canyon Spur Trail connects with the Upper Canyon Spur Trail and also leads to Inspiration Point, it is a steeper route. Continue on the Upper Canyon Spur Trail. (Those wishing to try out the Lower Canyon Spur Trail can check out the Switchback Trail in this guide.) There is another split in the trail at 0.68 mile. Bear right at the fork, heading east. The left side of the fork is a side trail.

The trail heads south after this point, and you head down some rocks a couple times before reconnecting with the Lower Canyon Spur Trail at 0.87 mile. Continue straight (south) to head toward Inspiration Point. The entrance to the Switchback Trail is to your right (south) at 0.94 mile. Bear left at the fork. That path will eventually turn around and head north to Inspiration Point. Descend some log steps before reaching a seasonal creek bed a little over 1.0 mile into the trail. Bear left (north) at the fork to continue on to Inspiration Point. The right side of the fork (south) goes back to the Switchback Trail. The trail winds west before reaching another fork at 1.06 miles. Head right (north) to continue to Inspiration Point. The other side of the fork is a washed-out side trail. Reach a bridge at 1.13 miles. (There is a shortcut to the north if you wish to circumvent the bridge.) A slight switchback occurs at 1.19 miles. Be mindful of unearthed tree roots at this point.

You reach the Mesa Loop and Lakeshore Loop Trails connection at 1.3 miles. Take the left side of the fork (northwest) to head onto the Lakeshore Loop Trail for some variety in scenery. An entrance to Bubba's Cutoff, a trail that connects with the Two Lakes Loop Trail, occurs to your left (south) at 1.4 miles. Continue straight (north) on the Lakeshore Loop Trail. Partial views of Lake Watonga begin to show up to your left (west) shortly

CHIEF HENRY ROMAN NOSE

Roman Nose State Park is named in honor of the late Southern Cheyenne council chief Henry Roman Nose. The park is situated on land that was allotted to his family by the US government in 1892. After suffering defeat with the Plains Indians at the Red River War and serving his prison term, Chief Henry Roman Nose received a formal education and worked as a government employee. He became council chief for the Southern Cheyenne in 1897. Highly regarded by his tribe, he was a champion of education and peace until his passing in 1917.

Bridge along the trail to Inspiration Point

after 1.6 miles. The trail then heads west before reaching a fork at 1.74 miles. The left side of the fork (north) is the remaining portion of the Lakeshore Loop Trail. (At the time of publication, the remaining segment tends to become overgrown and somewhat impassable.) Bear right (east) to head toward the Mesa Loop Trail. The route turns rocky and heads north, and then turns around and heads south for a majority of the way until you reach the Mesa Loop Trail connection at 1.94 miles. Continue straight (south) to follow the Mesa Loop Trail in a counterclockwise direction.

You encounter another fork at 2.31 miles. Bear left (north) to curve around and ascend the west side of the mesa. Views of Lake Watonga are available to your left (west). Achieve the rewards of Inspiration Point at the 2.81-mile mark. Feel free to take a break on the bench and be inspired by the 360-degree view before you. Once you have savored the landscape, turn around and head back on the left side of the loop. Continue south on the east side of the mesa. The trail turns around and heads back north at 3.32 miles. The trail then heads west for a short period at 3.6 miles, with a side trail to your right (north) before it winds south. At the fork at 3.63 miles, bear left (southeast) to continue on the Mesa Loop Trail. This portion of the trail narrows and can get overgrown, but it is not obstructed. The right side of the fork (southwest) leads to the impassable portion of the Lakeshore Loop Trail previously noted from the 1.74-mile mark. Head up some rocks before reaching an overlook to your right (west). The trail then heads south, and the path widens back up.

With no shortage of forks on this trail, another fork comes up at 3.75 miles. Bear right (west) to head back to the Lakeshore Loop Trail connection. The left side of the fork (south) goes back up the Mesa Loop Trail. At 3.96 miles you reach the Lakeshore Loop Trail connection. From this point, veer left (south) to head back the way you came to the Lodge Trailhead (without including the lollipop route to the vista).

MILES AND DIRECTIONS

0.0 Start at the Lodge Trailhead, southeast of the Roman Nose State Park Lodge. Head east across the footbridge.

0.05 Cross another, longer footbridge.

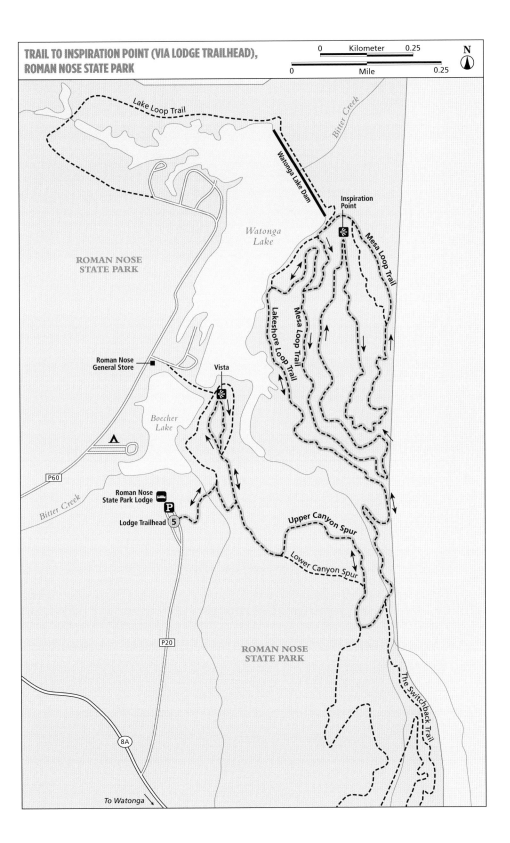

0   Kilometer   0.25

0   Mile   0.25

N

Lake Loop Trail

Bitter Creek

Watonga Lake Dam

Inspiration
Point

Watonga
Lake

ROMAN NOSE
STATE PARK

Mesa Loop Trail

Mesa Loop Trail

Roman Nose
General Store

Vista

Lakeshore Loop Trail

Boecher
Lake

P60

Bitter Creek

Roman Nose
State Park Lodge

Lodge Trailhead 5

Upper Canyon Spur

Lower Canyon Spur

P20

ROMAN NOSE
STATE PARK

The Switchback Trail

8A

To Watonga

0.08 Bypass a side trail to your right (east). Continue straight (north), up the stairs.

0.1 Reach the Two Lakes Loop connection. Veer right (south).

0.15 Traverse a switchback.

0.17 Reach a junction. Bear left (north) to continue on the lollipop to the vista.

0.24 Reach a fork. Continue straight (north) to the vista.

0.26 Reach the loop route to the vista. Take the loop in a clockwise direction.

0.34 Come upon a vista of Lake Watonga.

0.43 Reach the end of the loop. Head back south to the junction from the 0.17-mile mark.

0.51 Reach the Two Lakes Loop and Canyon Spur Trail connection. Continue straight (south) to head toward the Canyon Spur Trail (left side of fork).

0.56 Reach a fork. Bear left (east) at the fork.

0.63 Reach a junction. Bear left (north) to continue on the Upper Canyon Spur Trail.

0.68 Reach a fork. Take the right side of the fork, heading east.

0.87 Reconnect with the Lower Canyon Spur Trail. Continue straight (south) to head toward Inspiration Point.

0.94 Reach a fork. Take the left side of the fork, which will eventually turn around and head north to Inspiration Point.

0.95 Descend some log steps.

1.01 Bear (right) east across the seasonal creek bed to the fork. Veer left (north) at the fork to continue to Inspiration Point.

1.06 Reach a fork. Bear right (north) to continue to Inspiration Point.

1.14 Cross a bridge.

1.19 Traverse a switchback.

1.3 Reach the Mesa Loop and Lakeshore Loop Trails connection. Take the left side of the fork (northwest) onto the Lakeshore Loop Trail.

1.4 Reach a junction. Continue straight (north) on the Lakeshore Loop Trail.

1.61 Partial views of Lake Watonga and a side trail are to your left (west).

1.74 Reach a fork. Bear right (east) to head to the Mesa Loop Trail.

1.94 Reach the Mesa Loop Trail connection. Continue straight (south) to follow the Mesa Loop Trail in a counterclockwise direction.

2.31 Reach a fork. Bear left (north) to curve around toward the Mesa Loop Trail. Ascend the west side of the mesa.

2.81 Reach Inspiration Point. Turn around and head back on the left side of the loop to hike the east side of the mesa. Continue south.

3.63 Reach a fork. Bear left (southeast) to continue on the Mesa Loop Trail.

3.68 Come upon an overlook to your right (west).

3.75 Reach a fork. Bear right (west) to head back to the Lakeshore Loop Trail connection.

3.96 Reach the Lakeshore Loop Trail connection. Bear left (south) and head back the way you came to the Lodge Trailhead, without including the vista lollipop route.

5.32 Arrive back at the trailhead.

6 THE SWITCHBACK TRAIL (VIA TWO LAKES TRAILHEAD)

ROMAN NOSE STATE PARK

This trail allows the more adventurous hiker to meander back and forth through the Bitter Creek Canyon, with a wide range of ascents and descents. Scenes of Boecher Lake and Lake Watonga greet you at the beginning and at the end of the trail, while nonstop views of shale formations from millions of years ago surround you throughout the route.

Start: Two Lakes Trailhead, north of Boecher Lake
Elevation gain: 1,370 to 1,518 feet
Distance: 3.74-mile lollipop
Difficulty: Moderate to difficult due to steep and narrow ascents and descents
Hiking time: 2–3 hours
Seasons/schedule: Open year-round, sunrise to sunset
Fees and permits: None (subject to change)
Trail contacts: Roman Nose State Park Office & Lodge, 3236 S. Hwy. 8A, Watonga 73772; (580) 623-7281
Dog-friendly: Leashed dogs permitted

Trail surface: Dirt and rocky path
Land status: Oklahoma State Parks
Nearest town: Watonga
Other trail users: Mountain bikers, equestrians
Maps: USGS Watonga Lake; Roman Nose State Park map (available online at www.travelok.com/state -parks and via the Oklahoma State Parks mobile app)
Special considerations: Rattlesnakes may be present on this trail from spring to the beginning of the fall season.
    The Switchback Trail can also be accessed via the Lodge Trailhead.

FINDING THE TRAILHEAD

Heading west on I-40 from downtown Oklahoma City, exit onto US 281 Spur W/US 66 (exit 108) a little after 43 miles. After 4.2 miles US 281 Spur W becomes US 281 N; after 21 miles US 281 N becomes OK 8 N/S Clarence Nash Boulevard. Turn left (north) onto OK 8A N after traveling on OK 8 N for 4.3 miles. After 3.1 miles turn right (northeast) onto P60 Road and continue 0.5 mile. P60 Road then becomes P63 Road. The trailhead is to your right (east), past the general store and on the northern shoreline of Boecher Lake. Parking is available near the general store and the Two Lakes RV camping area. GPS: N35° 56.360' W98° 25.494'

THE HIKE

Aptly named, the Switchback Trail provides ridgeline views of the gypsum karst of Bitter Creek Canyon as well as sightings of Boecher Lake and Lake Watonga. It winds continuously through grassland and forested areas with full-spectrum views for most of its route, making it adventurous for both hikers and mountain bikers. The Switchback Trail is accessible via two trailheads. This guide uses the Two Lakes Trailhead. This trailhead is

nestled into the Two Lakes RV campground, just east of the general store and north of Boecher Lake.

The trail heads southeast before reaching a fork at 0.09 mile. Bear left (northeast) to continue on the Two Lakes Loop in a clockwise direction. The right side of the fork (southwest) goes to the Lodge Trailhead. Views of Lake Watonga will be to your left (north) as you head onto the Two Lakes Loop. The trail begins to head east at 0.11 mile and then winds south shortly after. At 0.14 mile there are side trails to your right (west) and to your left (east). Continue up the log steps after passing an overlook of Bitter Creek to your left (east) at the 0.19-mile mark. A connection to Bubba's Cutoff (which connects with the Lakeshore Loop Trail) appears shortly after. The path surface then turns rocky.

Less than 0.25 mile into the trail, you encounter the Vista Loop. Bear left (east) to head to the Canyon Spur Trail. The trail winds south shortly after. At 0.32 mile, you reach another fork that connects with the Two Lakes Loop Trail and the Lodge Trailhead. Continue straight (south) toward the Canyon Spur Trail. Reach another fork at 0.36 mile. Stay on the left side of the fork (south) to continue on the route. (The right side is a side trail that merges at the junction at 0.43 mile.) The trail heads east before you reach that junction. To the right (south) of the junction is the side trail. Straight ahead is the Lower Canyon Spur Trail. To the left (north) is a trail that leads to Inspiration Point and the Upper Canyon Spur Trail. Continue straight on the Lower Canyon Spur Trail for a more adventurous route. The Lower Canyon Spur portion has a slight rocky ascent of about 40 feet in elevation before it opens up to grassland. At 0.53 mile, there is a descent of 36 feet in elevation until you reach the fork at 0.58 mile. Bear right (south) to head toward the Switchback Trail. The left side of the fork (north) connects to the Upper Canyon Spur Trail.

You reach the Switchback Trail connection at 0.65 mile. The trail is full of what it is named for—riveting switchbacks. Take the right side of the fork (south) to head onto the Switchback Trail. The left side of the fork (east) heads to Inspiration Point. There is a rocky ascent of 45 feet in elevation from 0.68 mile to 0.72 mile. An overlook of the canyon is to your left (east) at 0.76 mile. From here until 1.65 miles, the trail primarily heads south in a series of switchbacks. The landscape interchanges between wooded areas and open grassland. Portions of the trail can get somewhat overgrown in the grassland areas. There is another ascent, this time of 45 feet in elevation, between 1.17 miles and 1.19 miles.

The trail begins to head north at 1.65 miles. There is one more switchback before the 2.04-mile mark. This section of the trail, at 1.95 miles, can get muddy after wet weather conditions. There is a point of interest to your left (west) just short of 2.0 miles. This cave, a common characteristic of karst topography, is thought to have provided shelter to American Indians in the past. Bear right (south) at the fork at 2.04 miles to continue on the Switchback Trail. The other side of the fork heads north and is a side trail. There is one more switchback before the 2.36-mile mark.

The trail then primarily heads north, with another series of switchbacks. Exercise caution at the steep descent that occurs at 2.82 miles. There is about a 41-foot drop in elevation until you reach the fork at 2.86 miles. Continue straight (north) on the Switchback Trail. The route that heads south from the fork is a side trail. There is another descent at 2.91 miles—about 29 feet in elevation until you reach a seasonal creek bed at 2.95 miles. The creek follows along to your left (west) and a barbed-wire fence to your right (east) for a short distance after this point.

At 3.02 miles, you reach another fork. Head left (southwest) to head back to the Lower Canyon Spur Trail. The right side of the fork (north) heads to Inspiration Point. You

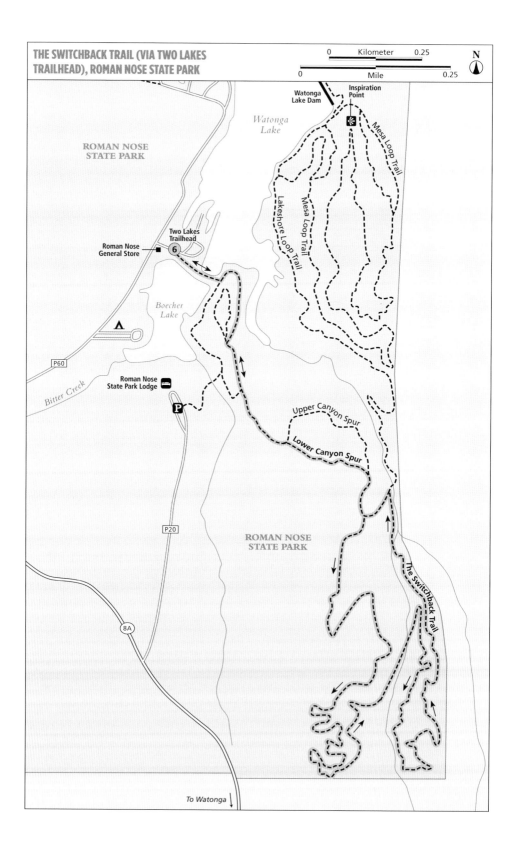

0   Kilometer   0.25

0   Mile   0.25

N

Watonga
Lake Dam

Inspiration
Point

Watonga
Lake

ROMAN NOSE
STATE PARK

Mesa Loop Trail

Two Lakes
Trailhead

Roman Nose
General Store

6

Lakeshore Loop Trail

Mesa Loop Trail

Boecher
Lake

P60

Roman Nose
State Park Lodge

P

Bitter Creek

Upper Canyon Spur

Lower Canyon Spur

P20

ROMAN NOSE
STATE PARK

The Switchback Trail

8A

To Watonga

will head up a series of log steps before reaching the Switchback Trail connection you initially came upon at 0.65 mile. From here, head back the way you came to the Two Lakes Trailhead.

Hawk along the bluffs

MILES AND DIRECTIONS

0.0 Start at the trailhead east of the general store and north of Boecher Lake.

0.09 Reach a fork. Bear left (north-east) to follow the Two Lakes Loop in a clockwise direction.

0.14 Bypass the side trails to your right (west) and to your left (east).

0.19 Reach an overlook of Bitter Creek to your left (east).

0.21 Bypass the Bubba's Cutoff connection to your left (east).

0.24 Reach the Vista Loop to your right (west). Bear left (east) to head to the Canyon Spur Trail.

0.32 Reach another fork. Continue straight (south) toward the Canyon Spur Trail.

0.36 Reach a fork. Stay on the left side of the fork (south) to continue the route.

0.43 Reach a junction. Continue straight onto the Lower Canyon Spur Trail.

0.58 Reach a fork. Bear right (south) to head toward the Switchback Trail.

0.65 Come to the Switchback Trail connection. Take the right side of the fork (south) to head onto the Switchback Trail. (A series of switchbacks occurs throughout this trail until the 2.86-mile mark.)

0.76 Reach an overlook to your left (east).

1.99 You will see a cave to your left (west).

2.04 Reach a fork. Bear right (south) to continue on the Switchback Trail. The trail eventually curves around and heads north in between switchbacks.

2.86 Reach a fork. Continue straight (north) on the Switchback Trail.

2.95 Cross a seasonal creek bed.

3.02 Reach a fork. Head left (southwest) to head back to the Lower Canyon Spur Trail.

3.09 Reach the Switchback Trail connection. Head right (north) to go back the way you came.

3.74 Arrive back at the trailhead.

HONORABLE MENTION
(RED CARPET COUNTRY, NORTHWEST OKLAHOMA)

Quiet waters of Middle Spring

A. **THREE SPRINGS TRAIL**

ROMAN NOSE STATE PARK

A relaxing stroll along trickling brooks and three echoing natural springs, the Three Springs Loop is one you should not bypass just because of its short length. It draws you into an unruffled canopy of eastern redcedar trees lingering over ethereal aquifers.

Start: Three Springs Trailhead, north of the CCC pavilion
Elevation gain: 1,444 to 1,477 feet
Distance: 0.29-mile loop
Difficulty: Easy
Hiking time: About 30 minutes
Seasons/schedule: Open year-round, sunrise to sunset
Fees and permits: None (subject to change)
Trail contacts: Roman Nose State Park Office & Lodge, 3236 S. Hwy. 8A, Watonga 73772; (580) 623-7281

Dog-friendly: Leashed dogs permitted
Trail surface: Dirt and rocky path
Land status: Oklahoma State Parks
Nearest town: Watonga
Other trail users: None
Maps: USGS Watonga Lake; Roman Nose State Park map (available online at www.travelok.com/state-parks and via the Oklahoma State Parks mobile app)

FINDING THE TRAILHEAD

Heading west on I-40 from downtown Oklahoma City, exit onto US 281 Spur W/US 66 (exit 108) a little after 43 miles. After 4.2 miles US 281 Spur W becomes US 281 N. After another 21 miles, US 281 N becomes OK 8 N/S Clarence Nash Boulevard. Turn left (north) onto OK 8A N after traveling on OK 8 N for 4.3 miles. After 3.5 miles, make a slight right (west) onto P10 Road and continue 0.2 mile toward the Big and Middle Springs. Parking is available in the parking lot east of the trailhead and CCC pavilion. After parking, walk toward the CCC pavilion. The trail begins north of the CCC pavilion. GPS: N35° 55.949' W98° 26.525'

GREAT PLAINS COUNTRY (SOUTHWEST OKLAHOMA)

SOUTHWEST OKLAHOMA is marked by arid landscape with the occasional body of water and cross-timber forest. Not as starkly different as northwest Oklahoma, it still is distinctive with its craggy granite mountains and drought-resistant greenery. Its lure mainly comes from the Wichita Mountains and the Quartz Mountain area. Both are composed of endless wilderness—havens for elk, hawks, lizards, and prairie dogs. They are also paradises for rappelers, providing fun challenges in extraordinary scenery. Southwest Oklahoma's narrow canyons, panoramic caves, waterfalls, and fascinating rock formations captivate visitors year-round.

Snow in the Wichita
Mountains (Hike 11)

7 WASHITA BATTLEFIELD PARK TRAIL

WASHITA BATTLEFIELD NATIONAL HISTORIC SITE

A relatively easy trail, the Washita Battlefield Park Trail is rich with history and culture. It pays homage to those who lost their lives in Lt. Col. George Armstrong Custer's attack on Chief Black Kettle's village and enriches trail users with accounts of what occurred in the area and along the Washita River.

Start: Washita Battlefield Park Trailhead, east of the parking lot (not the same as the visitor center parking lot; you will need to head farther west)

Elevation gain: 1,919 to 1,995 feet

Distance: 1.46-mile loop

Difficulty: Easy

Hiking time: About 1 hour

Seasons/schedule: Open year-round, 30 minutes before sunrise to 30 minutes after sunset; best during spring and fall

Fees and permits: None

Trail contacts: Washita Battlefield National Historic Site Visitor Center, 18555 Hwy. 47A, Ste. A, Cheyenne 73628; (580) 497-2742

Dog-friendly: No dogs allowed

Trail surface: Combination of paved, dirt, and mowed grass

Land status: National Park Service

Nearest town: Cheyenne

Other trail users: None

Maps: USGS Cheyenne; Washita Battlefield National Historic Site map (available online at www.nps.gov/waba/planyourvisit/maps.htm)

Special considerations: Areas surrounding and within this trail are considered sacred by the American Indian population. Please be respectful and do not venture off the trail.

The trail surface is not maintained during winter, so snow and ice are possible.

FINDING THE TRAILHEAD

From the US 283 intersection in Cheyenne, travel west on OK 47 for 0.9 mile. Turn right (north) on OK 47 Alt. You will pass the visitor center shared by the Black Kettle National Grassland and Washita Battlefield National Historic Site after 0.2 mile. Bear left (west) to stay on OK 47 Alt. After 1 mile, the parking lot to the trailhead is on your right (north). GPS: N35° 37.052' W99° 42.011'

THE HIKE

On a stark, wintry night in 1868, the Southern Cheyenne tribe in Chief Black Kettle's village near the Washita River was attacked without warning by Lt. Col. George Armstrong Custer and the 7th US Cavalry. More than 40 American Indians, including Chief Black Kettle and his wife, and 650 horses were killed that evening. The Washita Battlefield Park Trail takes you back to that fateful night and the atrocities that took place on this land.

Washita River

The Washita Battlefield Park Trail begins to the east of the trailhead's parking lot. There is an open structure housing historical information before you reach the trailhead. Fifteen points of interest are dispersed along the trail. (At time of publication, trail guides are planned to be available through the National Park System mobile app.) The trail begins with a paved surface and heads north into open grasslands.

You will encounter points of interest #1–#5 before reaching a fork at 0.33 mile. Places of note indicated by these markers include the escape routes of several American Indians, Custer's command post, and the site of Black Kettle's village. Once you reach the fork, continue straight (northwest) on the Lower Trail to start the loop. The right (east) side of the fork acts as a shortcut to the Upper Trail. (The Lower Trail does connect back with the Upper Trail.) Right before you reach the Washita River (point of interest #7 to your left [west] at the 0.61-mile mark), there is a tree adorned with American Indian prayer ties. These vibrant prayer ties are used in religious rites and are sacred to the American Indians. Please be respectful, and do not photograph the scene or touch the prayer ties. There are two benches to the left (west) beside the Washita River. The valley surrounding the Washita River was a refuge and gathering place for the Southern Plains tribes. Shielded from the harsh winds, it was also a wintering area where various tribes would get together to procure water and small game for food, as well as set up shelter and fire.

The path becomes a dirt surface after this point. Bear right (east) for a short distance before the trail heads south. At 0.93 mile, continue straight (southwest) to complete the loop and connect with the Upper Trail. Bear left (east) at 0.96 mile to continue on the Upper Trail. This is where the original fork you started the loop on is located. The trail returns to a paved surface and a forested area for a short distance. Mile mark 1.03 is another poignant point of interest (#12). This is the location where several hundred horses that belonged to the people of Black Kettle's village were slaughtered by Custer's troops. Prayer ties can also be seen on trees at this point. The trail returns to a dirt surface and then leads to log steps heading back into open grassland at 1.06 miles. At 1.1 miles, you reach a dead end. Bear right (west); the trail then begins to wind south. You reach several more points of interest before the trail returns to a paved surface at 1.41 miles, where there is a gate and a red granite trailhead marker. Reach the trailhead and complete the trail at 1.46 miles.

WASHITA BATTLEFIELD PARK TRAIL, WASHITA BATTLEFIELD NATIONAL HISTORIC SITE

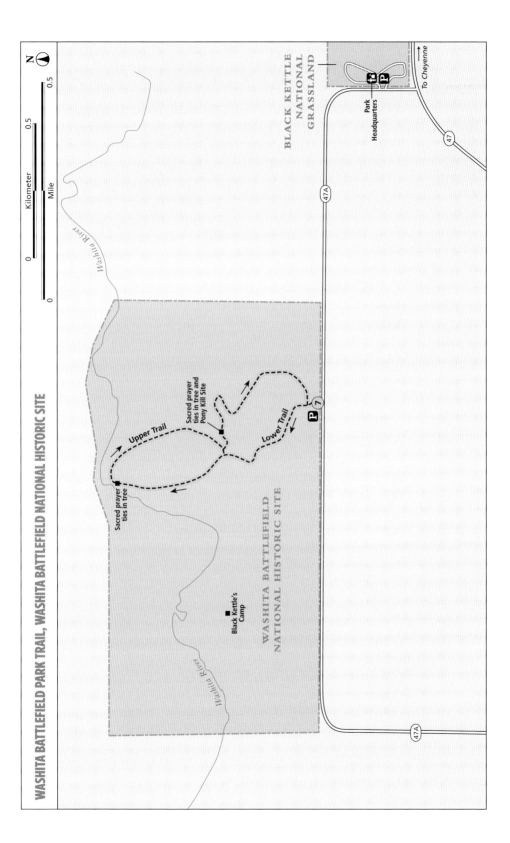

MILES AND DIRECTIONS

0.0 Start at the trailhead to the east of the parking lot.

0.33 Reach a fork. Continue straight (northwest) on the Lower Trail.

0.58 Come to sacred prayer ties on the trees from local American Indians. Do not touch the prayer ties or photograph the scene.

0.61 Arrive at the Washita River, to your left (west).

0.62 The path becomes a dirt surface.

0.93 Continue straight (southwest) to connect back with the Upper Trail.

0.96 Reach the Upper Trail. Veer left (east). The path returns to a paved surface for a short period.

1.03 The path turns back to a dirt surface.

1.06 Go up the log steps.

1.1 Reach a dead end. Veer right (west).

1.41 Head south, back toward the trailhead.

1.46 Arrive back at the trailhead.

8 BALDY POINT TRAIL

QUARTZ MOUNTAIN STATE PARK

Popular for its rock rappelling opportunities, Baldy Point is more than just a climber's haven. Hikers can enjoy winding around its south and eastern verges before heading up an overlook and taking in the views of the encompassing woodland valleys below.

Start: Baldy Point Trailhead, east of the Baldy Point Area parking lot
Elevation gain: 1,536 to 1,804 feet
Distance: 1.58 miles out and back
Difficulty: Easy to moderate due to ascending, narrow paths along the face of Baldy Point
Hiking time: 1–2 hours
Seasons/schedule: Open year-round, sunrise to sunset (strictly enforced)
Fees and permits: Parking pass required for day-use visitors
Trail contacts: Quartz Mountain State Park Office, 43393 Scissortail Rd., Lone Wolf 73655; (580) 563-2238. *Note:* At time of publication, a new office location within the park is being considered.
Dog-friendly: Leashed dogs permitted
Trail surface: Dirt and rocky path, becomes gravel and trodden grass on Cedar Creek Trail portion

Land status: Oklahoma State Parks
Nearest town: Hobart to the north, Altus to the south
Other trail users: Rock climbers
Maps: USGS Lake Altus; Quartz Mountain State Park maps (available online at www.travelok.com/state-parks and via the Oklahoma State Parks mobile app)
Special considerations: Portions of Baldy Point are private property. Some unofficial maps and trail guides indicate that the Baldy Point Trail is a loop; however, this would include trespassing on private property. Baldy Point Trail is an out and back trail. Once you stop at the overlook on Baldy Point, turn back the way you came.
  Rattlesnakes may be present on this trail from spring to the beginning of fall.

FINDING THE TRAILHEAD

From the US 138 and OK 9 intersection in Hobart, head west for 10 miles on OK 9 until you reach OK 44. Head south on OK 44 for 9.7 miles and then turn right (north) on OK 44A. After traveling 1.5 miles on OK 44A, turn left (west) at the fork onto E CR 1470. At the 0.7-mile mark on E CR 1470, the road becomes E CR 1465. Continue another 1.4 miles before turning right (north) on N2040 Road. Travel 0.5 mile on N2040 Road, and then turn right (east) onto E CR 1460. Continue on E CR 1460 for 0.3 mile. The road veers to the south and then back east before reaching the Baldy Point Area parking lot. GPS: N34° 53.867' W99° 20.047'

THE HIKE

Baldy Point is one of the many granite peaks that make up the Wichita Mountain Range in western Oklahoma. With its grand height and being surrounded by diverse forests and a wooded valley, it offers several rock climbing, hiking, and wildlife viewing opportunities. The Baldy Point Trail begins east of the Baldy Point area parking lot. You head left (north) toward Baldy Point. Heading right (south) leads to the Mesquite Forest Trail.

Wooded area around Baldy Point

Shortly after, the entrance to the Summit Trail is to your left (west). Bear right (east). Starting from this point and all around Baldy Point, there will be several diversions to the left (north and northeast) of the path. These are areas for climbers to reach the base of Baldy Point.

At 0.08 mile, pass a shortcut to the Mesquite Forest Trail to your right (south). Continue straight (east). Cross a small footbridge and then encounter the Mesquite Forest

Top: Cedar Valley
Bottom left and right: Views from Baldy Point Trail

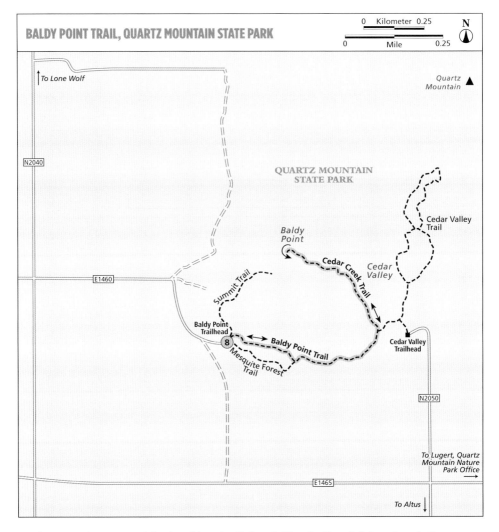

0   Kilometer 0.25

0   Mile   0.25

N

To Lone Wolf

Quartz
Mountain

N2040

QUARTZ MOUNTAIN
STATE PARK

Cedar Valley
Trail

Baldy
Point

E1460

Summit Trail

Cedar Creek Trail

Cedar
Valley

Baldy Point
Trailhead

8

Baldy Point Trail

Cedar Valley
Trailhead

Mesquite Forest
Trail

N2050

To Lugert, Quartz
Mountain Nature
Park Office
→

E1465

To Altus

Trail once again to your right (south) at the fork at 0.19 mile. Bear left (northeast). Cross
an old dead-end path before bearing left (north). The trail starts to wind in a southeast
direction. You cross a small seasonal creek bed at 0.44 mile before reaching a fork for the
Cedar Creek and the Cedar Valley Trails. Continue straight (north) on the Cedar Creek
Trail.

The Cedar Creek Trail segment narrows and starts to head northwest. You enter Cedar
Valley, with sweeping views of Quartz Mountain that continue all the way to the Baldy
Point overlook. You will have to step down off a large rock at the 0.58-mile mark. At
0.61 mile, there is a large boulder to your left (south) and evidence of a previous fire, as
you are surrounded by burnt timbers. Shortly after, reach a fork in the road that connects
with the Black Jack Pass Trail. Elevation at this point is 1,640 feet above sea level. Continue straight (west) up the face of the rock. Follow the gravel and trodden-grass surfaces
that wind to the left (south) of the large slabs of rock. Ascend several large slabs of rock
for a short distance before the trail surface interchanges between gravel and trodden grass.

At 0.79 mile, you reach an overlook. This is also the turnaround point. You will see a short lollipop route to your left (southeast) that will provide a more aerial, but not necessarily better, vantage point. Do not go past that point—you would be venturing onto private property. There are views of the Summit Trail and farmland to the west and portions of Baldy Point to the south. Elevation at this point is close to 1,800 feet. Once you have immersed yourself in the grand view, head back the way you came.

MILES AND DIRECTIONS

0.0   Start at the trailhead east of the Baldy Point area parking lot.

0.02 The Summit Trail entrance is to your left (west). Bear right (east).

0.08 Bypass the shortcut to the Mesquite Forest Trail to your right (south). Continue straight (east).

0.09 Cross a small footbridge.

0.19 Reach the Mesquite Forest Trail connection to your right (south). Bear left (northeast).

0.46 Reach a fork. The Cedar Valley Trail is to your right (east). Continue straight (north) on the Cedar Creek Trail.

0.62 Reach a fork in the path that connects to the Black Jack Pass Trail. Continue straight (west), up the face of the rock.

0.79 Come to an overlook of the Summit Trail, with farmland to the west and Baldy Point to the south. Head back the way you came.

1.58 Arrive back at the trailhead.

9 SUMMIT TRAIL (VIA CEDAR VALLEY TRAILHEAD)

QUARTZ MOUNTAIN STATE PARK

The Summit Trail traverses up the western face of Baldy Point. Before the ascent, the trail winds through a valley of large boulders, offering an experience as though you are wandering where ancient deities once dwelled. Accessing the Summit Trail from the Cedar Valley Trailhead allows you to enjoy Cedar Valley and the Mesquite Forest area as well.

Start: Cedar Valley Trailhead, north of the Cedar Valley area parking area

Elevation gain: 1,536 to 1,706 feet

Distance: 2.21 miles out and back with an additional loop

Difficulty: Moderate to difficult due to steep ascent and descent on Baldy Point

Hiking time: 1–2 hours

Seasons/schedule: Open year-round, sunrise to sunset (strictly enforced)

Fees and permits: Parking pass required for day-use visitors

Trail contacts: Quartz Mountain State Park Office, 43393 Scissortail Rd., Lone Wolf 73655; (580) 563-2238. *Note:* At time of publication, a new office location within the park is being considered.

Dog-friendly: Leashed dogs permitted

Trail surface: Dirt and rocky path

Land status: Oklahoma State Parks

Nearest town: Hobart to the north, Altus to the south

Other trail users: Rock climbers

Maps: USGS Lake Altus; Quartz Mountain State Park maps (available online at www.travelok.com/state-parks and via the Oklahoma State Parks mobile app)

Special considerations: This route begins with the Cedar Valley Trail and then takes the Baldy Point Trail for a short distance before connecting with the Mesquite Forest Trail. The Mesquite Forest Trail then connects to the Summit Trail. After coming back from the Summit Trail, this route leads you back on the Mesquite Forest Trail and then back to the Cedar Valley Trailhead without hiking the Cedar Valley Trail again. This route does not include the Cedar Creek Trail (not to be confused with the Cedar Valley Trail).

Rattlesnakes may be present on this trail from spring to the beginning of fall.

FINDING THE TRAILHEAD

From the US 138 and OK 9 intersection in Hobart, head west for 10 miles on OK 9 until you reach OK 44. Head south on OK 44 for 9.7 miles and then turn right (north) on OK 44A. After traveling 1.5 miles on OK 44A, turn left (west) on E CR 1470 for 0.7 mile. E CR 1470 becomes E1465 Road. Continue on E1465 Road for 0.4 mile before turning right (north) on N2050 Road to head into Cedar Valley. After another 0.4 mile you will reach the parking lot for the Cedar Valley area trailhead. GPS: N34° 53.883′ W99° 19.570′

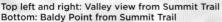
Top left and right: Valley view from Summit Trail
Bottom: Baldy Point from Summit Trail

THE HIKE

The Quartz Mountain area is popular for its granite peaks; however, it is also a remarkable place to encounter diverse vegetation, forests, wildlife, and terrain. The Summit Trail is accessible via the Baldy Point Trailhead. However, accessing the Summit Trail via the Cedar Valley Trailhead provides the geographical variety the Quartz Mountain area has to offer. The Summit Trail also covers the western side of Baldy Point.

The entrance to the Cedar Valley Trail is 0.02 mile from the Cedar Valley Trailhead. Bear right (north) to continue on the Cedar Valley Trail loop. This portion provides great panoramic views of Cedar Valley, Quartz Mountain, and Baldy Point. You reach a fork at 0.04 mile that serves as an exit for the Cedar Valley Trail loop. Continue straight (north). There is a shortcut at the 0.12-mile mark. Bear right (northeast). Enjoy the silence as you circle the valley with the mountains surrounding you. There is another fork in the trail at 0.3 mile. Continue straight (west). To the right (north) of the fork is an unofficial trail to the rocks. Continue straight (south) past the shortcut you encountered at the 0.12-mile mark. At 0.57 mile, bear right (southwest) at the original fork where you entered the Cedar Valley Trail. Then at 0.6 mile, bear right (west) to exit Cedar Valley. Head toward the Baldy Point Trail and Cedar Creek Trail junction at 0.66 mile.

From the junction, head left (south) on Baldy Point Trail. You cross a small seasonal creek bed shortly after. From this point to the Mesquite Forest Trail fork, there will be diversions on your right (north and northwest) for rock climbers to access the face of Baldy Point. The path surface also changes to gravel with unearthed tree roots. At 0.92 mile you cross an old, dead-end path. The fork for the Mesquite Forest Trail appears shortly after. Bear left (south) to follow the Mesquite Forest Trail.

The Mesquite Forest Trail starts to wind west at 0.96 mile. At 1.06 miles, there is a bench to your left (south) and a path connecting back to the Baldy Point Trail on your right (north). Continue straight (west). Take note of the mesquite, eastern redcedar, and hackberry trees as you wander through this area.

The Baldy Point area parking lot is to your left (west) at 1.12 miles. Bear right (north) and then reach the Summit Trail entrance at the left (northwest) side of the fork. The Summit Trail starts off with a narrow, trodden-grass surface and winds northwest through giant boulders before opening into a valley. Enjoy the view as the trail winds around the south side of the face of Baldy Point at 1.17 miles. The trail curves to the right (north) and turns to a gravel surface. The valley that surrounds you is quite impressive. Large boulders seemingly appear strewn here and there and piled atop one another. The scenery creates an aura as though you are walking on land where ancient deities roamed.

At the 1.25-mile mark, you cross a large slab of rock and head east. Shortly after, you go in between large boulders and then over another large slab of rock. Bear left (north) toward the gravel path again. The trail starts a steep ascent at 1.35 miles as you bear right (northeast) up the face of Baldy Point. The elevation ascends from 637 to 1,693 feet above sea level when you reach a vantage point around 1.4 miles. The path surface interchanges between gravel and trodden grass, dotted with prickly pear cactus. You do not have to go all the way up to the vantage point, but it is strongly advised not to ascend any higher, as it leads onto private property. Head back the way you came via the Mesquite Forest Trail, bypassing the Cedar Valley Trail.

MILES AND DIRECTIONS

0.0   Start at the trailhead north of the Cedar Valley area parking lot.

0.02 Reach a fork. Bear right (north) to continue on the Cedar Valley Trail.

0.04 Reach another fork. Continue straight (north).

0.12 Bear right (northeast) to bypass the shortcut.

0.24 Bear left (north).

0.3   Reach a fork. Continue straight (west).

0.49 Continue straight (south) past the previous shortcut route from the 0.12-mile mark.

0.57 Reach the original fork that included the entrance to the Cedar Valley Trail. Bear right (southwest).

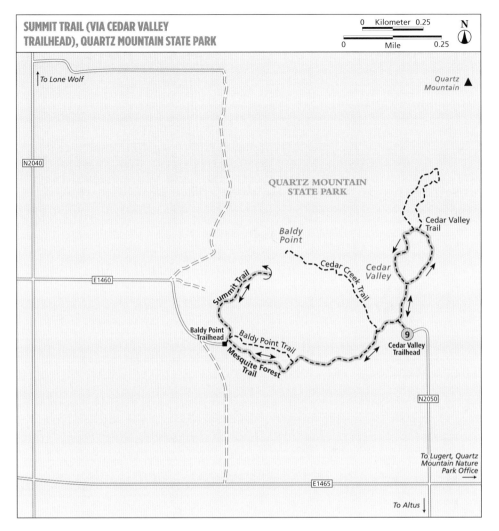

0.6 Bear right (west) to exit Cedar Valley and head toward the Baldy Point and Cedar Creek Trail junction.

0.66 Reach the Baldy Point and Cedar Creek Trail junction. Head left (south) on the Baldy Point Trail.

0.92 Bear left (south) for the Mesquite Forest Trail.

1.06 A path connecting back to the Baldy Point Trail is to your right (north). Continue straight (west) on the Mesquite Forest Trail.

1.12 Reach the Baldy Point area parking lot to your left (west). Continue on the trail by bearing right (north).

1.13 Reach the Summit Trail entrance at the left (northwest) side of the fork.

1.35 The trail begins a steep ascent. Bear right (northeast) up the face of Baldy Point.

1.4 Reach a vantage point. Head back the way you came via the Mesquite Forest Trail, bypassing the Cedar Valley Trail.

2.21 Arrive back at the trailhead.

10 LIGHT BLUE TRAIL (WEST AREA OF GRANITE HILLS TRAIL SYSTEM)

GREAT PLAINS STATE PARK

The Granite Hills Trail System lures hikers and mountain bikers alike with its rugged terrain and panoramic views of Tom Steed Reservoir. The Light Blue Trail, a recent addition to the route, lies in the western portion of the Granite Hills. It offers a good mix of rocky hills, dense forest, and lake views.

Start: Light Blue Trailhead
Elevation gain: 1,394 to 1,516 feet
Distance: 1.93-mile lollipop
Difficulty: Moderate due to uneven, rocky surfaces
Hiking time: 1.5–2 hours
Seasons/schedule: Open year-round, sunrise to sunset
Fees and permits: Parking pass required for day-use visitors
Trail contacts: Great Plains State Park Office, 22487 E 1566 Rd., Mountain Park 73559; (580) 569-2032
Dog-friendly: Leashed dogs permitted
Trail surface: Dirt and rocky path

Land status: Oklahoma State Parks
Nearest town: Snyder to the south, Roosevelt to the north
Other trail users: Mountain bikers
Maps: USGS Snyder; Great Plains State Park map (available online at www.travelok.com/state-parks and via the Oklahoma State Parks mobile app)
Special considerations: This lollipop trail connects with the Central Area of the Granite Hills Trail System (Light Green Trail and Green Trail).
Mountains bikers also use this trail. The path tends to get narrow; be courteous and yield to passersby.

FINDING THE TRAILHEAD

From the I-44 and US 62 junction in Lawton, head west for a little less than 33 miles on US 62. Turn right on US 138 N and continue 6.2 miles before turning left (west) on E1580 Road. You will see a huge sign indicating the Great Plains State Park entrance. Go 2 miles on E1580 Road before turning right (north) on N2440 Road. Continue 1.3 miles on N2440 Road to a small parking area next to the trailhead, on your right (east). GPS: N34° 44.565' W98° 59.165'

THE HIKE

The Granite Hills region of Great Plains State Park boasts several water sources, rocky mountains to climb and hike, and the historic Gold Bells Mill and Mine. Located within the Wichita Mountain Range, the Granite Hills Trail System navigates the diverse topography that makes southwestern Oklahoma so popular.

The Light Blue Trail begins in a forested area, with Tom Steed Reservoir and Snyder Lake behind you. There is a fork shortly after the entrance; bear right (south). The path on the other side is your return path. The view opens to arid grassland before you start to traverse over rocks at 0.1 mile. The trail then winds along the rocky path as views of Granite Mountain greet you to the right (west). Bear right (west) at 0.25 mile into the

trail. Views of Snyder Lake are on full display at 0.32 mile, and eventually you will cross over a couple of large rock slabs. You will see a Department of Interior marker in the ground shortly after. The trail starts to head south. At the rock cluster at 0.47 mile, bear right (west) before heading south again. The Mountain Park Dam is visible to your right (west) at 0.55 mile. A fallen tree branch might still be in the path. At 0.67 mile, bear left (west).

At 0.7 mile you will see Ranch Road as you face west. Follow the arrow on the post to head left (south). Stay on the grassy shoulder of the road and be aware of vehicles. After continuing for another 0.05 mile, bear left (southeast) uphill between two large rocks. It will be a wide grassy path with views of Snyder Lake showing up again to your right (west). Bear left (east) at 0.77 mile, and then bear left (north) at 1.02 miles to head back into the forested area. The trail interchanges between a rocky surface and dirt path after the 1.1-mile mark. Cross a small seasonal creek bed at 1.15 miles, possibly encountering a fallen tree trunk shortly after. The trail starts to wind and heads east again. The trail winds north at 1.32 miles, and you will cross a small creek bed once more. Pass over some wooden planks as the trail heads west at 1.37 miles. This area can get muddy after a decent rainfall.

As the path winds north at 1.4 miles, it returns to a rocky surface and you traverse through another forested area for a short period. Once you exit the forested area, bear right (east) and begin a slight rocky ascent of 60 feet in elevation. From this point the trail continues north back to the trailhead. At 1.7 miles the trail tops out and a grand view of Tom Steed Reservoir is right in front of you. The trail winds through a forested area for one last time at 1.84 miles. At 1.87 miles you encounter the initial fork you came to when you started the trail. The path that goes uphill to your right (northeast) heads into the Central Area of the Granite Hills Trail System. Continue straight, back to the trailhead to complete the lollipop portion of the trail at 1.94 miles.

Quiet moments on Tom Steed Reservoir

MILES AND DIRECTIONS

0.0 Start at the trailhead.

0.06 Reach a fork. Bear right (south).

0.17 Enjoy views of Granite Mountain to your right (west).

0.32 Come to views of Snyder Lake.

0.35 Reach the Department of Interior marker in the ground.

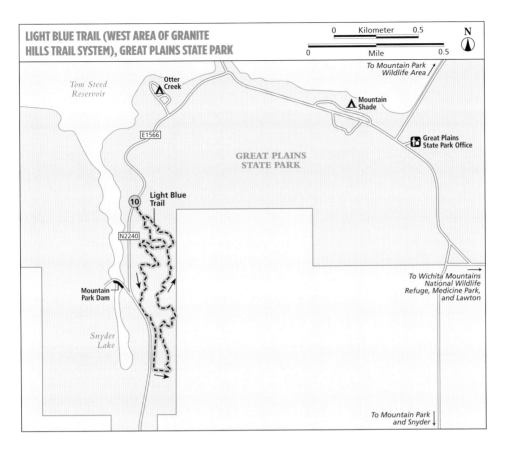

0   Kilometer   0.5

N

0   Mile   0.5

Tom Steed Reservoir

Otter Creek

To Mountain Park Wildlife Area

Mountain Shade

E1566

GREAT PLAINS STATE PARK

Great Plains State Park Office

Light Blue Trail

10

N2240

Mountain Park Dam

To Wichita Mountains National Wildlife Refuge, Medicine Park, and Lawton

Snyder Lake

To Mountain Park and Snyder

0.47 Come to a rock cluster. Bear right (west).

0.55 The Mountain Park Dam is to your right (west).

0.7 Approach Ranch Road to the west. Follow the arrow on the post to head left (south). Stay on the road's grassy shoulder.

0.75 Bear left (southeast) uphill between two large rocks.

1.15 Cross a small seasonal creek bed.

1.33 Cross another small seasonal creek bed.

1.37 Cross over some wooden planks. This area can get muddy.

1.7 The path flattens out after an ascent of 60 feet in elevation. Views of Tom Steed Reservoir are to the north.

1.87 Reach the fork from the 0.06-mile mark. Head straight back toward the trailhead.

1.94 Arrive back at the trailhead.

11 ELK MOUNTAIN TRAIL

WICHITA MOUNTAINS NATIONAL WILDLIFE REFUGE

Standing 2,270 feet above sea level, Elk Mountain provides hikers and climbers up-close experiences of oak and cedar forest, granite rock, and wildlife. The scenic Elk Mountain Trail leads you up one of the tallest features in the Wichita Mountains for a spectacular view.

Start: Elk Mountain/Charon's Garden Wilderness North Entrance Trailhead
Elevation gain: 1,641 to 2,219 feet
Distance: 2.44 miles out and back
Difficulty: Difficult due to steep inclines and uneven terrain
Hiking time: 1–2 hours
Seasons/schedule: Open year-round
Fees and permits: None
Trail contacts: Wichita Mountains National Wildlife Refuge Headquarters, 32 Refuge Headquarters, Indiahoma 73552; (580) 429-3222
Dog-friendly: Leashed dogs permitted
Trail surface: Dirt, gravel, and rocky path

Land status: US Fish and Wildlife Service
Nearest town: Medicine Park
Other trail users: Rappelers; no cyclists allowed
Maps: USGS Quanah Mountain; Wichita Mountains National Wildlife Refuge maps (available online at www.fws.gov/refuge/Wichita_ Mountains/maps.html)
Special considerations: Portions of this trail may be difficult to follow. Look ahead for areas with red dirt and gravel, which are usually where the trail continues.
There is no shade on this trail during summer. Make sure to bring adequate water.

FINDING THE TRAILHEAD

Heading south from Oklahoma City on I-44, take exit 45 to continue toward Wichita Mountains Wildlife Refuge on OK 49 W. Continue on OK 49 W for 20.3 miles to reach Indiahoma Road, on your left (south). Continue on OK 49 W for another 0.3 mile. You will see signage to turn onto the road toward Elk Mountain to your left (south). Travel 0.4 mile to the second parking lot. The trailhead to Elk Mountain begins at the bridge over Sunset Pool and Headquarters Creek. GPS: N34° 43.906' W98° 43.411'

THE HIKE

Its granite mountain ranges are what makes the Wichita Mountains so popular in Oklahoma. Elk Mountain is part of this system and provides year-round enjoyment for its scenery and topographical diversity. The Elk Mountain Trail allows you to summit Elk Mountain and take in grand, aerial views from the top. Hikers also have the chance to encounter gentle white-tailed deer, vibrant eastern collared lizards, soaring hawks, and other wildlife on the Elk Mountain Trail.

The Elk Mountain Trail begins at the bridge spanning Sunset Pool and Headquarters Creek. You then ascend some rocky steps, and the trail surface interchanges between

Top: Male white-tailed deer camouflaged with the scenery
Bottom left: Small waterfall stream
Bottom right: Wichita Mountains overlook

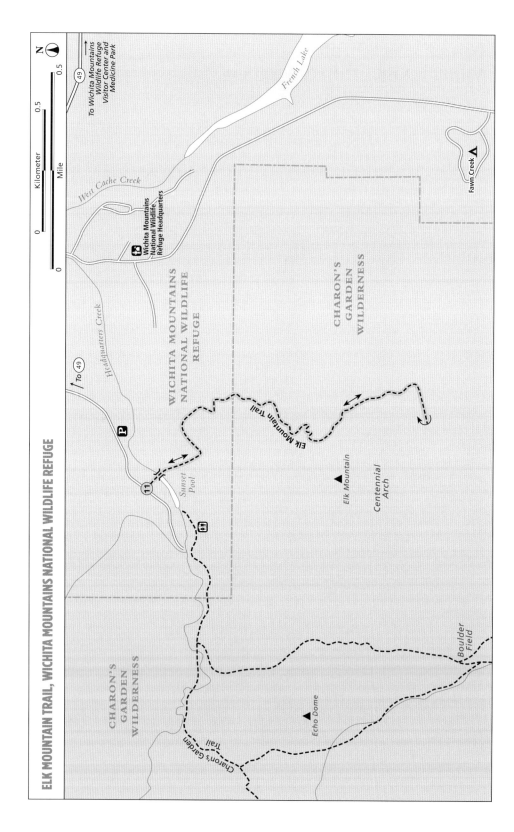

ELK MOUNTAIN TRAIL, WICHITA MOUNTAINS NATIONAL WILDLIFE REFUGE

To Wichita Mountains
Wildlife Refuge
Visitor Center and
Medicine Park

N

Kilometer

Mile

French Lake

Fawn Creek

West Cache Creek

Wichita Mountains
National Wildlife
Refuge Headquarters

WICHITA MOUNTAINS
NATIONAL WILDLIFE
REFUGE

CHARON'S
GARDEN
WILDERNESS

Headquarters Creek

To 49

P

11

Sunset
Pool

Elk Mountain Trail

Elk Mountain

Centennial
Arch

CHARON'S
GARDEN
WILDERNESS

Charon's Garden
Trail

Echo Dome

Boulder
Field

large rocks and a dirt path for the rest of the way up Elk Mountain. At 0.11 mile a small waterfall, stream, and view of Elk Mountain greet you to your right (west). Enter a forested area for a brief period before heading east at 0.15 mile. There is an unofficial trail to your right (south).

Overlooks of the Wichita Mountains are at the 0.24- and 0.35-mile marks. At 0.37 mile you reach a large boulder. Bear to the right (south). From this point there are several trail offshoots. Look ahead for the red-dirt path to be your guide when crossing the large slabs of rock, especially at 0.46 mile, where there is a diversion to your right (west). If you are heading south, you are going in the right direction. There are large slabs of rock, followed by rocky steps, then large slabs of rock again just short of 0.5 mile into the trail.

At 0.7 mile, veer right (west) to wind up the mountain from a westerly to a southerly direction. Reach another forested area at 0.78 mile. As this is the only area where there is adequate shade on the trail, feel free to rest here during the summer months. Before the forested area ends at 0.89 mile, head east up the rocky steps. Shortly after that, bear right (south), continuing up the face of Elk Mountain. At 1.06 miles, the trail levels out to a clearing offering panoramic views of the Wichita Mountains to your left (east).

Cross another large cluster of rocks at 1.08 miles, and at 1.1 miles reach the crest of Elk Mountain. Straight ahead (south) is a vista. You can turn back at this point. However, for a view of the Charon's Garden Wilderness Area, go right (west). Continue west until you reach a rock outcrop overlook at 1.2 miles. From this point you can see the east side of Charon's Garden Wilderness. After taking in the beautiful view, head back the way you came.

MILES AND DIRECTIONS

0.0   Start at the trailhead at the bridge.

0.11   Views of Elk Mountain appear to your right (west) along with a small seasonal waterfall and stream.

0.13   Reach a forested area.

0.24   Come to an overlook.

0.35   Reach another overlook.

0.37   Stay to the right (south) side of a large boulder.

0.7   Bear right (west), winding up the mountain from west to south.

0.78   Reach another forested area and then veer east up the rocky steps.

0.89   The forested area ends. Bear right (south).

1.06   The path levels out to a vista of the Wichita Mountains Wildlife Refuge to your left (east).

1.1   Reach the crest of Elk Mountain. Straight ahead (south) is an overlook. Bear right (west).

1.2   Reach a rock outcrop with an overlook of the east side of Charon's Garden Wilderness. Head back the way you came.

2.44   Arrive back at the trailhead.

12 POST OAK FALLS TRAIL

WICHITA MOUNTAINS NATIONAL WILDLIFE REFUGE

Post Oak Falls can be quite a gem after a decent rainfall, especially in the summer months, when the arid environment of the Wichita Mountains could use some relief from the heat. Surrounded by a serene pond, this small yet picturesque waterfall can be accessed by a short hike through the Charon's Garden Wilderness Area.

Start: Charon's Garden Wilderness south entrance/Post Oak Falls Trailhead in Spanish Canyon

Elevation gain: 1,444 to 1,604 feet

Distance: 1.28 miles out and back

Difficulty: Easy to moderate due to rocky ascents

Hiking time: 0.5–1 hour

Seasons/schedule: Open year-round; best after a rainfall

Fees and permits: None

Trail contacts: Wichita Mountains National Wildlife Refuge Headquarters, 32 Refuge Headquarters, Indiahoma 73552; (580) 429-3222

Dog-friendly: Leashed dogs permitted

Trail surface: Dirt and rocky path; two stream crossings

Land status: US Fish and Wildlife Service

Nearest town: Medicine Park

Other trail users: Rappelers; no cyclists allowed

Maps: USGS Quanah Mountain; Wichita Mountains National Wildlife Refuge maps (available online at www.fws.gov/refuge/Wichita _Mountains/maps.html)

Special considerations: Portions of this trail divert into several routes, but all eventually converge into the same trail near Post Oak Falls.
 There is no shade on this trail except at the waterfall. Make sure to bring adequate water.

FINDING THE TRAILHEAD

Heading south from Oklahoma City on I-44, take exit 45 to continue toward Wichita Mountains Wildlife Refuge on OK 49 W. Continue on OK 49 W for 20.3 miles to reach Indiahoma Road on your left (south). Signs for the Wichita Mountains Wildlife Refuge Headquarters and French Lake indicate where to turn. Continue on Indiahoma Road for 4.9 miles to the entrance for the Spanish Canyon/ Treasure Lake parking lot, on the right (north). Travel 0.4 mile to the parking lot. The trailhead for Post Oak Falls is the same as the trailhead for the Charon's Garden Wilderness south entrance, at the northern end of the parking lot. GPS: N34° 42.404' W98° 43.993'

THE HIKE

Whenever a decent rainfall showers on the dry, desert-like landscape of the Wichita Mountains, Post Oak Falls comes to life. Hidden in the crevices of Spanish Canyon in the Charon's Garden Wilderness Area, Post Oak Falls is a small yet stunning waterfall. It also features a tranquil pond—a sanctuary from the summer heat.

Post Oak Falls

Post Oak Falls can be accessed from the trailhead at the northern end of the Spanish Canyon/Treasure Lake parking lot. The path has a dirt surface until you reach the 0.08-mile mark, where you scramble up some large rocks. Stay to the left (west) to stay on track. At 0.34 mile, you reach a fork. Take the path farthest to the right. From here on out until you encounter the Post Oak Falls sign, there will be several split-offs from the path. All paths eventually converge. There is another fork at 0.36 mile. Again, keep to the right, and then keep to the left when you reach another fork at 0.4 mile. Cross a seasonal creek bed and reach more rocks to scramble at 0.45 mile before descending into a valley. A little after 0.5 mile, you reach an intersection of paths once again. Continue straight (north).

A sign directs you to Post Oak Falls at the 0.56-mile mark. Bear right (east) and walk across the rocky creek bed. Exercise caution—the rocks can be slippery. After the stream, the trail converts to a grassy path. Cross another rocky creek bed at 0.62 mile. Post Oak Falls becomes evident at 0.64 mile. After basking in the view, return the way you came.

MILES AND DIRECTIONS

0.0   Start at the trailhead at the northern end of the Spanish Canyon/Treasure Lake parking lot.

0.08 Scramble up the rocks and stay to the left (west).

0.34 Reach a fork. Take the path farthest to the right. All paths eventually converge.

Charon's Garden Wilderness Area

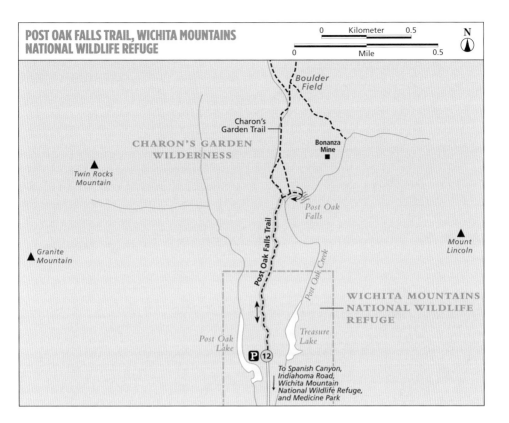

0.36 Reach another fork. Stay to the right.

0.4 Reach another fork. Stay to the left.

0.45 Cross a seasonal creek bed and reach more rocks to scramble.

0.51 Reach a junction. Continue straight (north).

0.56 Come to signage for Post Oak Falls. Bear right (east) and walk across the rocky creek bed. Exercise caution—the rocks can be slippery.

0.62 Cross another rocky creek bed.

0.64 Reach Post Oak Falls. Return the way you came.

1.28 Arrive back at the trailhead.

13 **KITE TRAIL**

WICHITA MOUNTAINS NATIONAL WILDLIFE REFUGE

The Kite Trail provides a variety in terrain as it traverses the narrows and also leads you around Lost Lake. The main draw of the Kite Trail, however, is its convenient access to vistas of Forty Foot Hole—a small yet spectacular feat of nature flowing down into the canyon.

Start: Kite Trailhead, west of the Boulder picnic area
Elevation gain: 1,417 to 1,562 feet
Distance: 2.27 miles out and back
Difficulty: Easy
Hiking time: 1–2 hours
Seasons/schedule: Open year-round
Fees and permits: None
Trail contacts: Wichita Mountains National Wildlife Refuge Headquarters, 32 Refuge Headquarters, Indiahoma 73552; (580) 429-3222
Dog-friendly: Leashed dogs permitted
Trail surface: Dirt, gravel, and rocky path
Land status: US Fish and Wildlife Service
Nearest town: Medicine Park

Other trail users: Rappelers; no cyclists allowed
Maps: USGS Quanah Mountain; Wichita Mountains National Wildlife Refuge maps (available online at www.fws.gov/refuge/Wichita_Mountains/maps.html)
Special considerations: There are several side trails, especially near the outlooks for West Cache Creek and Forty Foot Hole. Look ahead for areas with gravel, as these are usually where the trail continues. For help with navigation, the trail heads north short of 1.0 mile at Lost Lake and then heads east.
   There is no shade on this hike during summer. Make sure to bring adequate water.
   Markers with a white kite symbol serve as trail markers.

FINDING THE TRAILHEAD
Heading south from Oklahoma City on I-44, take exit 45 to continue toward Wichita Mountains National Wildlife Refuge on OK 49 W. Continue on OK 49 W for 18.3 miles; signs on your left (south) indicate to turn onto the road to Lost Lake. Continue 2.5 miles to the Boulder picnic area. The Kite Trailhead is to the west. GPS: N34° 42.071′ W98° 40.798′

THE HIKE
Not as tall in stature as its neighbor, Post Oak Falls, Forty Foot Hole is still a stunning panoramic sight to behold. This petite waterfall streams over several rock features into West Cache Creek and can be seen from different vantage points on the beginning portion of the Kite Trail. The Kite Trail can be accessed from either the Boulder picnic area or the Lost Lake picnic area. This trail description begins at the Boulder picnic area for quicker access to the Forty Foot Hole vista. There are a couple of diversions through the prairie to your left (west) before you reach the log steps at 0.11 mile. Views of West Cache Creek open up at this point as well. At 0.18 mile, you will scramble up some large

Top left: View at West Cache Creek
Top right: Forty Foot Hole
Bottom: Lost Lake

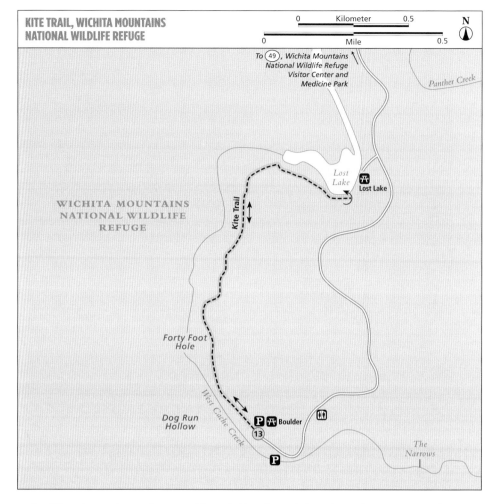

rocks. There is another rocky scramble at 0.29 mile, and then the path returns to a dirt surface.

Vistas of Forty Foot Hole begin at the 0.4-mile mark. Farther away from Forty Foot Hole, you will have panoramic views of West Cache Creek as well. There are several offshoots to vista points until the 0.45-mile mark, where the trail can become a bit overgrown. Head north up a rocky hillside at 0.53 mile. The path then levels out to a dirt surface and opens up to a valley shortly after. At 0.66 mile, continue straight (north) over the rocks and a seasonal creek bed. An overlook of the valley is to your left (west).

Cross another large rocky surface at 0.82 mile before reaching a vista for Lost Lake, to the north at 0.9 mile. Continue to bear right (east), winding along the east side of Lost Lake. Views of Lost Lake will be to your left (north). Be aware of the large stepdown at the 0.94-mile mark. The path surface becomes rocky again about 1.0 mile in, and there are various routes to descend back to the dirt trail. Follow the trail markers with the white kite symbol. Large rocks start to line the path, which will lead you to the Lost Lake picnic area at 1.14 miles. When you reach the Lost Lake picnic area, turn around and head back the way you came from the Boulder picnic area.

MILES AND DIRECTIONS

0.0   Start at the trailhead west of the Boulder picnic area.

0.11 Go up the log steps; views of West Cache Creek are to your left (west).

0.18 Scramble up the rocks. An overlook of West Cache Creek is to your left (west).

0.29 Start another rocky scramble.

0.4   Come to overlooks of Forty Foot Hole to your left (west).

0.53 The trail ascends north up a rocky hillside.

0.66 Reach an overlook to your left (west). Continue straight (north) over some rocks and a seasonal creek bed.

0.82 Cross over large slabs of rock.

0.9   To the north is an overlook for Lost Lake. Bear right (east).

1.04 The path turns rocky and starts to descend.

1.14 Reach the Lost Lake picnic area. Turn around and head back the way you came.

2.27 Arrive back at the trailhead.

14 JED JOHNSON TOWER TRAIL (INCLUDING CENTRAL PEAK VISTA)

WICHITA MOUNTAINS NATIONAL WILDLIFE REFUGE

The photo-worthy scene of the 60-foot-tall tower reflecting off Lake Jed Johnson makes this short but sweet hike something to add to your visit of the Wichita Mountains. On top of that, dramatic, all-encompassing views from the base of Central Peak are sure to make you stop in wonderment.

Start: Jed Johnson Tower Trailhead
Elevation gain: 1,601 to 1,703 feet
Distance: 1.5 miles out and back
Difficulty: Easy
Hiking time: 0.5–1 hour
Seasons/schedule: Open year-round
Fees and permits: None
Trail contacts: Wichita Mountains National Wildlife Refuge Headquarters, 32 Refuge Headquarters, Indiahoma 73552; (580) 429-3222
Dog-friendly: Leashed dogs permitted
Trail surface: Dirt and rocky path
Land status: US Fish and Wildlife Service

Nearest town: Medicine Park
Other trail users: Anglers; no cyclists allowed
Maps: USGS Mount Scott; Wichita Mountains National Wildlife Refuge maps (available online at www.fws .gov/refuge/Wichita_Mountains/ maps.html)
Special considerations: This trail guide includes additional hiking to the base of Central Peak. Feel free to turn around at Jed Johnson Tower if you need to cut the hike short.
There is limited shade coverage on this trail. Make sure to bring adequate water during the summer.

FINDING THE TRAILHEAD

 Heading south from Oklahoma City on I-44, take exit 45 to continue toward Wichita Mountains Wildlife Refuge on OK 49 W. Continue on OK 49 W for 11.5 miles and turn right (northwest) when you see signage for the Holy City and the Lake Jed Johnson Trailhead. (It will be the road after Meers Road.) Continue on this road for 0.6 mile, then make a left (south) to reach the Lake Jed Johnson Trailhead. GPS: N34° 44.035′ W98° 35.774′

THE HIKE

Named for a former US representative from Oklahoma, the glimmering lake surrounding the stately tower creates a picture-perfect visual. The Jed Johnson Tower Trail weaves primarily in a westerly direction through a mixture of grassland, scrub oak, and cedar trees, with astounding views all along the way. At 0.13 mile there is an overlook to your left (south). Come to a fork at the 0.17-mile mark. Stay on the right side of the fork (west)

Tower at Lake Jed Johnson

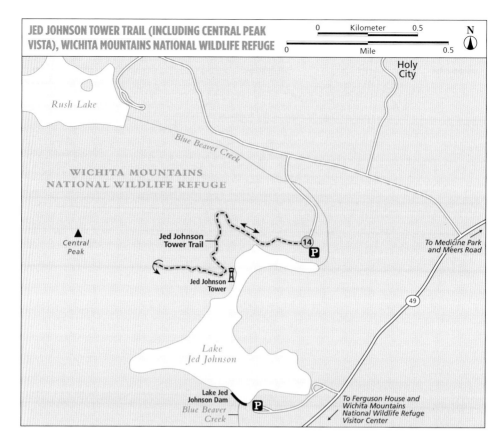

to continue on the trail. The left side of the fork that goes through the trees leads to an overlook of Lake Jed Johnson. At this point, take some time to venture to the shoreline of Lake Jed Johnson and see the tower from afar. After you have checked out the sights, continue straight (west). The trail begins to wind south at 0.3 mile, and then southeast at 0.45 mile. At the 0.5-mile point on the trail, head south toward Jed Johnson Tower, with views of Lake Jed Johnson to your left (east). Shortly after, at 0.52 mile, you reach Jed Johnson Tower. The tower was originally built as a fire watch tower by the Civilian Conservation Corps right before the United States entered World War II. Although the tower is now boarded up, you can still walk around it and surmise its history.

To shorten the hike, you can turn around and head back to the trailhead from this point. However, for an especially spectacular view, bear right (west) to head to the base of Central Peak. At 0.75 mile, the path heads north and becomes overgrown and less defined. It is suggested that you stop at this point and turn around, facing east. Survey the magnificent scene before you. Jed Johnson Tower is straight ahead of you (east). Lake Jed Johnson can be seen to your right (southeast), and the Holy City, though farther away, is visible to your left (northeast). Head back the way you came.

Central Peak

MILES AND DIRECTIONS

0.0   Start at the Jed Johnson Tower Trailhead.

0.13 Reach an overlook.

0.17 Reach a fork. The left side (south) leads to views of Lake Jed Johnson and Jed Johnson Tower. Stay on the right side (west) to continue on the trail.

0.5   The trail heads south toward Jed Johnson Tower. Views of Lake Jed Johnson are to your left (east).

0.52 Reach Jed Johnson Tower. Bear right (west) to head to the base of Central Peak.

0.75 The path becomes overgrown. Turn around, facing east, and enjoy the view before heading back the way you came.

1.5   Arrive back at the trailhead.

15 ORANGE TRAIL

LAKE LAWTONKA

Dotted with purple asters, gumweed, and prickly pear cactus, the Orange Trail excites with its continuous ascents and descents through desert-like landscape. It also offers remarkable views of Mount Scott and glistening Lake Lawtonka from various sections along the route.

Start: Orange Trailhead on East Lake Drive (Ranger Station Trailhead)
Elevation gain: 1,339 to 1,549 feet
Distance: 2.42-mile lollipop
Difficulty: Moderate to difficult due to uneven terrain and switchbacks
Hiking time: 2–3 hours
Seasons/schedule: Open year-round, sunrise to sunset
Fees and permits: None
Trail contacts: (Primary contact) Mountain Bike Club of the Wichitas, Chad Everett, (580) 591-1693, and Mark Ellis, (580) 574-8955; (secondary contact) City of Lawton Lake Division (580) 529-2663
Dog-friendly: Leashed dogs permitted
Trail surface: Dirt and rocky path
Land status: Owned by the City of Lawton; managed by the Mountain Bike Club of the Wichitas
Nearest town: Medicine Park to the east, Lawton to the south

Other trail users: Mountain bikers
Maps: USGS Mount Scott; Lake Lawtonka Trail System map (available at the trailhead); City of Lawton Lake Headquarters, 23510 OK 58, Lawton 73507; City of Medicine Park Town Hall, 154 E. Lake Dr., Medicine Park 73557; online at www.lawtonok.gov
Special considerations: This trail is also used by mountain bikers. Please be courteous to others while on the trail.
   Orange metal circles serve as trail markers.
   This trail can also be accessed by the School Slough Trailhead but involves going along a vehicle road. This description enters the trail from the Ranger Station Trailhead, with the route hiked in a counterclockwise direction.

FINDING THE TRAILHEAD

Heading south from Oklahoma City on I-44, take exit 45 to continue toward the Wichita Mountains Wildlife Refuge on OK 49 W. Continue on OK 49 W for 3.9 miles and turn right (northwest) on OK 58 N. After 1.4 miles, turn left (southwest) on Tackle Box Road. Tackle Box Road starts to head west after 0.1 mile and becomes Northwest Tackle Box Road. Continue west on Northwest Tackle Box Road for about 1.1 miles. The road changes to East Lake Drive and then starts to head south. After 0.3 mile, the trailhead is to your left (east). **Note:** This trailhead is also known as the Ranger Station Trailhead. GPS: N34° 44.212' W98° 30.109'

THE HIKE

The Orange Trail is quite an adventurous hike. It covers the Highlander and Diving Board sections and then comes back down on the Lower North Ridge, delivering encircling views at different points of elevation. Great spangled fritillary butterflies are common companions on this trail, as well as myriad colorful wildflowers and cacti.

A great spangled fritillary butterfly flutters around wild asters

Commencing with views of Mount Scott and Lake Lawtonka, the trail heads north from the Ranger Station Trailhead. At a little over 240 feet, you reach a fork. Bear right (northeast), following the orange trail marker. The left side (north) is the Orange Trail exit. Up until the 0.18-mile mark, there is a gain of 50 feet in elevation as you start heading up the Highlander section. Come to another fork at 0.07 mile. Bear right (south). The left side of the fork (north) connects to the Yellow Trail. A couple of switchbacks occur at the 0.18-mile mark, and views of Lake Lawtonka and Mount Scott reappear. Once the switchbacks end, the trail heads east into open grassland, alight with wildflowers during the blooming seasons.

After passing through a forested area, you reach a fork at 0.42 mile. Take the left side (east) of the fork to continue on the Orange Trail. You reach a Yellow Trail connection at 0.44 mile before reentering a brief forested area once again and then another Yellow Trail connection at 0.84 mile. You will head into the Diving Board section at this point. (The name will make sense once you pass the actual retro diving board on the trail.) Continue east before the trail heads northeast at 0.87 mile. Portions of the trail can get overgrown from 0.97 mile to the 1.13-mile mark. Proceed, heading north until you reach a fork at 1.18 miles. Bear left (west) to continue on the Orange Trail and the Lower North Ridge section. The right side of the fork (northeast) goes to the School Slough Trailhead. After the slabs of rock in the path at 1.25 miles, sections of the trail intermittently offer shade. After you cross the small footbridge at 1.31 miles, the trail can get overgrown for a while from 1.48 miles to 1.74 miles. Once the path clears up, magnificent lake views reemerge to your right (north). Be sure to savor the picture-perfect scenery.

The trail predominately heads south after 1.9 miles, with a few curves to the west and northwest. Continue straight (south) at the Yellow Trail intersection after the 2.0-mile mark. The final fork comes at 2.16 miles. Take the right side (northwest) of the fork, following the orange trail marker. The trail then curves back south to the trailhead.

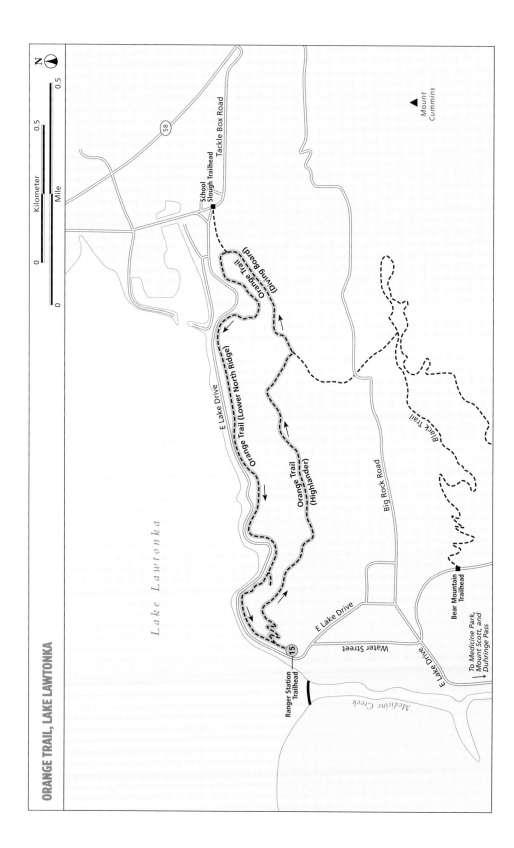

ORANGE TRAIL, LAKE LAWTONKA

N

Kilometer
0   0.5   0.5

Mile
0   0.5

Lake Lawtonka

School
Slough Trailhead

Tackle Box Road

58

Orange Trail
(Diving Board)

E Lake Drive

Orange Trail (Lower North Ridge)

Orange Trail
(Highlander)

Big Rock Road

Black Trail

Ranger Station
Trailhead

15

Water Street

E Lake Drive

E Lake Drive

Medicine Creek

Bear Mountain
Trailhead

To Medicine Park,
Mount Scott, and
Duhringe Pass

Mount
Cummins

Lake Lawtonka

MILES AND DIRECTIONS

0.0 Start at the Ranger Station Trailhead.

0.05 Reach a fork. Bear right (northeast).

0.07 Reach a fork. Bear right (south).

0.18 Start a series of switchbacks.

0.42 Reach a fork. Bear left (east) to continue on the Orange Trail.

0.44 Reach an intersection with the Yellow Trail. Continue straight (east) on the Orange Trail.

0.84 Reach another Yellow Trail connection. Head east, following the orange trail marker toward the Diving Board section.

0.97 Portions of the path can get overgrown from here to the 1.13-mile mark.

1.16 Reach an intersection. Continue straight (north), following the orange trail marker.

1.18 Reach a fork. Bear left (west) to continue on the Orange Trail.

1.31 Cross a small footbridge.

1.48 Portions of the trail can get overgrown from here until the 1.74-mile mark.

1.9 The trail heads south. Follow the orange trail marker.

2.01 Reach another intersection with the Yellow Trail. Continue straight (south) on the Orange Trail.

2.16 Reach a fork. Take the right side (northwest) of the fork.

2.42 Arrive back at the trailhead.

16 BLACK TRAIL

LAKE LAWTONKA

With cascading views of Medicine Park, Duhringe Pass, and Mount Cummins, the Black Trail curves around Bear Mountain and includes a vista of Lake Lawtonka. The trail is a testament to the beauty of the arid topography of western Oklahoma, with its abundance of sand-hued granite and rhyolite rocks and colorful succulents along its path.

Start: Black Trailhead on Merry Circle Drive (Bear Mountain Trailhead)
Elevation gain: 1,286 to 1,536 feet
Distance: 2.66-mile loop
Difficulty: Moderate to difficult due to uneven terrain and switchbacks
Hiking time: About 2 hours
Seasons/schedule: Open year-round, sunrise to sunset
Fees and permits: None
Trail contacts: Mountain Bike Club of the Wichitas, Chad Everett, (580) 591-1693, and Mark Ellis, (580) 574-8955
Dog-friendly: Leashed dogs permitted
Trail surface: Dirt and rocky path

Land status: Private property (not on land owned by the City of Lawton like the Orange Trail)
Nearest town: Medicine Park to the east, Lawton to the south
Other trail users: Mountain bikers
Maps: USGS Fort Sill; Lake Lawtonka Trail System map (available at the trailhead); City of Lawton Lake Headquarters, 23510 OK 58, Lawton 73507; City of Medicine Park Town Hall, 154 E. Lake Dr., Medicine Park 73557; online at www.lawtonok.gov
Special considerations: This trail is also used by mountain bikers. Please be courteous to others while on the trail.
Black metal circles serve as trail markers.

FINDING THE TRAILHEAD

 Heading south from Oklahoma City on I-44, take exit 45 to continue toward the Wichita Mountains Wildlife Refuge on OK 49 W. Continue on OK 49 W for 4.7 miles and turn right (northwest) on East Lake Drive. After 1.2 miles make a right (north) onto Merry Circle Drive. The trail is to your right (east), up the gravel road after about 0.2 mile. **Note:** This trailhead is also known as the Bear Mountain Trailhead. GPS: N34° 43.820' W98° 29.900'

THE HIKE

The Black Trail sits in the lower portion of the Lake Lawtonka Trail System, thus offering different scenic points from its counterparts. There is quite a bit of tree coverage on the trail, making it a favorite during the blazing Oklahoma summer months. The trailhead is also close to the heart of Medicine Park, a festive town full of dining and lodging options to delight both outdoor enthusiasts and tourists.

The trailhead is accessible via Merry Circle Drive. Head north on Merry Circle Drive (gravel road) for about 280 feet from the "Bear Mountain Trailhead" sign before bearing right (east) onto a dirt path. After about 450 feet, the trail heads north for a short distance before returning to an easterly direction. After this point, you access a series of switchbacks. The switchbacks conclude at the 0.45-mile mark, at which point the trail heads south. A little over 0.5 mile on the trail, you reach an overlook to your left (southeast). An alternate bike route connects back at 0.69 mile. Continue straight (south) and curve around the crest of Bear Mountain. Enjoy views of Lake Lawtonka and Mount Scott as you do. The trail starts to head northeast.

Continue straight (east) on the Black Trail when you reach the fork at 0.69 mile. This is where the alternate bike route converges. Continue east once again at the intersection at 0.92 mile. The trail wavers between heading south and west until you return to Merry Circle Drive at 2.5 miles. At the White Trail connection at 1.29 miles, continue straight (south) on the Black Trail. There is a series of switchbacks at 1.7 miles and 1.92 miles. Reach the most shaded portion of the trail at 2.2 miles. During the summer heat, you will be able to find some relief under the oak trees and shrubs here. The shade dissipates at 2.4 miles, and the trail heads west shortly after. Come to Bus Kamp, the incredibly fun-looking Mountain Bike Club of the Wichitas outpost, to your left (south) at 2.47 miles. Merry Circle Drive is adjacent to it. Once you reach Merry Circle Drive, at 2.5 miles, bear right (north) onto the side of the road to head back to the trailhead.

BLACK TRAIL, LAKE LAWTONKA

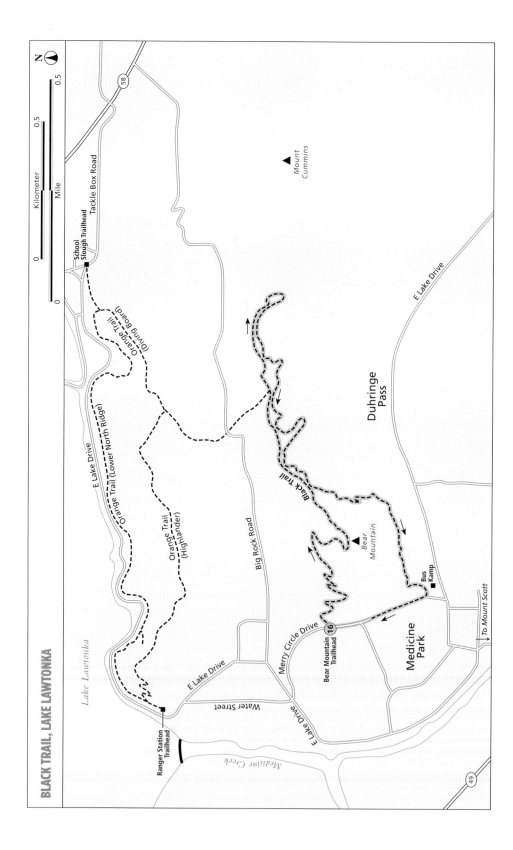

Mount Cummins

School
Slough Trailhead

Tackle Box Road

Orange Trail
(Diving Board)

Orange Trail (Lower North Ridge)

E Lake Drive

Orange Trail
(Highlander)

Lake Lawtonka

Big Rock Road

Black Trail

Duhringe Pass

Bear
Mountain

E Lake Drive

Bus
Kamp

Ranger Station
Trailhead

Merry Circle Drive

Bear Mountain
Trailhead 16

Medicine
Park

E Lake Drive

Water Street

To Mount Scott

Medicine Creek

49

58

N

Kilometer   0.5

0

0   Mile   0.5

View of Mount Scott

MILES AND DIRECTIONS

0.0 Start by heading north on Merry Circle Drive.

0.05 Bear right (east) onto the dirt path.

0.09 Traverse a series of switchbacks until the 0.45-mile mark.

0.17 Cross over large slabs of rock.

0.52 Reach an overlook to your left (southeast). Bypass the alternate biking route, and continue straight (south) to curve around the top of Bear Mountain.

0.54 Head northeast toward a fork.

0.69 Reach a fork that merges with the alternate biking route. Continue straight (east).

0.92 Reach an intersection. Continue straight (east).

1.29 Reach a fork. Continue straight (south).

1.7 Traverse a series of switchbacks until the 1.8-mile mark.

1.92 Traverse another series of switchbacks until 2.2 miles.

2.2 The most shaded portion of the trail starts here and ends at 2.4 miles.

2.47 Reach Bus Kamp (the Mountain Bike Club of the Wichitas outpost) to your left (south).

2.5 Reach the gravel surface of Merry Circle Drive. Bear right (north) onto the side of road to head back and complete the loop.

2.66 Arrive back at the trailhead.

Sunrise view of the cove near
the Mountain Pass Trail

HONORABLE MENTION

(GREAT PLAINS COUNTRY, SOUTHWEST OKLAHOMA)

B. MOUNTAIN PASS TRAIL

QUARTZ MOUNTAIN STATE PARK

The Mountain Pass Trail is a short but worthwhile hike up Twin Peaks and then down to a picturesque cove of Lake Altus-Lugert. All along the way you are greeted by the occasional blue-hued berries of the eastern redcedar, the distinctive Texas live oak, and the desert prickly pear. You may even see a great blue heron finding respite in the cove during sunrise.

Start: Mountain Pass Trailhead, west of cabins #10 and #11
Elevation gain: 1,549 to 1,680 feet
Distance: 0.44 mile out and back
Difficulty: Moderate to difficult due to steep ascent and decline
Hiking time: 1–2 hours
Seasons/schedule: Open year-round, sunrise to sunset (strictly enforced)
Fees and permits: Parking pass required for day-use visitors
Trail contacts: Quartz Mountain State Park Office, 43393 Scissortail Rd., Lone Wolf 73655; (580) 563-2238. **Note:** At time of publication, a new office location within the park is being considered.

Dog-friendly: Leashed dogs permitted
Trail surface: Dirt and rocky path
Land status: Oklahoma State Parks
Nearest town: Hobart to the north, Altus to the south
Other trail users: Rock climbers
Maps: USGS Lake Altus; Quartz Mountain State Park maps (available online at www.travelok.com/state-parks and via the Oklahoma State Parks mobile app)
Special considerations: Blue painted diamonds serve as trail markers.

FINDING THE TRAILHEAD

From the US 138 and OK 9 intersection in Hobart, head west for 10 miles on OK 9 until you reach OK 44. Head south on OK 44 for 9.7 miles, then turn right (north) on OK 44A. After traveling 1.5 miles on OK 44A, turn right (east) at the River Road Tent Campground. Continue from there a little over 1.5 miles; you will see a road to your right (northeast) before the Robert M. Kerr Performance Hall that leads you to cabins #10 and #11. The Mountain Pass Trailhead is east of the cabins. GPS: N34° 54.104' W99° 18.197'

FRONTIER COUNTRY (CENTRAL OKLAHOMA)

Although most of **FRONTIER COUNTRY** is a concrete jungle, the Oklahoma City area is home to many wonderful areas reserved for outdoor activities and experiences with nature. Unpaved multiuse trails are usually primitive and provide the most exposure to wooded areas and creeks. Do not disregard the paved trails though—most of them provide a similar feeling of separation from the crowded city life and offer a host of greenery and interesting sights as well. Head outside the Oklahoma City area and you will have access to beautiful lakes such as Liberty Lake and Lake McMurtry.

Sunset at Lake McMurtry (Hikes 22 & 23)

17 STINCHCOMB EAST TRAIL

STINCHCOMB WILDLIFE REFUGE

A bird-watcher's paradise, the Stinchcomb Wildlife Refuge is home to all sorts of incredible fowl species. It also shelters turtles, butterflies, fish, and other woodland creatures. This uncomplicated trail that runs through the east side of the refuge extends opportune moments to witness varied wildlife.

Start: Stinchcomb East Trailhead, Main Gate/Gate 1 entrance to East Lake Road/River Road
Elevation gain: 1,227 to 1,270 feet
Distance: 5.18 miles out and back
Difficulty: Easy
Hiking time: 2–3 hours
Seasons/schedule: Open year-round, sunrise to sunset
Fees and permits: None
Trail contacts: City of Oklahoma City Parks Administration, 420 W. Main St., Ste. 210, Oklahoma City 73102; (405) 297-3882

Dog-friendly: Leashed dogs permitted
Trail surface: Dirt
Land status: Managed by the Oklahoma City Water Trust, owned by the City of Oklahoma City
Nearest town: Oklahoma City
Other trail users: Cyclists, anglers
Maps: USGS Bethany; Stinchcomb Wildlife Refuge map (available at the trailhead and online at www.okc-audobon.org)

FINDING THE TRAILHEAD

From downtown Oklahoma City, get onto I-40 W from South Shields Boulevard. After 7.4 miles on I-40 W, take exit 142 for Council Road. Turn right (north) on North Council Road and continue 4.2 miles. Turn left (west) on NW 50th Street and continue 0.5 mile. Turn right (north) onto North Stinchcomb Avenue. The parking lot and trailhead are to your left (west). GPS: N35° 31.384' W97° 39.805'

THE HIKE

The Stinchcomb Wildlife Refuge is named in remembrance of Lee Stinchcomb, whose family donated the homesteaded land on which the refuge lies. The trail that traverses the east section of the refuge demonstrates that the refuge is a sanctuary brimming with wildlife and why it is beloved by locals. Myriad sparrows and kinglets will warble around you as you head down the trail. Wood ducks parade on the water in the early morning, and you might catch various fauna scurrying around in the tall grasses and trees.

Once you get past the gravel surface leading up to the Main Gate (Gate 1), the path becomes a wide dirt path. It will remain so until the end of the trail. Right off the bat, an unofficial trail to your left (west) leads to Street Car Lake in 90 feet. At 0.06 mile, you come to a Stinchcomb memorial marker to your left (west). From here on out, you will notice several side trails to your left (west). This guide only points out the ones that have the most accessible views. The trail heads north at 0.3 mile. At 0.48 mile, a side trail of about 195 feet in length leads to an outlook of the North Canadian River to your left (west). The trail winds northeast shortly after.

Top: Stinchcomb Lake
Left: An American robin perched in a cedar tree
Right: Mother turtle with her baby in the North Canadian River

Partial views of the North Canadian River and Stinchcomb Lake materialize to your left (west) at 0.81 mile as the trail heads northwest. Right after 1.0 mile on the trail, come to a small pond to your left (southwest). The trail heads west at 1.4 miles before heading back northwest for a final time at 1.65 miles. There is one more overlook of the North Canadian River right by the trail to your left (west) at 1.8 miles. At times, turtles can be seen here resting on fallen branches under the warm sun. Reach Gate 2 at 1.91 miles. The path can get overgrown from this point. Be cautious of erosion on the sides of the trail. When you reach the large cylindrical blocks and the John Kilpatrick Turnpike comes into view, you have reached the end of the trail. The mile marker at this point is 2.59 miles. Turn around and return to the trailhead.

MILES AND DIRECTIONS

0.0 Start at the trailhead at Main Gate/Gate 1, north of the parking lot. A 90-foot-long side trail to Street Car Lake is to your left (west).

0.06 The Stinchcomb memorial marker is to your left (west).

0.48 A side trail (195 feet in length) to an overlook of the North Canadian River is to your left (west).

1.02 Come to a small pond to your left (southwest).

1.8 Reach another overlook of the North Canadian River, right by the trail to your left (west).

1.91 Pass through Gate 2. The path can get overgrown from this point. Be cautious of eroded sides of the trail.

2.59 Reach several large cylindrical blocks with the John Kilpatrick Turnpike in view. Turn around and return to the trailhead.

5.18 Arrive back at the trailhead.

18 JIM THORPE REHABILITATION COURAGE TRAIL (COMBINED WITH TRAIL B, TRAIL C, AND MEADOW TRAIL)

MARTIN PARK NATURE CENTER

The Martin Park Nature Center is a real delight for both individuals and families who are looking to get some exercise in the outdoors and want to enjoy the beauty of the area, where an array of wildlife can be spotted. It has a variety of topography, including ponds, creeks, forests, and open meadows.

Start: Jim Thorpe Rehabilitation Courage Trailhead, at the southeast corner of the Martin Park Nature Center parking lot
Elevation gain: 1,024 to 1,096 feet
Distance: 2.06 miles of multiple loops
Difficulty: Easy
Hiking time: About 1 hour
Seasons/schedule: Apr–Sept, 5 a.m.–9 p.m.; Oct–Mar, 5 a.m.–6 p.m.
Fees and permits: None
Trail contacts: Martin Park Nature Center Visitor Center, 5000 W. Memorial Rd., Oklahoma City 73142; (405) 297-1429
Dog-friendly: Service dogs only

Trail surface: Decomposed granite (ADA compliant)
Land status: City of Oklahoma City
Nearest town: Oklahoma City
Other trail users: None
Maps: USGS Britton; Martin Park Nature Center map (available at the park and online at www.okc.gov/departments/parks-recreation/martin-park-nature-center/integris-courage-trail)
Special considerations: The described route includes the Trail B, Trail C, and Meadow Trail loops, which all connect with the Jim Thorpe Rehabilitation Courage Trail.

FINDING THE TRAILHEAD

Heading west on the John Kilpatrick Turnpike from the OK 74 junction, take the Meridian Avenue exit. Then head west onto Memorial Avenue for 1 mile before turning left (south) on Martin Park Boulevard. Make a quick left (east) back onto Memorial Avenue; the entrance to the Martin Nature Park Center is to your right (south). GPS: N35° 36.443' W 97° 36.569'

THE HIKE

The Martin Park Nature Center is a beautiful gem in the heart of the city. As the pioneer for wheelchair-accessible trails in the Oklahoma City area, the Jim Thorpe Rehabilitation Courage Trail allows all nature enthusiasts to experience various areas of the Martin Park Nature Center. The described route includes the more primitive, yet still easy to navigate trails—Trail B, Trail C, and the Meadow Trail—for additional adventure and sightseeing. All three trails connect back to the Courage Trail.

The Courage Trail begins at Storytime Circle. If you have young ones with you, crossing Turtle Bridge might be an exciting chance for them to see turtles and water landing fowl. After crossing Turtle Bridge, you will see the visitor center ahead of you. Stay on the left side of the fork and head into the wooded area. The trail winds along the north side of the visitor center, and views of Turtle Pond will be to your left (south). At 0.06 mile, make sure to go around the observation deck as part of your route. After that, stay on the left side of the fork. A wild bird observation station is to your right (west) at 0.14 mile. A meadow is also visible for a brief period.

At 0.2 mile, come to an elevated observation deck. Go around to the left (east) of the deck to head to Trail B. Continue straight (north) at the fork at 0.24 mile to start on Trail B. There is a service road at 0.3 mile. Continue straight (southeast) to start the Trail B loop in a clockwise direction. You go down a few wooden steps and reach a meadow again at 0.32 mile. At 0.44 mile, the trail starts to wind south, before heading northwest at the 0.5-mile point. A riparian overlook of Spring Creek presents worthy views to your left (southwest).

Reach a junction with the service road at 0.57 mile, with a couple paths leading back to the elevated observation deck. Continue straight (northwest) toward the wooden steps to head back. Once you reach the elevated observation deck again, veer left (south) along the fence posts to continue on the Courage Trail. Reach another intersection with the service road at 0.65 mile. Follow the Courage Trail marker fastened to a post and continue straight (south).

You reach a junction at 0.77 mile. Head left (south) to cross the Iron Turtle Bridge. Come to another junction at 0.8 mile. Bear left (east) to start on Trail C in a clockwise direction. Cross a couple footbridges and views of Spring Creek will be to your left (north). Reach another fork at 0.97 mile. Veer right (east) to continue on the loop. At

Left: View of Turtle Pond
Right: Deer sighting in the meadow

1.15 miles you close out the loop for Trail C and go north to head back across the Iron Turtle Bridge. Once across the bridge, bear left (west) toward the Courage Trail marker.

Along the way back to Storytime Circle, there will be a footbridge, entrances to the Dry Creek Bridge and Cottonwood Trail to your left (west), and a wildlife viewing station to your right (east). The Courage Trail markers are your guides. You reach Storytime Circle at 1.5 miles. For additional wildlife sightings, bear left (west) toward the fence posts to start the Meadow Trail. You soon reach the Cottonwood Trail fork. Bear right (west) to head to the Meadow Trail loop. At the starting point of the Meadow Trail loop, bear left (south) to complete the trail in a clockwise direction. At the 1.93-mile mark, come to another fork. Steer to the right (southeast) side of the fork to continue on the loop. You reach the starting point of Meadow Trail at 2.02 miles. Veer left (east) to head back to Storytime Circle.

MILES AND DIRECTIONS

0.0   Start at Storytime Circle. Cross the Turtle Bridge.

0.02 Stay on the left side of the fork.

0.2   Reach an elevated observation deck. Bear left (east) of the deck to head to Trail B.

0.24 Reach a fork. Continue straight (north) to start on Trail B.

0.3   Reach a service road. Continue straight (southeast) on the loop.

0.5   Come to a riparian overlook of Spring Creek to your left (southwest).

0.57 Reach a junction with the service road. Continue straight (northwest) toward some wood steps.

0.62 Reach the elevated observation deck again. Bear left (south) along the fence posts to continue on the Courage Trail.

0.77 Reach a junction. Bear left (south) to go across the Iron Turtle Bridge and head toward Trail C.

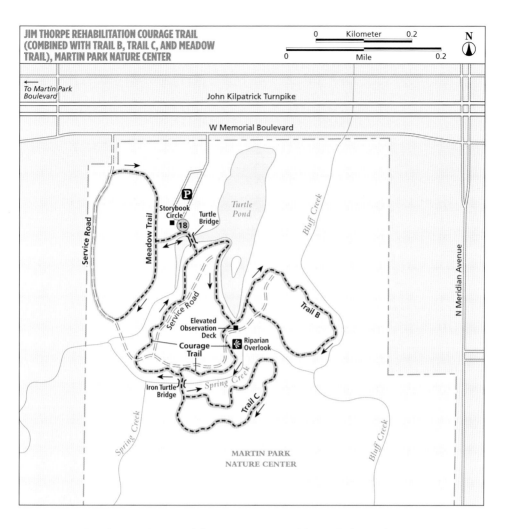

0.8 Reach a junction. Bear left (east) to start Trail C in a clockwise direction.

1.15 Reach a fork. Go north and head back to the Courage Trail.

1.23 Reach a junction again after the Iron Turtle Bridge. Bear left (west) toward the Courage Trail marker.

1.5 Reach Storytime Circle. Bear left (west) toward the fence posts to start the Meadow Trail.

1.53 Reach the Cottonwood Trail connection. Bear right (west) to head to the Meadow Trail loop.

1.55 Reach the Meadow Trail. Bear left (south) to complete the trail in a clockwise direction.

1.93 Reach a fork. Take the right (southeast) side of the fork to continue on the loop.

2.02 Reach the original fork at the starting point of the Meadow Trail. Head back to Storytime Circle.

2.06 Arrive back at the trailhead.

19 SUTTON WILDERNESS TRAIL

GEORGE MIKSCH SUTTON URBAN WILDERNESS PARK (CITY OF NORMAN)

George Miksch Sutton Urban Wilderness Park is a serene reprieve from your daily, urban routine. The short but rewarding trail that meanders through the area takes you away from the hustle and bustle and lets you enjoy the sounds of nature.

Start: Sutton Wilderness Trailhead, north of the George Miksch Sutton Urban Wilderness Park parking lot
Elevation gain: 1,165 to 1,216 feet
Distance: 1.37-mile loop
Difficulty: Easy
Hiking time: About 1 hour
Seasons/schedule: Open year-round, sunrise to sunset
Fees and permits: None
Trail contacts: Norman Chamber of Commerce Parks and Recreation, 115 E. Gray St., Norman 73069; (405) 366-5472

Dog-friendly: Leashed dogs permitted
Trail surface: Dirt and gravel path
Land status: Leased by the City of Norman; owned by the Oklahoma Department of Mental Health and Substance Abuse Services
Nearest town: Norman
Other trail users: None
Maps: USGS Norman; City of Norman Sutton Wilderness Trail map (available on-site; information online at www.visitnorman.com/places-to-go/sutton-wilderness-park)

FINDING THE TRAILHEAD

From the South Jenkins Avenue and Boyd Street intersection at the University of Oklahoma, head west on Boyd Street for 1 mile. Turn left (north) on 12th Avenue SE (later changes to 12th Avenue NE) for about 2.1 miles before turning left (west) into the George Miksch Sutton Urban Wilderness Park parking lot. The trailhead is to the north of the parking lot. GPS: N35° 14.558' W97° 25.456'

THE HIKE

The Sutton Wilderness Trail is a leisurely loop that takes you through several woods, along the shores of the Hospital Lake Reservoir and areas teeming with wildlife. Sutton Urban Wilderness Park is named in honor of the late, world-renowned ornithologist George Miksch Sutton. Sutton, who was also an artist and author, spent a great deal of time studying the birdlife around the Hospital Lake Reservoir.

The trail commences at the northern end of the parking lot. You will take the trail in a counterclockwise direction. At 0.13 mile, you cross a small creek bed. Starting from this point, several side trails lead to overlooks of the Hospital Lake Reservoir. Come to a bench to your right (north) at 0.17 mile.

You reach views of the prairie to your right (north) at the 0.42-mile mark. Shortly after, the trail begins to head north before heading west and then southwest. At 0.69

Top: Overlook of Hospital Lake Reservoir
Left: Wildflowers and greenery along the Sutton Wilderness Trail
Right: Rabbit sighting along Sutton Wilderness Trail

mile, the trail starts to travel in a southern direction and the trail surface becomes paved for a short distance. You can see a decent portion of the Hospital Lake Reservoir to your left (east). A bench as well as a scenic turnaround are at the 0.84–mile mark; both are to your right (west). This guide's route stays on the Sutton Wilderness Trail loop and does not include the scenic turnaround. As you continue straight (southeast), the path returns to a gravel surface.

The trail eventually heads north at 0.97 mile. There will be another bench to your left (west). Cross an earth dam, which establishes the western boundary of the lake. The trail starts to wind east after the dam. At 1.17 miles you encounter another scenic turnaround, this time to your left (north). Again, the described route stays on the Sutton Wilderness Trail loop. Continue straight on the paved road before returning to the parking lot at 1.37 miles.

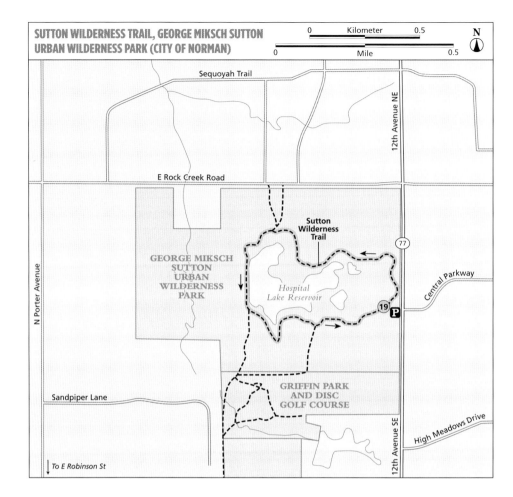

MILES AND DIRECTIONS

0.0 Start at the trailhead north of the parking lot and bear right.

0.13 Cross a seasonal creek bed. There are numerous side trails that lead to overlooks of the Hospital Lake Reservoir.

0.17 Come to a bench to your right (north).

0.42 Views of the prairie are to your right (north).

0.69 The path becomes a paved surface for a short distance. Views of the Hospital Lake Reservoir are to your left (east).

0.84 Reach a scenic turnaround and a bench to your right (west). Continue straight on the gravel path (southeast).

1.03 Come to a bench to your left (west).

1.17 Reach a scenic turnaround to your left (north). Continue straight on the paved road.

1.37 Arrive back at the trailhead.

20 LIBERTY LAKE TRAIL

LIBERTY LAKE (CITY OF GUTHRIE)

This trail is a quintessential hike through cedar and oak blended forests, and it is likely you will encounter nine-banded armadillos and white-tailed deer scampering around the whispering trees. Included halfway through the route is a grand vista of Liberty Lake.

Start: Liberty Lake Trailhead, at the equestrian parking area southwest of the pay station
Elevation gain: 935 to 1,043 feet
Distance: 6.51-mile loop with additional spurs to overlooks
Difficulty: Easy
Hiking time: At least 3 hours
Seasons/schedule: Open year-round, sunrise to sunset
Fees and permits: Day-use fee (self-pay)
Trail contacts: City of Guthrie Municipal Services, 407 Commerce Blvd., Guthrie 73044; (405) 282-8400
Dog-friendly: Leashed dogs permitted
Trail surface: Dirt and mowed grass; occasional unearthed tree roots in the path
Land status: City of Guthrie
Nearest town: Guthrie
Other trail users: Cyclists, equestrians, anglers
Maps: USGS Guthrie South; Liberty Lake Trail map (available at the trailhead and online at www.travelok.com)

Special considerations: The south and north sides of the loop involve walking along vehicular roads. Please exercise caution when traversing the road.

Portions of this trail can get muddy after decent precipitation.

White rectangular trail markers showing "LLT—Liberty Lake Trail," orange ties, and white blazes on trees serve as trail guides. Yellow diamonds with arrows also provide directional guidance.

Note: At the time of publication, a new side trail called Freedom Loop has been added to the Liberty Lake Trail. It totals 1.3 miles in length. It occurs after the fork to Rocky Point Vista and right before the trail heads north, in between the 4.25- and 4.5-mile marks. Additional side trails and outlooks are being considered. Any new side trails will not affect the Liberty Lake Trail's total mileage but hopefully will offer more opportunities to explore the beauty of Liberty Lake.

FINDING THE TRAILHEAD

From downtown Oklahoma City, get on I-235 S. Take exit 1A for I-40 E toward I-35 N/US 62 E. Make sure to keep right (north) at the fork to continue on I-35 N/US 62 E. After 25 miles, take exit 151 for Seward Road. Turn left (west) onto East Seward Road. After 2.7 miles (the last 0.5 mile, after passing the Coltrane Road intersection, is a gravel and packed dirt road) the road eventually heads north. The entrance to Liberty Lake is to your left (west). After making a one-way loop around the pay station, head east into the equestrian parking area; the trailhead is to your right (south). GPS: N35° 48.082' W97° 27.700'

Prairie area of Liberty Lake

THE HIKE

The trail that surrounds the graceful and glassy-surfaced Liberty Lake is meant to be taken in a clockwise direction. The topography that encompasses the trail interchanges between forest and open grassland. It predominately heads south, with a few changes in course bearing west until the 1.1-mile mark. You reach a fork about 85 feet into the trail. Take the left side (south) of the fork to continue on the trail. The right side (southwest) of the fork goes to a campground. Partial views of the campground and Liberty Lake are to your right (west). You cross a vehicle road coming from the campground at 0.2 mile. Continue straight (south). There is an unofficial trail to your right (west) shortly after. At 0.41 mile, barbed-wire fencing appears to your left (east); the trail then parallels West Seward Road at 0.48 mile.

You go over some unearthed tree roots at 0.58 mile as you head away from Liberty Lake. Head down a ditch before reaching a fork at 0.75 mile on the trail. Take the left side of the fork and continue south. Shortly after crossing the first of several creek beds at 0.87 mile, pass a side trail to your left (east). Continue south until partial views of Liberty Lake emerge to your right (west) a little over 1.0 mile on the trail. The lake views dwindle at 1.1 miles as the trail heads east. The trail eventually heads back south at 1.34 miles until you reach Forrest Hills Road at 2.11 miles. As you head down a small ditch at 1.4 miles, there is a seasonal creek bed to your right (east). You eventually cross this creek bed as it curves toward the trail at 1.44 miles. After a small footbridge at 1.9 miles, there is a side trail to your right (southwest) at 1.97 miles, and then an old structure to your left (east) at 2.06 miles.

As you near Forrest Hills Road, the terrain turns marshy and the path surface becomes mowed grass. Head west along the side (mowed-grass portion) of West Forrest Hills Road. Be cautious of passing vehicles. At 2.15 miles you need to cross a short, single-lane bridge. Quickly return to the mowed grass and then bear right (north), back into a grassy area at 2.24 miles. The trail heads west again. The path surface returns to dirt once again at 2.35 miles and then the trail winds north. After this point, there are a few opportunities to head down some side trails to get close to the shores of Liberty Lake; one is at 2.52 miles. Side trails at 2.58 miles and 2.6 miles eventually merge to the same viewpoint. After checking out the side trails, continue straight (southwest) at the fork at 2.6 miles. The trail heads north at 2.95 miles and continues in this direction for the majority of the route until you reach the fork to Rocky Point Vista at 3.93 miles.

Rocky Point Vista

Vista of woodland area

Cross another small footbridge at 2.96 miles. After a few mild dips in the path at 3.17 miles, you come to a picnic bench to your left (west) at 3.56 miles. Bypass the side trail to your left (northwest) at 3.74 miles and continue toward the Rocky Point Vista. Partial views of Lake Liberty become available again to your right (east). The side trail to the Rocky Point Vista is at the fork at 3.93 miles. Bear left (north) to the Rocky Point Vista. Take in the extravaganza that surrounds you as you are offered multiple vantage points of Liberty Lake. Once you are done relishing the view, turn around and head back to the fork at the 3.93-mile mark. At this point take what would have been the left side of the fork (southwest) to move forward on the loop.

Bypass another side trail coming from the left (south) at 4.2 miles. The entrance to the Freedom Loop occurs shortly after from the right (north). (**Note:** You may continue on the Freedom Loop if you would like to add mileage to your hiking trip. It will reconnect with the Liberty Lake Loop after 1.3 miles.) The Liberty Lake Loop trail then heads

predominantly north from the 4.49-mile mark until you reach the dam at 5.6 miles. Before the trail bottoms out at 4.78 miles, there is another scenery viewing opportunity. The view this time is of the diverse trees surrounding the lake. Cross another seasonal creek bed at 4.98 miles, and then walk across an old stone structure at 5.0 miles into the trail. After crossing your last seasonal creek bed at 5.43 miles, you reach a fork that leads toward the dam and lake at 5.54 miles. Bear right (east) at the fork.

You will come to the dam at 5.6 miles. Head toward the stop sign so that you can go around the dam's concrete barrier. Be aware of vehicles traveling on the dam, as you will be walking along the side of West Seward Road. You reach the end of the dam at 6.0 miles. Veer around the concrete barrier and head south back onto the dirt path. The trail then winds east along the concrete barrier across an open area. Head southeast, back into the forested area, at 6.08 miles. From here until you exit the forest, the trail eventually winds west and then curves east. The forest ends at 6.46 miles. Go across the one-way vehicle road (coming from the pay station) at 6.49 miles, and then head back toward the trailhead and equestrian parking area.

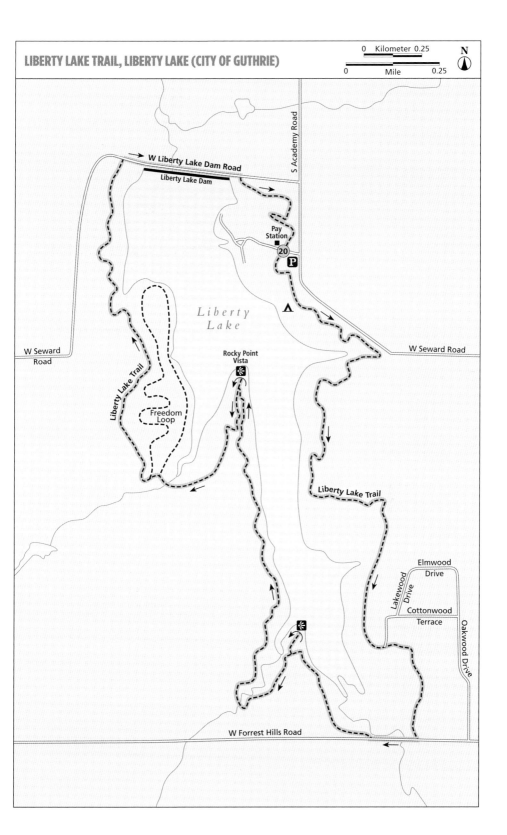

LIBERTY LAKE TRAIL, LIBERTY LAKE (CITY OF GUTHRIE)

0   Kilometer   0.25

0   Mile   0.25

N

W Liberty Lake Dam Road

Liberty Lake Dam

S Academy Road

Pay Station

20

P

Liberty Lake

W Seward Road

W Seward Road

Rocky Point Vista

Liberty Lake Trail

Freedom Loop

Liberty Lake Trail

Elmwood Drive

Lakewood Drive

Cottonwood Terrace

Oakwood Drive

W Forrest Hills Road

MILES AND DIRECTIONS

0.0 Start at the equestrian parking area. Hike the trail in a clockwise direction.

0.2 Cross the vehicle road. Continue straight (south).

0.24 Bypass the side trail to your right (west).

0.75 Reach a fork. Take the left side of the fork and continue south.

0.87 Cross a seasonal creek bed. Bypass the side trail to your left (east) shortly after.

1.4 Head down a small ditch. A seasonal creek bed is to your right (east).

1.44 Cross the seasonal creek bed that was to your right (east).

1.9 Reach a small footbridge over a small seasonal creek.

1.97 Bypass the side trail to your right (southwest).

2.06 Pass an old structure to your left (east).

2.11 Head west along the mowed-grass portion of West Forrest Hills Road. Be cautious of passing vehicles.

2.15 Cross the single-lane bridge and return to the mowed-grass path.

2.24 Bear right (north), back into a grassy area.

2.52 Come to an outlook of Liberty Lake to your right (east).

2.58 A side trail to an outlook is straight ahead (north).

2.6 Reach a fork. To your right (north) is another side trail that merges with the side trail from the 2.58-mile mark. Continue straight (southwest).

2.96 Reach a small footbridge over a seasonal creek bed.

3.56 A picnic bench is to your left (west).

3.74 Bypass the side trail to your left (northwest).

3.93 Reach a fork. Bear left (north) toward the Rocky Point Vista.

3.96 Reach Rocky Point Vista. Turn around and head back to the fork from the 3.93-mile mark. Head southwest to continue the loop.

4.2 A side trail merges from the left (south). The entrance to the new Freedom Loop occurs to the right (north) shortly after. (*Option:* You may take the Freedom Loop route for additional mileage. It reconnects with the Liberty Lake Loop trail after 1.3 miles.)

4.78 Reach a plateau area with a vista of trees.

4.98 Cross a seasonal creek bed.

5.0 Pass over an old structure.

5.43 Cross a seasonal creek bed.

5.54 Bear right (east) at the fork toward the dam and the lake.

5.6 Reach the dam. Head west toward the stop sign.

5.64 Bear around the stop sign to head east across the dam.

6.0 Bear around the edge of the dam to head south, back onto the dirt path.

6.04 The trail winds east along the concrete barrier and across an open area.

6.08 Head southeast, back into a forested area.

6.49 Reach the one-way vehicle road coming from the pay station. Go across to head back toward the trailhead.

6.51 Arrive back at the trailhead.

21 **SCIP NORTH TRAILS SYSTEM**

SOLDIER CREEK INDUSTRIAL PARK (CITY OF MIDWEST CITY)

The North Trails System of SCIP is quirky and free spirited. It includes breezing through a tunnel formed by bursting sunflowers, seeing whimsical toys lounging in the tree branches above you, and passing an abandoned boat named the SS *Broken Derailleur*. For a fun workout experience, this trail system does not disappoint.

Start: White Trailhead, east of the parking lot and south of the informational signage
Elevation gain: 1,132 to 1,172 feet
Distance: 3.6 miles of stacked loops
Difficulty: Easy
Hiking time: About 2 hours
Seasons/schedule: Open year-round, sunrise to sunset; best in spring through fall for wildflowers
Fees and permits: None
Trail contacts: City of Midwest Parks and Recreation, 200 N. Midwest Blvd., Midwest City 73110; (405) 739-1291
Dog-friendly: Leashed dogs permitted
Trail surface: Dirt
Land status: Maintained in partnership with the Oklahoma

Earthbike Fellowship, owned by the City of Midwest City
Nearest town: Midwest City
Other trail users: Cyclists
Maps: USGS Midwest City; City of Midwest City Soldier Creek Industrial Park Recreational Trails map (available online at www.midwestcityok.org)
Special considerations: This trail is also used by cyclists. Please be courteous to others while on the trail.

The North Trails System comprises the Green Trail, Yellow Trail, and Red Trail. To access the Green Trail, this guide uses the trailhead starting at the White Trail (which is part of the South Trails System).

FINDING THE TRAILHEAD

From downtown Oklahoma City, get on I-235 S. Take exit 1A for I-40 E toward I-35 N/U S62 E. Make sure to keep right (north) at the fork to continue on I-35 N/US 62 E. After 2 miles, take exit 130 for NE 23rd Street/US 62 E and head east. The parking lot and trailhead are to your right (south) after traveling on NE 23rd Street/US 62 E for about 3.8 miles. The parking lot and trailhead are at 7250 NE 23rd Street in Midwest City. GPS: N35° 29.569′ W97° 24.033′

THE HIKE

The North Trails System consists of three easy yet stimulating trails, complete with switchbacks, and boasts a wide range of greenery. Once you step foot on this part of the Soldier Creek Industrial Park (SCIP) trail system, you can already gather how unique it is. The route begins with an entrance to the White Trail (part of the SCIP South Trails System) east of the parking lot. Take the White Trail in a counterclockwise direction and head west into the "pollinator habitat" brimming with looming sunflowers, milkweed,

Indian paintbrush, and coneflowers. A little over 500 feet into the trail, you reach the North Trails System's entrance. The North Trails System consists of the Green Trail, Yellow Trail, and Red Trail. A spectacular tunnel of sunflowers during the blooming season invites you through at 0.14 mile.

You reach pavement at 0.19 mile. The trail surface returns to dirt at the road overpass at 0.27 mile. Once you head north under the road overpass, you reach the Green Trail entrance and, shortly after, a forested area. The Green, Yellow, and Red Trails are all meant to be taken in a clockwise direction. For entertainment, look for eccentric toys placed in the trees above you at each of the trails' connections. Crutcho Creek is to your left as you continue north. Short of 0.5 mile on the trail, you reach a fork. Continue north (straight) and reach another fork at 0.52 mile. Take the left side of the fork to continue the trail in a clockwise direction. Views open up to a prairie before the trail winds west, back into a forested area at 0.6 mile.

Prior to reaching the Yellow Trail entrance at 0.88 mile, the trail changes from heading north to east and back to north again. A junction leading to the Yellow Trail shows up at 0.8 mile. Bear left (north) to head toward the Yellow Trail. The surroundings open up to a prairie landscape once again. At the Yellow Trail entrance at 0.88 mile, bear left to hike the Yellow Trail in a clockwise direction. Crutcho Creek reappears at the 0.92-mile mark, this time to your left (south) as the trail heads west. You reach the Red Trail entrance at 1.18 miles. Continue west onto the Red Trail. From this point until the 1.63-mile mark, the trail winds back and forth from north to west, with one turnabout in between at 1.61 miles. Pass a side trail to your right (north) at 1.29 miles. Continue straight (west) on the Red Trail. Rocks may be present in the path at 1.4 miles. Ruins of an old two-story home that was hit by an A-7D Corsair fighter jet from Tinker Air Force Base in 1985 is visible to your right (east).

The trail begins heading east before you bear right (south) onto the gravel-based Old Air Depot Boulevard at 1.78 miles. A side trail to the old house you saw at the 1.4-mile mark shows up to your right (west) at 1.94 miles. Continue straight (southeast) on the Red Trail. At 2.06 miles you reach the Yellow Trail connection. Stay on the left side of the loop to continue in a clockwise direction, heading east. For the majority of the route until you head back to the White Trail connection, with the exception of a couple turn-abouts at 2.48 and 2.55 miles, you head south. You will reach the Green Trail connection at 2.43 miles. Stay on the left side to continue in a clockwise direction.

At 2.58 miles, an abandoned boat dubbed the SS *Broken Derailleur* is to your left (north). The SS *Broken Derailleur* is another ode to the trail system's quirkiness. There is a break in the forest scenery and some rocks in the path prior to reaching the Green Trail connection at 2.67 miles. At the next couple of forks, continue south to take the trail in a clockwise direction. After heading back into a wooded area and crossing a seasonal creek bed, you reach the North Trails System entrance at 2.86 miles. From here, head back south under the overpass, across the pavement, through the sunflower "tunnel," and back to the White Trail connection.

You will reach the White Trail connection at 3.06 miles. Bear right (south) to complete the trail in a counterclockwise direction. Enter a wooded area, cross a seasonal creek bed, and head east before encountering the Orange Trail connection (part of the South Trails System) at 3.3 miles. Take the left side of the fork to continue on the White Trail.

Fairytale forests on the North Trails System

Sunflower tunnel on the White Trail

Cross another seasonal creek bed as the trail heads primarily north after this point. At 3.35 miles you reach the other end of the Orange Trail. Take the left side of the fork to continue on the White Trail. At 3.4 miles, you are again welcomed by the bursting sunflowers. Enjoy these sun-beaming flora as you reach the White Trail entrance at 3.58 miles. From here, continue straight (north) back to the trailhead and parking lot.

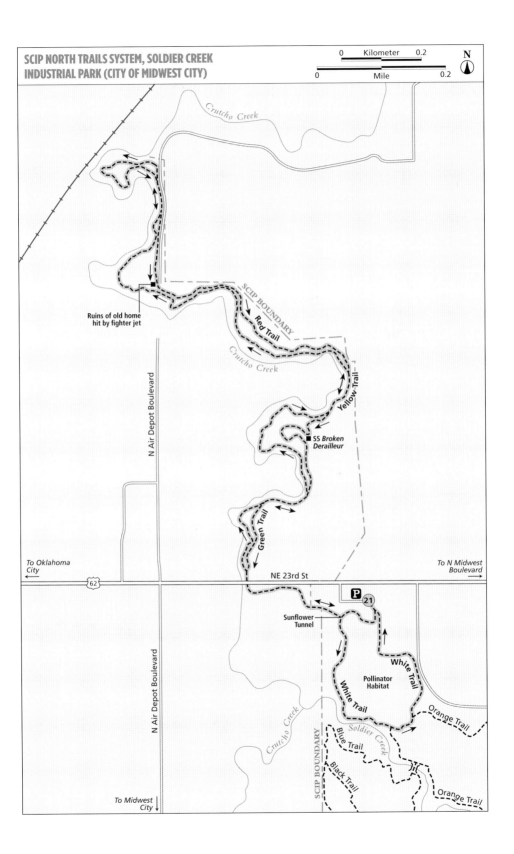

0   Kilometer   0.2

0   Mile   0.2

N

Crutcho Creek

SCIP BOUNDARY

Red Trail

Ruins of old home
hit by fighter jet

Crutcho Creek

Yellow Trail

■ SS Broken
Derailleur

N Air Depot Boulevard

Green Trail

To Oklahoma
City

62

NE 23rd St

To N Midwest
Boulevard

P 21

Sunflower
Tunnel

White Trail

Pollinator
Habitat

White Trail

Orange Trail

N Air Depot Boulevard

Crutcho Creek

SCIP BOUNDARY

Soldier Creek

Blue Trail

Black Trail

Orange Trail

To Midwest
City

MILES AND DIRECTIONS

0.0   Start at the trailhead east of the parking lot.

0.02 Reach the White Trail and hike it in a counterclockwise direction.

0.1   Reach the North Trails System entrance.

0.14 Go through a tunnel of sunflowers in the blooming season.

0.19 Head out of the wooded area and onto the pavement.

0.27 Head north under the overpass. The path returns to a dirt surface.

0.29 Reach the Green Trail entrance and take it in a clockwise direction.

0.49 Reach a fork. Continue north.

0.52 Reach another fork. Take the left side to continue the Green Trail in a clockwise direction.

0.8   Reach a junction. Bear left (north) to head to the Yellow Trail.

0.88 Reach the Yellow Trail entrance. Take the left side to follow the Yellow Trail in a clockwise direction.

1.18   Reach the Red Trail entrance. Continue west.

1.29 Bypass the side trail to your right (north). Continue straight (west) on the Red Trail.

1.4   Watch for rocks in the path. Ruins of a two-story home hit by a fighter jet from Tinker Air Force Base are to your right (east).

1.78   Bear right (south) onto the gravel path to continue on the loop.

1.94 Bypass the side trail to the old house from the 1.4-mile mark on your right (west). Continue straight (southeast) on the Red Trail.

2.06 Reach the Yellow Trail connection. Stay on the left side of the loop (east) to continue in a clockwise direction.

2.43 Reach the Green Trail connection. Stay on the left side to follow the trail in a clockwise direction. The trail heads south, back to the North Trails System and White Trail junction.

2.58 Come to the SS *Broken Derailleur* to your left (north).

2.67 Reach a fork with the Green Trail entrance. Continue straight (south).

2.69 Reach a fork. Take the left side to continue in a clockwise direction.

2.81   Cross a seasonal creek bed.

2.86 Reach the North Trails System entrance. Continue south under the overpass back to the White Trail connection.

3.06 Reach the White Trail connection. Bear right (south) to complete the loop in a counterclockwise direction.

3.23 Cross a seasonal creek bed.

3.3   Reach the Orange Trail connection. Take the left side of the fork to continue on the White Trail.

3.32 Cross a seasonal creek bed.

3.35 Reach the Orange Trail exit. Take the left side of the fork to continue on the White Trail.

3.4   The trail opens back up into a sunflower field.

3.58 Reach the White Trail entrance. Continue straight (north), back to the trailhead.

3.6   Arrive back at the trailhead.

22 BLUE (SOUTHWEST) TRAIL

LAKE MCMURTRY NATURAL RESOURCE AND RECREATION AREA

The easiest of all the trails at Lake McMurtry, the Blue Trail also rewards with continuous lake views. Beguiling oak-cedar forests with mossy ravines trade off with undulating meadows blooming with thistles. You might even encounter a three-toed box turtle along the trail.

Start: Blue (Southwest) Trailhead
Elevation gain: 919 to 1,004 feet
Distance: 6.93-mile lollipop
Difficulty: Easy to moderate due to uneven terrain
Hiking time: At least 3 hours
Seasons/schedule: Open year-round, sunrise to sunset
Fees and permits: Day-use fee
Trail contacts: Lake McMurtry Friends, 30285 Bronco Curve, Stillwater 74075; (405) 747-8085
Dog-friendly: Leashed dogs permitted
Trail surface: Dirt and rocky path with intermittent, unearthed tree roots
Land status: City of Stillwater in partnership with Lake McMurtry Friends

Nearest town: Stillwater
Other trail users: Mountain bikers, anglers
Maps: USGS Lake Carl Blackwell; Lake McMurtry Friends Trail System map (available at the trailhead and online at www.lakemcmurtry.org/maps.html)
Special considerations: This trail is also used by mountain bikers. Please be courteous to others while on the trail.
Blue metal trail markers and blue blazes serve as guides for this trail.
There are trail mileage signs posted throughout this trail. Mileage calculations in this guide differ from the trail mileage signs, but the trail mileage signs are also useful.

FINDING THE TRAILHEAD

From the Main Street and OK 51 W/West 6th Avenue intersection in Stillwater, head west on OK 51 W/West 6th Avenue for 6.6 miles. Turn right (north) on N3270 Road/Redland Road and continue about 3 miles. Turn left (west) on Airport Road/E0590 Road. After 0.9 mile, make a right (north) into the Lake McMurtry West Recreation Area. The road winds around for about 2.4 miles before you reach Bronco Curve. Turn right (southeast) onto Bronco Curve; 0.2 mile later, make another right (southwest). The Blue Trailhead is north, across the road from the bait shop. Parking is available next to the bait shop. GPS: N36° 10.265' W97° 11.353'

THE HIKE

Multifaceted Lake McMurtry is a water source for many of its neighboring ecosystems. Migratory birds as well as northern cardinals, Carolina chickadees, and Carolina wrens frequent the surrounding meadows and cedar-oak forests. Bass, saugeye, catfish, and crappie create ringlets in the waters at dawn and dusk. When you are not out hiking on

Lake McMurtry's engaging trail system, its waters can produce a lot of activities, such as kayaking and stand-up paddling. Other area recreation includes disc golf and lakefront camping.

The Blue Trail shines a light on the beauty of Lake McMurtry in several sections. The trail commences by heading west into an oak forest. You come to a clearing before reentering a forested area, this time composed mainly of eastern redcedar trees. From this point on, the topography interchanges between wooded areas and prairielands. In the grassy areas, lilac-hued thistles flourish in spring and summer. The trail winds in a northwesterly direction with a small footbridge in between before curving south and then west at 0.54 mile. Prior to heading left (south) on a paved road, you come to a dip in the path as well as some large slabs of rock. The paved road, which you will walk on for about 0.7 mile, is the entrance road to the Lake McMurtry West Recreation Area. Be aware of passing vehicles. Bear left (east) at the 0.69-mile mark to reenter the Blue Trail. Unearthed tree roots become more frequent at this point as the trail winds south. An inlet is visible to your left (east) at 0.84 mile. After 1.0 mile on the trail, you will head away from the water.

The trail interchanges between winding west and south all the way up to the 1.54-mile mark. Things to notice during this segment are an enchanting ravine blanketed with moss and a seasonal creek bed at 1.13 miles, a rocky alcove to the southwest at 1.36 miles, and another seasonal creek bed at 1.49 miles. The trail begins to head east at 1.54 miles before heading northeast. Lake views and seasonal creek beds occur before the trail heads in a southeast direction at 1.95 miles. It continues to wind south for the majority of the trail until the route curves northeast toward the loop portion of the lollipop. Bypass the side trail coming from your left (east) at 2.07 miles, and stay on the trail when it intersects a dirt road at the 2.13- and 2.62-mile marks. You will cross a seasonal creek bed and a couple footbridges prior to reaching the loop. Lake viewing opportunities are in abundance in this section of the trail.

Start the loop in a clockwise direction at 3.24 miles. There are partial views of an inlet of Lake McMurtry along the way. The latest addition to the Lake McMurtry trail system is the Green Trail. The Blue Trail connects with the Green Trail at 3.44 miles. If you wish to get to the Red Trail, the Green Trail is your ticket there. To stay on the Blue Trail loop, continue straight (east). The loop concludes at 3.7 miles. Bear left (south) to return to the trailhead.

MILES AND DIRECTIONS

0.0   Start at the Blue Trailhead.

0.43 Cross a small footbridge.

0.58 Encounter a dip in the path with unearthed tree roots.

0.62 Bear left (south) onto the paved road.

0.65 Cross a small seasonal creek bed.

0.69 Reenter the Blue Trail by bearing left (east).

0.75 Bear right (south).

0.84 There is an inlet of Lake McMurtry to your left (east).

1.13   Pass a small moss-covered ravine to your left (east). The trail descends over a seasonal creek bed shortly after.

1.36   Pass an alcove to your left (southwest).

1.49   Cross a small seasonal creek bed.

1.63   Cross a small seasonal creek bed.

Three-toed box turtle along the Blue Trail

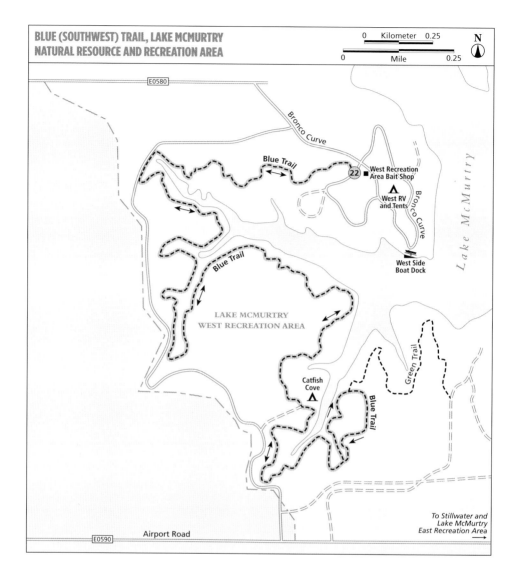

BLUE (SOUTHWEST) TRAIL, LAKE MCMURTRY NATURAL RESOURCE AND RECREATION AREA

1.67 Cross large slabs of rock in the path. There is a slight ascent up some unearthed tree roots shortly after. You will encounter a dip in the path before the slight ascent.

1.7 Cross a small seasonal creek bed.

1.89 Views of Lake McMurtry are ahead of you.

2.07 Bypass the side trail to your left (east).

2.13 The trail intersects a dirt road. Continue straight (east).

2.2 Lake views open up.

2.27 There is an outlook to the lake to your left (south).

2.45 Encounter a dip in the path that is also part of a seasonal creek bed.

2.62 The trail intersects a dirt road. Continue straight (east).

2.72 Bypass the signage by curving left (west).

Mossy ravine

2.9 Cross a small footbridge.

2.93 Cross a small seasonal creek bed.

2.94 Reach a fork. Take the right side (east) of the fork.

2.97 Reach a fork. Continue straight (east).

3.02 Cross a small footbridge. The trail heads north shortly after.

3.1 Partial views of the lake are available to your left (north).

3.24 Reach a loop. Follow it in a clockwise direction.

3.44 Reach the Green Trail entrance to your left (north). Continue straight (east) on the Blue Trail loop.

3.7 Reach the end of the loop. Bear left (south) to head back the way you came.

6.93 Arrive back at the trailhead.

23 RED (SOUTHEAST) TRAIL

LAKE MCMURTRY NATURAL RESOURCE AND RECREATION AREA

The Red Trail may not have as many lake views as its southwest counterpart, the Blue Trail, but it does have the multiplicity in terrain and elevation changes that makes it an invigorating hike. As it courses through the dense forests, the Red Trail includes sightings of quaint ponds and windswept meadows.

Start: Red (Southeast) Trailhead
Elevation gain: 943 to 1,024 feet
Distance: 7.16-mile loop
Difficulty: Moderate due to uneven terrain and switchbacks
Hiking time: At least 3 hours
Seasons/schedule: Open year-round; sunrise to sunset
Fees and permits: Day-use fee
Trail contacts: Lake McMurtry Friends, 30285 Bronco Curve, Stillwater 74075; (405) 747-8085
Dog-friendly: Leashed dogs permitted
Trail surface: Dirt and rocky path with intermittent, unearthed tree roots
Land status: City of Stillwater in partnership with Lake McMurtry Friends

Nearest town: Stillwater
Other trail users: Mountain bikers, anglers
Maps: USGS Lake Carl Blackwell; Lake McMurtry Friends Trail System map (available at the trailhead and online at www.lakemcmurtry.org/maps.html)
Special considerations: This trail is also used by mountain bikers. Please be courteous to others while on the trail.
   Red metal trail markers serve as guides for this trail.
   There are trail mileage signs posted throughout this trail. Mileage calculations in this guide differ from the trail mileage signs, but the trail mileage signs are also useful.

FINDING THE TRAILHEAD

From the Main Street and 3rd Avenue intersection in Stillwater, head north on South Main Street for 0.8 mile. South Main Street becomes North Boomer Road at this point and then changes to North Washington Street after 1 mile. Continue on North Washington Street for 3.1 miles and then turn left (west) onto E0570 Road/McMurtry Road. E0570 Road/McMurtry Road changes to Chisholm in 4 miles. After 1.5 miles on Chisholm, turn left (southwest) onto Burris Road. After 0.8 mile, Burris Road changes to Chisholm Curve. Continue on Chisholm Curve for about 430 feet and then turn left (south), passing the East Tent Campsites area. After 0.1 mile you will see a pavilion and parking lot to your left (east). The Red Trailhead is to the east of the parking lot. GPS: N36° 10.852' W97° 10.496'

Vista of Lake McMurtry

THE HIKE

The trail system at Lake McMurtry is a favorite among mountain bikers. With its switch-backs, variation in topography, and the feeling of "being away from the city," the Red Trail appeals to hikers as well. Although it does not showcase Lake McMurtry as much as the Blue Trail, it does begin and end near the lake's shoreline. It also exhibits different kinds of natural scenery, all just as unspoiled and noteworthy.

The Red Trail originates close to the shoreline of Lake McMurtry, east of a parking lot and a pavilion. Within 600 feet of the entrance, you reach a fork. Bear right to continue east, past a modest pond. After this point, you will come across a couple side trails to your right, one heading west and another heading south, respectively. Bypass those and continue toward the old footbridge at 0.38 mile. The trail starts to head south, and you encounter a series of switchbacks until the 1.75-mile mark. Close to the 0.5-mile mark, cross a seasonal creek bed. A couple more side trails will be to the west and southeast of you. At 0.66 mile, partial views of Lake McMurtry come into sight. Bear right (south-west) at the fork at 0.67 mile. An alternate route sign appears at 1.82 miles. This sign indicates that the trail will split in two directions at the upcoming fork. The right side (west) of the fork leads to the "downhill" section, covering a distance of 0.4 mile. The left side (southwest) of the fork continues through the "meadow" section, which is 0.9 mile in length. The "downhill" section is more maintained and includes a tree-framed vista of Lake McMurtry at 1.88 miles. This is perhaps the best and most distinctive view of the lake on the Red Trail, even if the view is not panoramic.

The trail heads south and then east before the route from the "meadow" section merges with the trail you are currently on. This concurrence will occur at 2.17 miles. There is

a mild dip in the path before the trail proceeds south into another series of switchbacks. The switchbacks conclude at 2.8 miles, with a small footbridge and additional partial lake views in between. The trail heads east before reaching the Green Trail connection at 2.89 miles. The Green Trail is a relatively new trail that connects the Red and Blue Trails. Bear left (north) to continue on the Red Trail. You again embark on a series of switchbacks that finish up at the 5.65-mile mark. During these switchbacks, you will encounter a seasonal creek bed, several footbridges, downed trees, and ditches. Take care at the footbridge at 4.93 miles—this one in particular is a bit old and unstable. Also be aware of the private property to your right (east) at 5.35 miles; make sure to stay on the trail.

After the switchbacks, the trail heads east, then north, and then west before you see a much larger pond through the trees at 5.9 miles. Reach the final series of switchbacks, this time milder in nature, as the trail heads north. There is another unstable footbridge to be careful of at 6.0 miles. After bypassing a couple more side trails to your left (northwest and west), another pond comes into view to your left (west). You will also see an intriguing alcove in the rocks as the trail heads west. After crossing another small footbridge, the trail winds south. You come to another footbridge at 6.7 miles. This footbridge is also unsteady, so be careful going across it. The trail heads predominately west for the remainder of the hike. Take a break and enjoy a meal at the pavilion by the lake once you have completed the hike.

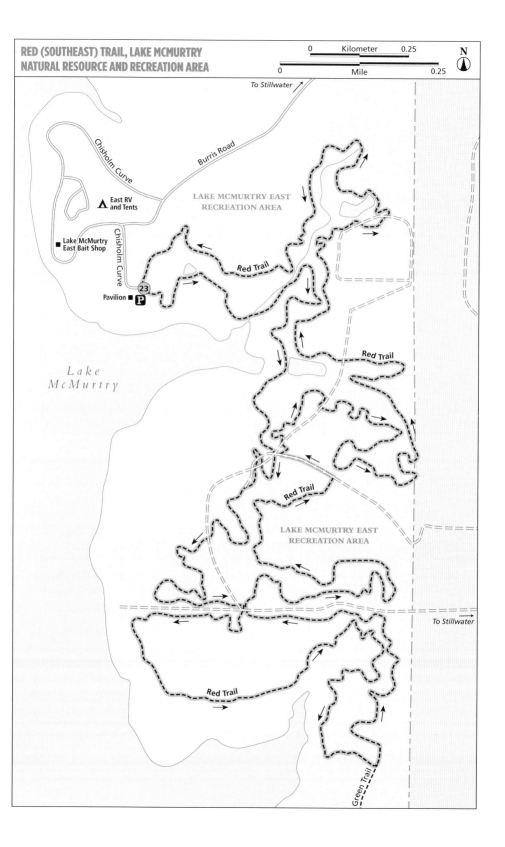

RED (SOUTHEAST) TRAIL, LAKE MCMURTRY
NATURAL RESOURCE AND RECREATION AREA

Kilometer

Mile

N

To Stillwater

Chisholm Curve

Burris Road

East RV
and Tents

LAKE MCMURTRY EAST
RECREATION AREA

Lake McMurtry
East Bait Shop

Chisholm Curve

23

Pavilion ■ P

Red Trail

Red Trail

Lake
McMurtry

Red Trail

LAKE MCMURTRY EAST
RECREATION AREA

To Stillwater

Red Trail

Green Trail

MILES AND DIRECTIONS

0.0   Start at the trailhead east of the parking lot and pavilion.

0.11 Reach a fork. Bear right (east) to continue past a pond.

0.2   Bypass the side trail to your right (west).

0.31 Bypass the side trail to your right (south).

0.38 Reach an old footbridge. Go around it if possible.

0.4   Traverse a series of switchbacks until the 1.75-mile mark.

0.48 Cross a small seasonal creek bed.

0.54 Bypass the side trail to your right (west).

0.58 Bypass the side trail to your left (southeast).

0.66 Partial views of Lake McMurtry emerge.

0.67 Reach a fork. Bear right (southwest).

1.84 Reach a fork. To the right (west) is the "downhill" section (0.4 mile). To the left (southwest) is the "meadow" section (0.9 mile). Take the more-maintained route to the "downhill" section.

1.88 A tree-framed vista of Lake McMurtry becomes available.

2.37 Encounter a mild dip in the path.

2.4   Traverse a series of switchbacks until the 2.8-mile mark.

2.49 Cross a small footbridge.

2.75 Partial views of Lake McMurtry are available to your right (west).

2.89 Reach the Green Trail connection. Bear left (north) to continue on the Red Trail. Traverse a series of switchbacks until the 5.65-mile mark.

3.21 Cross a small seasonal creek bed.

3.29 Cross a small footbridge.

4.51 There is a ditch to your right (east). Bear left (northwest).

4.75 Bypass the side trail to your left (west).

4.93 Proceed over the unstable bridge with caution.

5.35 Private property is to your right (east).

5.5   Cross a small footbridge.

5.9   Come to a view of the pond. The trail heads north with a series of switchbacks.

6.0   Proceed over the unstable bridge with caution.

6.15 Bypass the side trail to your left (northwest).

6.17 A side trail merges with the path from the left (west).

6.21 A pond becomes visible to your left (west).

6.5   Pass an alcove in the rocks to your left (west).

6.56 Cross a small footbridge.

6.7   Proceed over the unsteady bridge with caution.

7.16 Arrive back at the trailhead.

HONORABLE MENTIONS
(FRONTIER COUNTRY, CENTRAL OKLAHOMA)

Geese swimming along
Bluff Creek

C. **BLUFF CREEK (MOUNTAIN BIKE) TRAIL**

BLUFF CREEK PARK (CITY OF OKLAHOMA CITY)

Complete with enough switchbacks and mixture in terrain to delight hikers and bikers alike, the Bluff Creek Mountain Bike Trail is open to both. Occasional rafts of ducks and unique, tent-shaped primitive shelters can also be seen along the route.

Start: Bluff Creek (Mountain Bike) Trailhead, west of the Bluff Creek Park parking lot
Elevation gain: 1,023 to 1,129 feet
Distance: 3.93-mile loop
Difficulty: Moderate due to uneven, rocky trail with steep ascents and descents and multiple side trails
Hiking time: About 3 hours
Seasons/schedule: Open year-round; park hours 5 a.m.–11 p.m.
Fees and permits: None
Trail contacts: City of Oklahoma City Parks Administration, 420 W. Main St., Ste. 210, Oklahoma City 73102; (405) 297-3882
Dog-friendly: Leashed dogs permitted
Trail surface: Dirt and rocky terrain

Land status: Trail maintained in partnership with Earth Bike Fellowship; land owned by the Oklahoma City Parks & Recreation Department
Nearest town: Oklahoma City
Other trail users: Mountain bikers
Maps: USGS Britton; Bluff Creek Park map (at the trailhead)
Special considerations: The Bluff Creek Mountain Bike Trail is widely used by mountain bikers and offers a lot of side trails. Please be courteous to others while on the trail. Be alert for mountain bikers headed your way or coming from behind you, especially on narrow portions of the trail.

FINDING THE TRAILHEAD

Heading from downtown Oklahoma City, use I-235 S to connect with I-40 W. Take exit 1B onto I-40. After 4.4 miles, merge onto I-44 E/OK 3 W. Continue on I-44 E/OK 3 W (which later changes to OK 74 N) for 8.5 miles. Turn left (west) onto Hefner Road. Travel 1.5 miles and turn right (north) onto North Meridian Avenue. Continue 0.1 mile on North Meridian Avenue then turn left (west) into Bluff Creek Park. The mountain bike (unpaved) trailhead is the farthest to the north, on the west side of the parking lot. GPS: N35° 35.115′ W97° 36.339′

D. BERT COOPER TRAIL

LAKE HEFNER
(CITY OF OKLAHOMA CITY)

With a working lighthouse by its path and sweeping views of the Oklahoma City skyline, the Bert Cooper Trail loops through stout trees and along Lake Hefner's ocean-like waves to give you a work-out just shy of 10 miles.

Start: Pedestrian trail accessible from any of the parking lots surrounding Lake Hefner
Elevation gain: 1,165 to 1,225 feet
Distance: 9.57-mile loop
Difficulty: Easy
Hiking time: About 4 hours
Seasons/schedule: Open year-round, 5 a.m.–11 p.m.
Fees and permits: None
Trail contacts: City of Oklahoma City Parks Administration, 420 W. Main St., Ste. 210, Oklahoma City 73102; (405) 297-3882
Dog-friendly: Leashed dogs permitted
Trail surface: Paved

Land status: City of Oklahoma City
Nearest town: Oklahoma City
Other trail users: Cyclists (Hikers, please use designated pedestrian paths.)
Maps: USGS Britton; City of Oklahoma City trails map (available online at www.okc.gov/departments/parks-recreation/trails/trails-map)
Special considerations: This trail is also used by cyclists. Please use pathways designated for pedestrians.
   A few sections of the trail cross vehicular roads. Please be aware of and yield to vehicles.

FINDING THE TRAILHEAD

From the I-40 and I-44 junction west of downtown Oklahoma City, head onto I-44/OK 74 N. After 7.3 miles, take the Britton Road exit. Head west for 0.6 mile on Britton Road and then turn right (north) onto Lake Hefner Parkway. Park in any available parking lot to access the pedestrian trail. The trail is accessible from several points surrounding the lake. GPS: N35° 34.266' W97° 34.657'

Lighthouse near Lake Hefner

Greenthreads in full bloom along the Spring Creek Trail

E. SPRING CREEK TRAIL

SPRING CREEK PARK (CITY OF EDMOND)

A quick jaunt from the hub of Oklahoma City, the Spring Creek Trail is a relatively easy trail that offers decent mileage and respite from the busyness of the city. Surrounded by greenery, inlets, and wildflowers, trail users can also enjoy nearby Arcadia Lake.

Start: Spring Creek Trailhead, on the south end of North Midwest Boulevard
Elevation gain: 1,011 to 1,053 feet
Distance: 5.07 miles out and back
Difficulty: Easy
Hiking time: About 2 hours
Seasons/schedule: Open year-round, 7 a.m.–10 p.m.
Fees and permits: No day-use fee required if using the trail only
Trail contacts: City of Edmond Department of Parks and Recreation, 2733 Marilyn Williams Dr., Edmond 73034; (405) 359-4630

Dog-friendly: Leashed dogs permitted
Trail surface: Paved
Land status: City of Edmond
Nearest town: Edmond
Other trail users: Cyclists
Maps: USGS Edmond; City of Edmond Spring Creek map (available online at www.edmondok.com/418/Trails)
Special considerations: This trail is also used by cyclists. The left lane is designated for cyclists; the right lane is for pedestrians.
   Another trailhead is located near the Integris Health facilities.

FINDING THE TRAILHEAD

From the 15th Street exit off I-35 N, head east for 2 miles on 15th Street until you reach the Spring Creek Park entrance. You can park to the right (south) of the Spring Creek Park entrance. If you chose to spend the day at Spring Creek Park, pay the day-use fee at the entrance and then turn left onto North Midwest Boulevard for 0.5 mile. North Midwest Boulevard loops around, and you can find several parking spots. After parking, head toward the five yellow barrier poles. The paved Spring Creek Trail begins at the barrier poles and heads south. Parking is also available outside the Spring Creek Park entrance or at the Integris Health facilities (for the other trailhead). GPS: N35° 38.530' W97° 23.514'

CHICKASAW COUNTRY (SOUTH CENTRAL OKLAHOMA)

The south central region of Oklahoma is most recognizable by its abundance of rejuvenating water sources. Refreshing clear creeks, natural springs, and ocean-hued lakes all make up the topography of the region. One of Oklahoma's tallest waterfalls, Turner Falls, thunders with nearby views of the Arbuckle Mountains. Mineral springs bubble with life, and American bison graze among the verdant forests of the Chickasaw National Recreation Area. Visitors can find a restful getaway at the floating cabins on the shores of the grand Lake Murray.

Small waterfall on the way to Buffalo and Antelope Springs (Hike 27)

24 VETERANS LAKE TRAIL

CHICKASAW NATIONAL RECREATION AREA

This trail encircles Veterans Lake, granting lake views from numerous angles. Picture-perfect, especially at sunrise, the beauty of the lake can be enjoyed by everyone because of the path's paved surface. Be delighted by a combination of woodlands with bridges and grasslands abloom with wildflowers on this trail.

Start: Veterans Lake Trailhead
Elevation gain: 945 to 997 feet
Distance: 2.8-mile loop
Difficulty: Easy
Hiking time: 1–2 hours
Seasons/schedule: Open year-round, sunrise to sunset
Fees and permits: None
Trail contacts: Chickasaw National Recreation Area Headquarters, 901 W. 1st St., Sulphur 73086; (580) 622-7234
Dog-friendly: Leashed dogs permitted; no dogs allowed on trails east of the Travertine Nature Center, inside the nature center, and any areas where visitors can swim (exceptions for service and law enforcement animals)
Trail surface: Paved (ADA accessible)
Land status: National Park Service
Nearest town: Sulphur
Other trail users: Anglers
Maps: USGS Sulphur South; Chickasaw National Recreation Area map (available online at www.nps .gov/chic/planyourvisit/maps.htm)

FINDING THE TRAILHEAD

From the Travertine Nature Center, head down Southeast Perimeter Road until you reach the US 177 N to OK 7/Broadway Avenue intersection. After stopping at the stop sign, continue straight (west) through the intersection. Travel on Southwest Perimeter Road for 1.2 miles before making a left (south) onto Veterans Lake Road. You will reach the Veterans Lake parking lot in 0.3 mile. The trailhead is at the south end of the parking lot. GPS: N34° 29.516' W96° 59.252'

THE HIKE

With the ease of a flat and paved surface, the Veterans Lake Trail provides a good workout of almost 3 miles along with alluring displays of the 67–acre lake. Its surface also allows everyone to experience the trail, including the disabled. The route is relatively simple as it travels in a giant loop around the lake. The trail winds through oak-cedar forests and prairies flowing with bluestem grass, Leavenworth's eryngo, coneflower, and black-eyed Susan. Benches are perched all along the path, adding to its relaxing nature. The optimal time to capture the serenity of Veterans Lake is at sunrise, right before anglers embark on the waters to make their catch.

The Veterans Lake Trail starts off in a southeast direction across the dam. It continues in this direction after the dam until 0.35 mile. At 0.35 mile, the trail curves and starts to head north. There is a bridge to cross at 0.92 mile. The trail continues heading primarily

Top: Veterans Lake at dawn
Left: Leavenworth's eryngo along the Veterans Lake Trail
Right: Late summer glow on the Veterans Lake Trail

VETERANS LAKE TRAIL, CHICKASAW NATIONAL RECREATION AREA

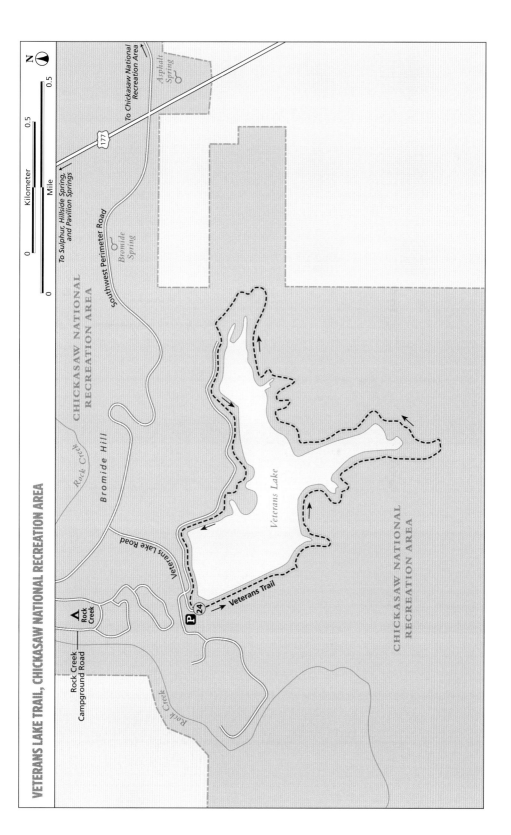

Still waters of Veterans Lake

north until 1.31 miles, when the trail heads east. Views of Veterans Lake become less visible at this point.

At 1.54 miles the trail curves around onto a bridge and then starts to head back north. You traverse through an oak–cedar wooded area at 1.76 miles and then cross another bridge at 1.89 miles. Lake views reappear to your left (west) at 1.87 miles. After the 1.89-mile mark, the trail heads west all the way back to the trailhead.

You reach a parking lot at 2.03 miles, a picnic area at 2.2 miles, and then another parking lot at 2.41 miles. At the latter mile point, go across the crosswalk northeast of the pavilion to reconnect with the paved trail. Once you pass a fishing dock to your left (south) at 2.73 miles, return to the parking lot where you started.

MILES AND DIRECTIONS

0.0   Start at the trailhead south of the parking lot and bear right (southeast).

0.35 The trail curves and starts to head north.

0.92 Cross the bridge.

1.31 The trail heads east. Views of Veterans Lake diminish.

1.54 The trail curves north. Go across the bridge.

1.76 Reach an oak-cedar wooded area.

1.89 Cross the bridge.

1.87 Lake views emerge once again to your left (west).

2.03 Reach a parking lot.

2.2   Reach a picnic area.

2.41 Reach another parking lot. Go across the crosswalk northeast of the pavilion to reconnect with the paved trail.

2.73 Pass a fishing dock to your left (south).

2.76 Reach the parking lot where you started.

2.8   Arrive back at the trailhead.

25 BISON PASTURE TRAIL (INCLUDING BROMIDE HILL OVERLOOK)

CHICKASAW NATIONAL RECREATION AREA

A herd of American bison can be seen resting and grazing at the center point of this trail, making this a fun hike for adults and children alike. The enchanting Hillside Springs can be accessed from this trail as well. For the more ambitious, a hike to the top of Bromide Hill for spectacular aerial views of the Rock Creek area and Arbuckle Mountains is included.

Start: Bison Pasture Trailhead
Elevation gain: 902 to 1,070 feet
Distance: 3.12-mile lollipop with an additional spur to an overlook
Difficulty: Moderate due to a couple switchbacks and changes in elevation
Hiking time: 1–2 hours
Seasons/schedule: Open year-round, sunrise to sunset
Fees and permits: None
Trail contacts: Chickasaw National Recreation Area Headquarters, 901 W. 1st St., Sulphur 73086; (580) 622-7234

Dog-friendly: Leashed dogs permitted; no dogs allowed on trails east of the Travertine Nature Center, inside the nature center, and any areas where visitors can swim (exceptions for service and law enforcement animals)
Trail surface: Dirt and gravel
Land status: National Park Service
Nearest town: Sulphur
Other trail users: None
Maps: USGS Sulphur South; Chickasaw National Recreation Area map (available online at www.nps .gov/chic/planyourvisit/maps.htm)

FINDING THE TRAILHEAD

From the Travertine Nature Center, head down Northeast Perimeter Road via the one-way exit route for about 1.7 miles. Once you reach US 177 S, stop at the stop sign and then turn left (southwest). After 300 feet, turn right (west) onto Northwest Perimeter Road. The trailhead is to your left (south) after 1.1 miles. Parking is available at the Rock Creek Campground, across Northwest Perimeter Road to your left (northwest). GPS: N34° 29.869' W96° 59.137'

THE HIKE

The iconic American bison is the country's national mammal. The bison's population dwindled after the 1800s due to habitat loss, hunting, and epidemics. Endeavors to stabilize the population, including species reintroduction and preservation on national land, have helped the population rebound. Chickasaw National Recreation Area is one of the special places in Oklahoma that provides sanctuary to this great animal. In 1920, a herd from the Wichita Mountains National Wildlife Refuge was transferred to the area that includes Bison Viewpoint. The Bison Pasture Trail winds around this region, with Bison Viewpoint as one of its stopping points.

Rock Creek, the largest creek in the Chickasaw National Recreation Area, neighbors the trail on the left (north). The trail winds around the north face of Bromide Hill after about 600 feet from the trailhead. At 0.16 mile, you head up a switchback. There is an ascent of 115 feet in elevation from this point to the 0.37-mile mark. Panoramic views of the Chickasaw National Recreation Area are available to your left (north) during this segment. Continue the ascent on the right-hand side (southeast) of the fork at 0.33 mile to get to the Bromide Hill Overlook. The left side (east) of the fork continues to Bison Viewpoint. The trail curves and winds southwest at 0.37 mile. There are a couple short-cuts to the Bromide Hill Overlook parking lot and Southwest Perimeter Road to your left (south) before you reach the Bromide Hill Overlook at 0.46 mile. The area where the nearly 140-foot-tall Bromide Hill stands also holds the name "Robbers' Roost"—old tales claim that outlaws used to seek refuge among the bluffs. The view from Bromide Hill is breathtaking. Astounding at any time of day, hikers can see quite a bit. The scene before you includes the endless greenery of Chickasaw National Recreation Area, the lively town of Sulphur, the traversing of Rock Creek, and, on a clear day, the Arbuckle Mountains and Washita River Valley.

After your break at the Bromide Hill Overlook, head back down to the fork from the 0.33-mile mark to move forward onto the Bison Pasture Trail. When you reach that fork,

View from Bromide Hill Overlook

Left: Hillside Springs
Right: Bison grazing at Bison Viewpoint

it will clock in at 0.6 mile. Curve around and head east toward the Bison Viewpoint. The trail predominately heads east, with a curve to the north and south in between. At 0.75 mile on the trail, take the right side of the fork (northeast) to continue to the Bison Viewpoint. This begins the loop portion of the lollipop, with the loop meant to be taken in a counterclockwise direction. A lily pond appears to your left (east), and there is a pause from the tree shade at 0.82 mile. Tree cover returns at the 0.89-mile mark. You will cross four footbridges before reaching the Bison Viewpoint at 1.5 miles. Chances of seeing bison at the viewpoint are greater in early morning or late afternoon. Bison calves are born in spring and can be seen throughout the summer. If you do not see any bison during your hike, a parking lot right off US 177 for the viewpoint gives you another chance without having to do the hike again.

Heading north from the Bison Viewpoint, you come to your first series of rock stairs at 1.69 miles. You also need to cross Bison Road (the road that leads to the ranger station), so be aware of passing vehicles. Another series of stairs occurs at 1.73 miles; the fairy tale–like Hillside Springs is to your left (west) shortly after. Nicknamed "Beauty Spring," this cistern-held mineral spring is extremely beautiful to look at, but its water is not to be consumed because of its bacteria content. Pavilion Springs, originally known as "Big

BISON PASTURE TRAIL (INCLUDING BROMIDE HILL OVERLOOK), CHICKASAW NATIONAL RECREATION AREA

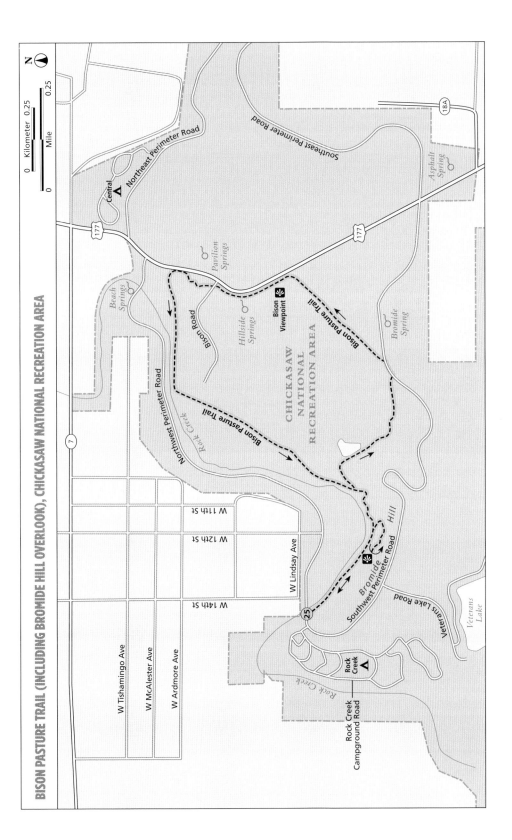

Tom" before it was renamed for the pavilion built over it, can be seen to your north at 1.82 miles. Bear left (west) to continue on the loop.

Before reaching the end of the loop, you will bypass a couple side trails and cross four more footbridges. At 2.65 miles, where the loop ends, continue straight (southwest). Continue past the Bromide Hill Overlook connection to your left (south) and head northwest, back to the trailhead.

MILES AND DIRECTIONS

0.0   Start at the trailhead southeast of the Rock Creek Campground.

0.16 Reach a switchback. There will be an ascent of 115 feet in elevation until the 0.37-mile mark.

0.33 Reach a fork. Continue the ascent on the right-hand side (southeast) of the fork to get to the Bromide Hill Overlook.

0.4   A shortcut to the Bromide Hill Overlook parking lot and Southwest Perimeter Road is to your left (south). Continue west.

0.43 Another shortcut to the parking lot and road is to your left (south).

0.46 Reach the Bromide Hill Overlook, to your right (north). Head back down to the fork to continue on the Bison Pasture Trail.

0.6   Reach the Bison Pasture Trail. Curve around and head east toward the Bison Viewpoint.

0.75 Reach a fork. Take the right side of the fork (northeast) to start the loop portion of the lollipop in a counterclockwise direction.

0.82 A lily pond is to your left (east).

0.89 Cross the footbridge.

0.97 Cross the footbridge.

1.0   Cross the footbridge.

1.1   Cross the footbridge.

1.5   Reach the Bison Viewpoint.

1.69 Use the rock stairs and cross Bison Road. Head north.

1.73 Go down the rock stairs.

1.75 Hillside Springs is to your left (west).

1.82 Pavilion Springs can be seen to your north. Bear left (west).

1.98 Cross the footbridge.

2.04 Cross the footbridge.

2.11 Cross the footbridge.

2.17 Bypass the side trail to your left (east). Cross the footbridge.

2.19 Bypass the side trail to your left (east).

2.57 Cross the footbridge.

2.65 Reach a fork to close the loop. Continue straight (southwest).

2.8   Bypass the Bromide Hill Overlook connection to your left (south) as you head northwest, back to the trailhead.

3.12 Arrive back at the trailhead.

26 TRAVERTINE CREEK TRAIL (INCLUDING LITTLE NIAGARA FALLS)

CHICKASAW NATIONAL RECREATION AREA

While Little Niagara Falls is the main draw of this route, the Travertine Creek Trail itself is a delightful path surrounded by eastern redcedar trees and miniature waterfalls. It follows along Travertine Creek, ending with views of Little Niagara and limestone-based Travertine Island.

Start: Travertine Creek Trailhead, south of Central Campground
Elevation gain: 945 to 1,053 feet
Distance: 2.95 miles out and back
Difficulty: Easy
Hiking time: 1–2 hours
Seasons/schedule: Open year-round, sunrise to sunset
Fees and permits: None
Trail contacts: Chickasaw National Recreation Area Headquarters, 901 W. 1st St., Sulphur 73086; (580) 622-7234
Dog-friendly: No dogs allowed on trails east of the Travertine Nature Center, inside the nature center, and any areas where visitors can swim (exceptions for service and law enforcement animals)

Trail surface: Dirt and gravel
Land status: National Park Service
Nearest town: Sulphur
Other trail users: None
Maps: USGS Sulphur North; Chickasaw National Recreation Area map (available online at www.nps.gov/chic/planyourvisit/maps.htm)
Special considerations: There are options when it comes to trailheads for this trail. The trail can be accessed from the northeast near the Travertine Nature Center and Little Niagara area or from the west near the Central Campground and Pavilion Springs area. This guide uses the latter trailhead.

FINDING THE TRAILHEAD

From the Travertine Nature Center, head down the one-way Northeast Perimeter Road for about 1.7 miles. The trailhead is to your left (south), right before you reach US 177 N. There is a parking area 375 feet east of the trailhead and south of Central Campground. GPS: N34° 30.257' W96° 58.150'

THE HIKE

If you want to hike to Little Niagara Falls, the Travertine Creek Trail is the perfect route to get there. Along the way you will get to experience the noticeable beauty of the Chickasaw National Recreation Area, with its bountiful forests and flowing waters. Travertine Creek travels alongside the trail for the majority of its length. The creek sources its water from both Buffalo Springs and Antelope Springs. Limestone from the

Travertine Creek

springs' water gets redeposited as travertine, which is how the creek got its name. Interestingly enough, the creek was initially named Sulphur Creek.

Starting at the rock steps south of Central Campground, the trail heads southeast until you reach Cold Creek Campground. Continue straight (southeast) at the fork at 0.19 mile. The right side (south) of the fork connects with Pavilion Springs, which lies along the Bison Pasture Trail. After crossing a few seasonal creek beds stemming from Travertine Creek, bypass the side trail to your right (south) at 0.46 mile. Travertine Creek becomes more visible to your left (north), with a couple short waterfalls along the way.

A connector trail to Cold Creek Campground becomes available to your left (north) at 0.61 mile. Shortly after, you cross a bridge and the trail starts to wind in a northeasterly direction. Come to another footbridge and side creek bed at the 0.88-mile mark and a subsequent bridge at 1.04 miles. When you come to the fork at 1.12 miles, continue straight (northeast). You encounter Southeast Perimeter Road at 1.15 miles. Watch for moving vehicles before crossing the road. There is a fork immediately after. Take the left side (northeast) of the fork to Little Niagara Falls. The right side (east) heads to the Travertine Nature Center.

You must cross another road (use the pedestrian crosswalk) and the Travertine Nature Center parking lot to reach the Little Niagara Falls area at 1.36 miles. Feel free to have a packed lunch at one of the adjoining picnic tables or take a dip in the refreshing waters. It is not advisable to shortcut across the large rocks lying within Little Niagara Falls—they are very slippery and dangerous. Use designated pathways to get to the other side. After resting for a little bit, bear left (northwest) of Little Niagara Falls and connect with the trail behind the restroom building. Reach a junction at 1.42 miles; bear right (south) to go to Travertine Island. Straight (west) leads to Lost Cave Falls. To the left (north) is a

Little Niagara

TRAVERTINE CREEK TRAIL (INCLUDING LITTLE NIAGARA FALLS), CHICKASAW NATIONAL RECREATION AREA

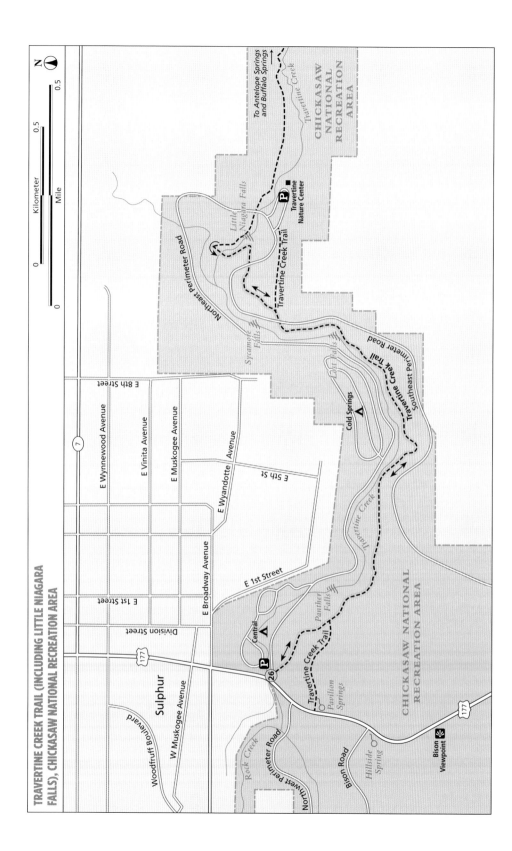

shortcut back to the Travertine Nature Center parking lot. Cross a footbridge at 1.43 miles to reach Travertine Island. A large sign on the "island" describes the composition of the rock that forms it. After learning about the geology and wandering around Travertine Island for a bit, head back to the fork from the 1.15-mile mark. Bear right (southwest) and cross Southeast Perimeter Road to return the way you came.

MILES AND DIRECTIONS

0.0   Start at the rock steps south of Central Campground.

0.19 Reach a fork. Continue straight (southeast).

0.38 Cross a seasonal creek bed.

0.44 Cross a seasonal creek bed.

0.46 Bypass the side trail to your right (south). Continue straight (southeast).

0.55 Travertine Creek parallels the trail on your left (north).

0.61 Reach a fork. Continue straight (southeast).

0.69 Bear left (north) and go across the bridge.

0.73 Views of Travertine Creek continue to your left (north).

0.88 Cross the footbridge and then a seasonal creek bed shortly after.

1.04 Go over the bridge.

1.12 Reach a fork. Continue straight (northeast).

1.15 Cross Southeast Perimeter Road (watch for moving vehicles). Reach a fork shortly after. Take the left side (northeast) of the fork to Little Niagara.

1.31 Cross the road and the parking lot to head east toward Little Niagara.

1.36 Reach little Niagara. Bear left (north). It is not advisable to shortcut across the large rocks lying within Little Niagara Falls—they are very slippery. Connect with the trail behind the restroom building.

1.42 Reach a junction. Bear right (northeast) to go to Travertine Island.

1.43 Cross a footbridge.

1.46 Reach Travertine Island. Turn around and head back to the fork from the 1.15-mile mark.

1.74 Reach the fork from the 1.15-mile mark. Bear right (southwest). Cross Southeast Perimeter Road and head back to the trailhead.

2.95 Arrive back at the trailhead.

27 BUFFALO AND ANTELOPE SPRINGS TRAIL

CHICKASAW NATIONAL RECREATION AREA

Perhaps the favorite trail of visitors to the Chickasaw National Recreation Area, the Buffalo and Antelope Springs Trail has a lot of qualities that make it so. It features a melodic creek, sacred natural springs, a charming stone bridge, and mesmerizing side trails lush with wide-ranging greenery—cedar and oak forests, horsetail, prickly pear, and coneflowers, to name just a few.

Start: Buffalo and Antelope Springs Trailhead
Elevation gain: 1,034 to 1,142 feet
Distance: 3.2 miles out and back with three side loops
Difficulty: Easy
Hiking time: 1–2 hours
Seasons/schedule: Open year-round, sunrise to sunset
Fees and permits: None
Trail contacts: Chickasaw National Recreation Area Headquarters, 901 W. 1st St., Sulphur 73086; (580) 622-7234

Dog-friendly: No dogs allowed on trails east of the Travertine Nature Center, inside the nature center, and any areas where visitors can swim (exceptions for service and law enforcement animals)
Trail surface: Dirt and gravel
Land status: National Park Service
Nearest town: Sulphur
Other trail users: None
Maps: USGS Sulphur North; Chickasaw National Recreation Area map (available online at www.nps .gov/chic/planyourvisit/maps.htm)

FINDING THE TRAILHEAD

The Buffalo and Antelope Springs Trailhead is south of the Travertine Nature Center. To get to the Travertine Nature Center from the Chickasaw Visitor Center in Sulphur, head south on US 177 S/West 1st Street for 1 mile. Turn left (east) on Southeast Perimeter Road and continue for 1.6 miles until you reach a fork. Continue straight (northeast) onto the one-way road leading to the Travertine Nature Center parking lot. The trailhead is on the right side (east) of the road after 0.2 mile. Park in the parking lot south of the trailhead. GPS: N34° 30.296' W96° 57.038'

THE HIKE

The Buffalo and Antelope Springs Trail is quite a delight. Not only is it family-friendly, but it also has photogenic scenery and is rich with history. It heads primarily east all the way to its turnaround point, with the exception of three side loops.

The trail surface is wide and composed of gravel from the trailhead to the 0.17-mile mark. There is a bench to your right (south) before the Travertine Nature Center comes into view at 0.1 mile. The entrance for the first of the three side loops, the Prairie Loop Trail, is at 0.17 mile. The trail surface changes to dirt at this point. Bear right (south) to hike the Prairie Loop Trail. Head across the rock steps in Travertine Creek at 0.21 mile

and take the loop in a counterclockwise direction. The landscape interchanges between clusters of horsetail, cedar–oak woodlands, and then arid geography dotted with prickly pear and yucca. Be aware of downed trees on this trail. The Prairie Loop Trail ends at 0.73 mile, and you reconnect with the Buffalo and Antelope Springs Trail at 0.8 mile. Bear right (east) to continue. After passing a side trail and a bench to your right (southwest), views of Travertine Creek emerge short of the 1.0-mile mark.

The entrance to the second side trail, the Tall Oaks Loop Trail, occurs at 1.03 miles. Similar in topography to the Prairie Loop Trail, it stays true to its name with its abundance of towering oaks and other hardwood trees. It is also meant to be taken in a counterclockwise direction. After crossing Travertine Creek, the Tall Oaks Loop Trail ends at 1.49 miles. You connect back with the Buffalo and Antelope Springs Trail at 1.5 miles. Bear right (northeast) to move forward on the main trail.

At 1.63 miles you reach the entrance and exit for the final loop. This loop includes the Dry Creek Loop Trail entrance as well as access to Buffalo Springs and Antelope Springs. Bear right (south) across the rock slab to start the loop in a counterclockwise direction. Travertine Creek, with its ebbing current, refreshing aura, and miniature waterfalls, are to your right (south), paralleling the trail. A rocky footbridge popular for photographs is at the 1.73-mile mark. Cross it to reach the Dry Creek Loop Trail entrance at 1.88 miles. Bear right (south) to complete the loop in a counterclockwise direction. This trail is similar in nature to the Prairie and Tall Oaks Loop Trails, but contains more cedar woodlands and meadows. The Dry Creek Loop Trail ends at 2.41 miles. Continue straight (north) toward Buffalo Springs and Antelope Springs.

Buffalo Springs and Antelope Springs are the key sources of water for Travertine Creek. They are also freshwater springs, while the other springs in the Chickasaw

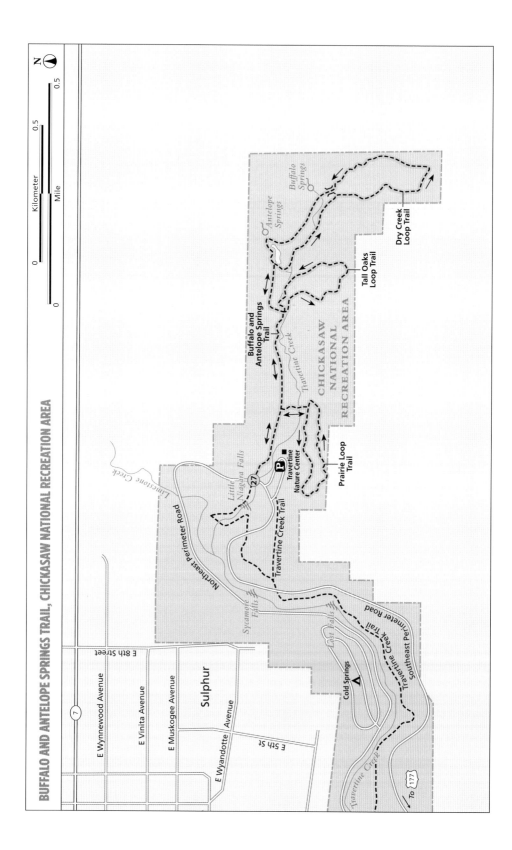

BUFFALO AND ANTELOPE SPRINGS TRAIL, CHICKASAW NATIONAL RECREATION AREA

Sulphur

E 8th Street
E Wynnewood Avenue
E Vinita Avenue
E Muskogee Avenue
E Wyandotte Avenue
E 5th St

Limestone Creek
Northeast Perimeter Road
Little Niagara Falls
Sycamore Falls
Lost Falls
Cold Springs
Travertine Creek

Travertine Creek Trail
Travertine Nature Center
Travertine Creek
Prairie Loop Trail
Buffalo and Antelope Springs Trail
Antelope Springs
Buffalo Springs

CHICKASAW NATIONAL RECREATION AREA
Tall Oaks Loop Trail
Dry Creek Loop Trail
Southeast Perimeter Road
Travertine Creek Trail

To 177

N

Kilometer
0   0.5
Mile
0   0.5

National Recreation Area are mineral springs. You reach the life-giving Buffalo Springs (*Yunush Kulli*) at 2.43 miles. Its emerald-hued waters are encircled by a stone basin as a safeguard. Please respect the fragility of the natural spring and do not touch or enter it. After taking a break and marveling at the significance of Buffalo Springs, head toward the footbridge at 2.45 miles. Bypass the side trail to your right (north) shortly after. Continue straight (west) to Antelope Springs. Come to a fork at 2.58 miles and another at 2.59 miles. Stay on the right side (northwest) of the fork each time to continue toward Antelope Springs. The equally beautiful Antelope Springs (*Issibulba Kulli*) is at 2.62 miles. After admiring the flow of water coming from the rocky hillsides, bear left (southwest). At 2.67 miles you reach the entrance to the final loop that was originally at the 1.63-mile mark. From here, head back west to the Travertine Nature Center and the trailhead.

Bridge before Dry Creek Loop Trail

MILES AND DIRECTIONS

0.0 Start at the Buffalo and Antelope Springs Trailhead.

0.08 Come to a bench to your right (south).

0.1 Travertine Nature Center is to your right (south).

0.17 Reach the Prairie Loop Trail entrance. Bear right (south). The path surface turns to dirt.

0.21 Cross the rock steps in Travertine Creek.

0.24 Bear right (west) to hike the loop in a counterclockwise direction. Watch for large rocks in the path.

0.6 Bypass the side trail to your right (east).

0.73 The Prairie Loop Trail ends. Bear right (north) to head back to the main trail.

0.8 Reach the Buffalo and Antelope Springs Trail (main trail). Bear right (east).

0.9 Bypass the side trail to your right (southwest). Come to a bench on your right (north) shortly after.

0.97 Views of Travertine Creek are to your right (south).

0.98 Come to another outlook to your right (south).

1.03 Reach the Tall Oaks Loop Trail entrance. Bear right (southeast) across the rock steps to take the loop in a counterclockwise direction.

1.25 Cross a seasonal creek bed.

Buffalo Springs (*Yunush Kulli*)

1.4   Cross a seasonal creek bed. Travertine Creek then parallels to your right (north).

1.49 The Tall Oaks Loop Trail ends. Bear right (north) to head back onto the main trail.

1.5   Reach the Buffalo and Antelope Springs Trail (main trail). Bear right (northeast).

1.62 Come to an outlook on your right (south).

1.63 Reach a fork that heads toward the Dry Creek Loop Trail. Bear right (south) across the rock slab.

1.64 Bear right (west) to take the Dry Creek Loop Trail in a counterclockwise direction.

1.73 Cross a photo-worthy footbridge.

1 88 Reach the Dry Creek Loop Trail entrance. Bear right (south).

2.41 The Dry Creek Loop Trail ends. Continue straight (north) toward Buffalo Springs.

2.43 Reach Buffalo Springs (*Yunush Kulli*).

2.45 Cross a footbridge. Bypass a side trail to your right (north) shortly after. Continue straight (west) to Antelope Springs.

2.58 Reach a fork. Stay on the right side (northwest) of the fork to head toward Antelope Springs.

2.59 Reach another fork. Continue straight (west) to Antelope Springs.

2.62 Reach Antelope Springs (*Issibulba Kulli*). Bear left (southwest) to head back to the trailhead.

3.2   Arrive back at the trailhead.

28 BUCKHORN HIKING TRAIL

LAKE MURRAY STATE PARK

With myriad footbridges, quiet forest bends, and incredible lake views, the Buckhorn Trail showcases a tiny corner of all the magnificence the Lake Murray area has to offer.

Start: Buckhorn Hiking Trailhead, west of the Lake Murray cabins
Elevation gain: 725 to 801 feet
Distance: 3.3 miles out and back
Difficulty: Easy to moderate due to uneven terrain
Hiking time: 2–3 hours
Seasons/schedule: Open year-round, sunrise to sunset
Fees and permits: Parking pass required for day-use visitors
Trail contacts: Lake Murray State Park Office, 13528 Scenic State Hwy. 77, Ardmore 73401; (580) 223-4044
Dog-friendly: Leashed dogs permitted
Trail surface: Dirt and rocky path
Land status: Oklahoma State Parks

Nearest town: Ardmore
Other trail users: Cyclists
Maps: USGS Lake Murray; Lake Murray State Park map (available online at www.travelok.com/state-parks and via the Oklahoma State Parks mobile app)
Special considerations: The actual trail ends at Tipps Point Road next to the Tipps Point parking lot. To see additional views of Lake Murray, proceed across Tipps Point Road to the shoreline.
  This trail intersects the biking trail. Be aware of multiple side trails; follow signage for "Big Loop" and "Tipps Point."

FINDING THE TRAILHEAD

From the US 77 S/South Commerce Street and OK 199/West Broadway Street junction in Ardmore, head south on US 77 S for 7 miles. Turn left (east) on OK 77/Lodge Road. After traveling 2.5 miles on OK 77/Lodge Road, turn left (northeast) on Holly Road. The trailhead is to your left (north), just short of 100 feet down the road and west of the cabins. Parking is available right at the trailhead. GPS: N34° 04.354' W97° 06.034'

THE HIKE

The mighty and jewel-toned Lake Murray is quite a sight to see. There are several opportunities to see the lake from different angles on the Buckhorn Hiking Trail—first a cove, then an inlet, and then its extensive shoreline. From the trailhead, the trail starts off heading west. After a couple hundred feet, there are large rocks in the path until you reach the footbridge at 0.08 mile. There is a side trail to an overlook of a cove in Lake Murray that is worth visiting. Head west across the footbridge. The trail quickly heads north as you go up the log steps. Partial views of Lake Murray continue to your right (east). After 0.18 mile the path surface interchanges between dirt and rock. Just shy of 0.25 mile, you reach a junction. Alternate biking trails are to your left (west) and straight ahead (northwest). Bear right (north) to continue on the path that has more lake views. Cross a footbridge shortly after, and then the trail winds northwest. The alternate bike trail heading northwest eventually merges at 0.33 mile.

Vista of inlet

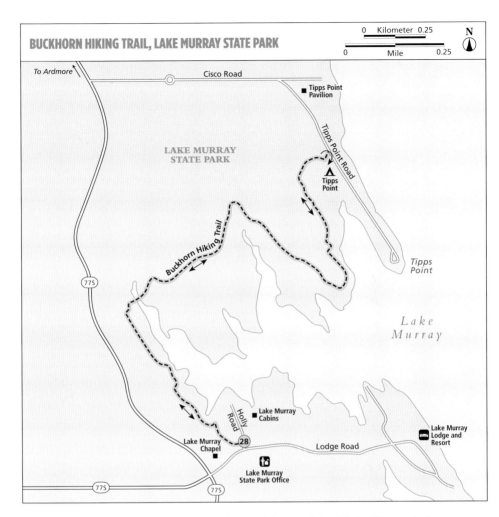

Head straight (north) to continue on the Buckhorn Hiking Trail. Close to being on the trail for 0.5 mile, you reach a fork. Bear right (northeast) toward Tipps Point. The path straight ahead (northwest) is another alternate bike route. Come to another fork shortly after, with another alternate bike route straight ahead (northeast). Bear right (east) toward the footbridge. There is a bench to your left (north) before you cross the footbridge. The bridge is a bit rickety and spans a beautiful inlet portion of Lake Murray; try not to be distracted, and find a safe spot to take in the view. Go down some rocks after the footbridge, and then come to another bench, this time to your left (north). The trail then heads northeast. Be aware of unearthed tree roots in the path surface starting at 0.57 mile.

After the log steps at 0.6 mile, the trail curves back and forth from south to north all the way to 1.25 miles. During this part of the trail, there are several footbridges and sections with log steps and large rocks in the path. Be mindful of the ditch at 0.9 mile, as well as the alternate bike trail that occurs to your left (northeast) at 0.94 mile. Bear right (northeast) toward Tipps Point at the fork at 1.23 miles. Straight ahead (north) is another alternate bike route. You are greeted with partial views of Lake Murray to your right (east) at this point.

Bear right (east) when you reach the barbed-wire fence at 1.54 miles. Come to another fork shortly after. Continue straight (east) to Tipps Point. The left side of the fork (north) is the final alternate bike route. At 1.63 miles you reach a dead end into Tipps Point Campground. Bear left (north) to get to Tipps Point and reach Tipps Point Road at 1.65 miles. The trail ends at this point, but feel free to cross Tipps Point Road (with caution) to enjoy the rewarding shoreline view of Lake Murray. Once you finish soaking in the scenery, turn around and head back the way you came.

MILES AND DIRECTIONS

0.0   Start at the trailhead west of the cabins.

0.08 The trail heads west across a footbridge. A side trail to a worthwhile overlook of Lake Murray is to your right (north). Go up the log steps where the trail heads north. Partial views of Lake Murray are to your right (east).

0.18 Come to a couple overlooks of Lake Murray.

0.24 Reach a junction. Head right (north) for more lake views.

0.27 Cross a footbridge.

0.33 Head straight (north) to continue on the Buckhorn Trail. The path from the 0.18-mile mark merges.

0.49 Reach a fork. Bear right (northeast) toward Tipps Point.

0.51 Reach a fork. Bear right (east) toward a footbridge.

0.53 Come to a bench on your left (north). Cross a footbridge and go down some rocks.

0.57 Another bench is to your right (southeast).

0.6 Go up some log steps.

0.7 There are logs in the path at this point.

0.73 Go over a couple footbridges and some log steps.

0.9 Be aware of the ditch.

0.92 Cross a footbridge. Continue up the log steps.

0.94 Bypass the alternate bike trail to your left (northeast). Continue straight (south).

0.96 Go over a small footbridge.

1.22 Partial views of Lake Murray emerge to your right (east).

1.23 Reach a fork. Bear right (northeast) to Tipps Point.

1.58 Reach a fork. Continue straight (east) to Tipps Point.

1.63 Bear left (north) to get to Tipps Point.

1.65 The trail ends at Tipps Point. Cross Tipps Point Road to get shoreline views of Lake Murray. Head back the way you came.

3.3 Arrive back at the trailhead.

29 SKI JUMP TO TUCKER TOWER TRAIL

LAKE MURRAY STATE PARK

Reminiscent of European-style castles photographed by former Oklahoma state senator Fred Tucker, majestic limestone Tucker Tower serves as a beacon from the 1930s. The dazzling turquoise-hued waters of Lake Murray that surround the tower add the perfect touch of enchantment.

Start: Ski Jump Trailhead, in the southwest section of Ski Jump Campground
Elevation gain: 709 to 815 feet
Distance: 6.12 miles out and back
Difficulty: Moderate due to uneven terrain
Hiking time: 3–4 hours
Seasons/schedule: Open year-round, sunrise to sunset
Fees and permits: Parking pass required for day-use visitors
Trail contacts: Lake Murray State Park Office, 13528 Scenic State Hwy. 77, Ardmore 73401; (580) 223-4044
Dog-friendly: Leashed dogs permitted

Trail surface: Dirt and rocky path
Land status: Oklahoma State Parks
Nearest town: Ardmore
Other trail users: Cyclists
Maps: USGS Lake Murray; Lake Murray State Park map (available online at www.travelok.com/state-parks and via the Oklahoma State Parks mobile app)
Special considerations: The actual trail ends at the Tucker Tower parking lot. This guide includes hiking to Tucker Tower for additional vantage points.
  Blue metal circles with an arrow in the middle serve as trail markers.

FINDING THE TRAILHEAD
From the US 77 S/South Commerce Street and OK 199/West Broadway Street junction in Ardmore, head south on US 77 S for 7 miles. Turn left (east) on OK 77/Lodge Road and make a right (south) on OK 77 S after 2.4 miles. Continue 2.4 miles on OK 77 S and turn left (east) into the Ski Jump Campground. The trailhead is to your right (south) before you reach any of the campsites. Due to limited parking in the Ski Jump Campground, it is best to reserve a camping spot at the campground or come from the Buzzards Roost to Ski Jump Trail. GPS: N34° 02.672' W97° 05.777'

THE HIKE
From a potential retreat for Oklahoma governors to a geological museum and, most recently, a nature center, Tucker Tower echoes with ambitious aspirations. Although it was never actually occupied due to lack of funding by the Works Progress Administration, the tower was eventually completed by the State of Oklahoma as a memorial for the public. With outstanding panoptic views of Lake Murray from its observation deck, Tucker Tower serves as a wondrous reward for those venturing on the Ski Jump Trail.

Vista of Tucker Tower

The trail begins near the entrance of the Ski Jump Campground and initially heads south. The route is comparable to a giant switchback. Before the trail winds east, you cross your first seasonal creek bed at 0.14 mile. From 0.19 to 1.0 mile, the scenery interchanges between cedar landscapes and wildflower-flourishing grasslands. Note the vivid

colors of canary-hued bitterweeds and pastel-tinted asters while on the trail's grassy areas. The trail parallels Lake Murray to its north at around 0.3 mile and heads south again. Before you reach the last grassland portion of the trail, the trail curves around and heads north at 0.8 mile. After this point, you traverse several seasonal creek beds and areas with fallen tree branches and tree trunks. There are several large rocks you need to cross over as well, at 1.61, 1.9, and 1.92 miles. Between these points, the trail curves back around and heads southeast at 1.5 miles before heading north again at 2.1 miles. You encounter a series of dips in the path shortly after. Most of them are mild in their elevation changes (only a couple feet), and they do provide a break in the monotony of the trail.

At 2.27 miles you reach a fork. Take the left side (north) of the fork to head to Tucker Tower. The right side of the fork leads to a vehicle road to Tucker Tower. After a few more rocky surfaces and another seasonal creek bed, you are greeted with views of the glacial-like waters of Lake Murray to your left (west) starting at the 2.49-mile mark. A switchback occurs at 2.72 miles, where the trail heads south and then back north around the inlet. At 2.82 miles, the trail ends at the Tucker Tower parking lot. Head north through the parking lot and continue 0.75 mile to the Lake Murray Nature Center and Tucker Tower to attain additional views of Lake Murray. Remember to be aware of and yield to vehicles.

Reach the Lake Murray Nature Center at 2.95 miles. Head around the left side (east) of the nature center toward Tucker Tower. There are some stairs to climb before you reach Tucker Tower at 3.05 miles. Venture to the top of Tucker Tower for incredible aerial views of Lake Murray. Also, take time inside the tower to peruse some of the history of the Civilian Conservation Corps projects conducted at the lake and be fascinated by the exhibits on display in the Lake Murray Nature Center. Once you are finished, head back to the Ski Jump Campground.

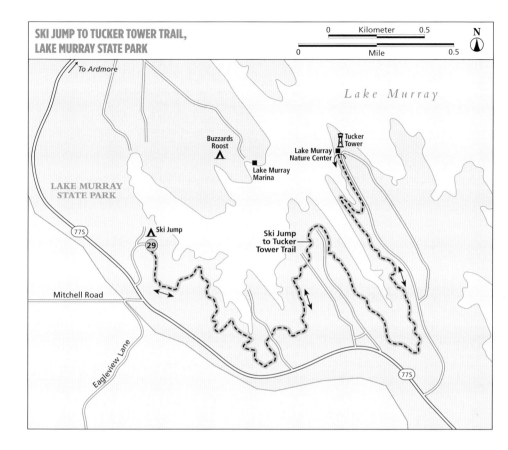

MILES AND DIRECTIONS

0.0 Start at the trailhead southwest of Ski Jump Campground.

1.33 Watch for any downed trees.

2.27 Reach a fork. Take the left side (north) of the fork to head to Tucker Tower.

2.7 Views of Lake Murray open up to your left (west).

2.72 Reach a switchback that heads south and then back north around an inlet of Lake Murray.

2.82 The trail ends at the Tucker Tower parking lot. Walk across the parking lot to visit the tower and nature center.

2.95 Reach the Lake Murray Nature Center. Head around the left side (east) of the nature center toward Tucker Tower.

3.05 Reach Tucker Tower. After enjoying the views from the top, take time to read the historical displays inside the tower and check out the exhibits at the Lake Murray Nature Center. Return the way you came.

6.12 Arrive back at the trailhead.

HONORABLE MENTIONS
(CHICKASAW COUNTRY, SOUTH CENTRAL OKLAHOMA)

F. LAKEVIEW (OF THE ARBUCKLES) TRAIL

CHICKASAW NATIONAL RECREATION AREA

With captivating views of the Lake of the Arbuckles surrounding you, this short and sweet trail presents beautiful panoramas at both sunrise and sunset.

Start: Lakeview (of the Arbuckles) Trailhead, on the east side of N3360 Road and north of the swimming area
Elevation gain: 866 to 906 feet
Distance: 0.98 mile out and back
Difficulty: Easy
Hiking time: 0.5–1 hour, depending on the time spent viewing the scenery
Seasons/schedule: Open year-round, sunrise to sunset
Fees and permits: None
Trail contacts: Chickasaw National Recreation Area Headquarters, 901 W. 1st St., Sulphur 73086; (580) 622-7234

Dog-friendly: Leashed dogs permitted; no dogs allowed on trails east of the Travertine Nature Center, inside the nature center, and any areas where visitors can swim (exceptions for service and law enforcement animals)
Trail surface: Dirt
Land status: National Park Service
Nearest town: Sulphur
Other trail users: Anglers
Maps: USGS Dougherty; Chickasaw National Recreation Area map (available online at www.okc.gov/departments/parks-recreation/trails/trails-map)

FINDING THE TRAILHEAD

From the Travertine Nature Center, head down Northeast Perimeter Road before turning right (north) onto US 177 N to OK 7/Broadway Avenue for a total of 1.8 miles. Head west on OK 7/Broadway Avenue for 2.1 miles before turning left (south) on Cooper Memorial Road. Cooper Memorial Road becomes N3360 Road after passing The Point Campground. Continue 5.5 miles to the trailhead, on your left (east). GPS: N34° 26.716′ W97° 01.254′

Sunset at Lake of the Arbuckles

G. **CRAVEN NATURE TRAIL**

TISHOMINGO NATIONAL WILDLIFE REFUGE

The focal point of this trail is the remarkable stillness of Dick's Pond, named in honor of the son of the refuge's first manager, Earl Craven. This watery sanctuary can be home to herons, otters, and ducks. The Craven Nature Trail allows you to experience the varied wildlife that has found a haven in the beguiling ambience of the eastern cross-timber forest.

Start: Craven Nature Trailhead
Elevation gain: 620 to 683 feet
Distance: 0.84-mile lollipop
Difficulty: Easy
Hiking time: 0.5–1 hour, depending on the time spent enjoying the scenery
Seasons/schedule: Open year-round, sunrise to sunset (strictly enforced)
Fees and permits: None
Trail contacts: Tishomingo National Wildlife Refuge Visitor Center, 11766 S. Refuge Rd., Tishomingo 73460; (580) 371-2402

Dog-friendly: Leashed dogs permitted
Trail surface: Asphalt up to boardwalk, dirt path for remainder of trail
Land status: US Fish and Wildlife Service
Nearest town: Tishomingo
Other trail users: None
Maps: USGS Tishomingo; Tishomingo National Wildlife Refuge map (available at the trailhead and park office)

FINDING THE TRAILHEAD

From East Main Street in Tishomingo, travel east for a little over 1 mile before making a right (southeast) onto South Refuge Road. Continue 1.9 miles to the trailhead, on your right (west). Parking is available at the trailhead. GPS: N34° 12.512' W96° 38.603'

View from the boardwalk at Dick's Pond

GREEN COUNTRY
(NORTHEAST OKLAHOMA)

NORTHEAST OKLAHOMA is aptly named "Green Country" because of the multitude of hardwood forests that decorate its riveting escarpments and winding rivers. Everywhere you look, you are bound to find trees, possibly some species of oak, cedar, elm, or dogwood. Tallgrass prairie can also be found in this region, with an abundance of vibrant wildflowers in the mix. White-tailed deer, butterflies, and armadillos call this area home, as do the residents of Oklahoma's second-largest city, Tulsa. Green Country is also home to the state's other largest waterfall, the iconic Dripping Springs Waterfall.

Forested area at Sparrow Hawk Mountain (Hike 39)

30 LESS TRAVELED TRAIL

KEYSTONE ANCIENT FOREST PRESERVE

True to its name, this latest addition to the Ancient Keystone Forest has an alluring ambience of solitude. Wild berries grow untamed among the age-old trees. Even if there is not a soul in sight, a handful of charming 12-spotted skimmer dragonflies, red-spotted purple butterflies, and buckeye butterflies may accompany you along the trail.

Start: Main trailhead, west of the Keystone Ancient Forest Preserve visitor center
Elevation gain: 748 to 1,056 feet
Distance: 5.01-mile lollipop
Difficulty: Moderate due to uneven terrain
Hiking time: 2–3 hours
Seasons/schedule: Open Thurs 7 a.m.–2 p.m., Fri–Sun 7 a.m.–6 p.m.; hours subject to change. (Check the City of Sand Springs website and Keystone Ancient Forest's social media for official open hiking dates.)
Fees and permits: None
Trail contacts: (Main contact) Keystone Ancient Forest Visitor Center, (918) 246-7795; (secondary contact) City of Sand Springs Parks and Recreation, 1050 W. Wekiwa Rd., Sand Springs 74063; (918) 246-2500, ext. 2661 (**Note:** At time of publication, a visitor center has been constructed to the east of the main trailhead. Staff is available during hours mentioned above for any questions and/or assistance.)
Dog-friendly: Leashed dogs permitted only on designated "Hike with Your Dog Dates." Check the City of Sand Springs website and Keystone Ancient Forest's social media for official dog-friendly dates.
Trail surface: Dirt and rocky path
Land status: City of Sand Springs in partnership with The Nature Conservancy
Nearest town: Sand Springs
Other trail users: None
Maps: USGS Wekiwa; Keystone Ancient Forest Trail System map (available at the trailhead and online at www.sandspringsok.org and on Keystone Ancient Forest's social media page)

FINDING THE TRAILHEAD

From North Wilson Avenue in Sand Springs, merge onto US 412 W/US 64 W. Continue a little over 6 miles and take the exit for 209th West Avenue. Turn right (north) onto 209th West Avenue/New Prue Road and travel 2.1 miles. The road leading to the Keystone Ancient Forest main trailhead and visitor center is on your left (west). GPS: N36° 10.868′ W96° 13.786′

THE HIKE

Going along the Less Traveled Trail, you get the feeling of how it got its name. It is by no means a forsaken route, but it does provide the tranquility of a trail with fewer travelers. There is an idiosyncratic serenity in the air, and the trail setting is lush with enchanting greenery and beautiful winged insects during the warmer seasons. It does have its share of ascents and descents. All will be noted in the trail description. The Less Traveled

View of Less Traveled Trail

Trail also serves as a firebreak for roughly 400 acres of the preserve. Those portions of the preserve are periodically managed with controlled burns to promote healthy growth of the native landscape.

The Less Traveled Trail begins at the same trailhead as the Frank Trail. Instead of heading straight toward the Frank and the Childers Trails, take the gravel path to the left and continue about 60 feet to the fire road. The trail starts to head west up to the fork at 400 feet. Bear right (northwest) to follow the fire road. At 0.12 mile, the path surface turns rocky with a mild ascent of 10 feet to the 0.5-mile mark. Between these two points, you will bear left (south) at the Frank Trail connection at 0.23 mile and then cross a seasonal creek bed at 0.38 mile. The trail starts to wind south and then east. At the 0.5-mile mark, there is a mild descent of 15 feet over a length of 0.03 mile.

After crossing a couple seasonal creek beds, you ascend about 30 feet in elevation from the 0.59-mile mark to the 0.62-mile mark. You then enter a cross-timber forest at 0.73 mile and encounter some large slabs of rock in the path. There is a mild dip in between 0.76 mile and 0.87 mile. Cross another seasonal creek bed and descend about 90 feet until the 1.38-mile mark. Your surroundings open up to a prairie for a short distance at 1.64 miles. The trail eventually bears west at 1.81 miles, followed by a small switchback involving a change of 15 feet in elevation.

A power line clearing is to your left (south) at 2.15 miles; you shortly embark on another series of switchbacks until the 2.56-mile mark. In between these switchbacks are a couple more seasonal creek beds. Exercise additional caution after the switchbacks. That portion of the trail can get overgrown and muddy after decent precipitation. The final noticeable ascent occurs at 2.73 miles, where the trail starts to head north. You ascend about 65 feet in elevation until the 2.9-mile mark. At 2.85 miles, the trail heads west. After the 3.12-mile mark, shaded areas begin to dissipate.

Bear right (north) at 3.28 miles to continue on the trail. The other direction is a dirt road, West 9th Street. Continue straight (north) at the fork at 3.48 miles, and then head east, back onto the fire road, at 4.29 miles. You return to some shade at this point, which will provide relief during the Oklahoman summers. Resume heading east at the fork at 4.64 and 4.77 miles. Head back the way you came after the fork at 4.77 miles, the same fork you encountered about 400 feet from the trailhead.

Left: Small creek along Less Traveled Trail
Right: Buckeye butterfly sighting

MILES AND DIRECTIONS

0.0   Start at the main trailhead. Take the left side on the gravel path.

0.01   Reach a fire road. Continue straight (north).

0.08   Reach a fork. Bear right (northwest) to follow the fire road.

0.12   There is a slight ascent of 10 feet to the 0.5-mile mark.

0.23   Reach an intersection. Bear left (south).

0.38   Cross a small seasonal creek bed.

0.5   Descend about 15 feet to the 0.53-mile mark.

0.53   Cross a small seasonal creek bed.

0.54   Cross a small seasonal creek bed.

0.59   Ascend 27 feet to the 0.62-mile mark.

0.76   Encounter a dip in the path until the 0.87-mile mark.

0.84   Cross a small seasonal creek bed.

0.87   Descend 89 feet to the 1.38-mile mark.

1.85   Traverse a small switchback. The elevation fluctuates up and down between 15 feet to the 2.04-mile mark.

2.15   See a power line clearing to your left (south).

2.24   Head north for a couple switchbacks.

2.27   Cross a small seasonal creek bed.

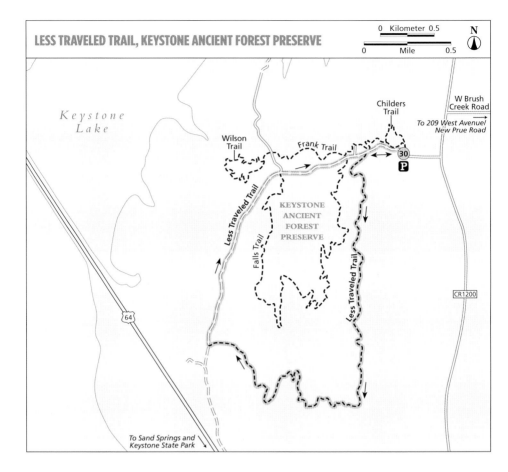

LESS TRAVELED TRAIL, KEYSTONE ANCIENT FOREST PRESERVE

2.39 Traverse a small switchback.

2.5 Traverse a small switchback.

2.56 Cross a small seasonal creek bed. This part of the path can get overgrown.

2.6 The path can get muddy here after decent precipitation.

2.73 The trail ascends 65 feet to the 2.9-mile mark.

2.85 Bear left (west).

3.28 Bear right (north). The other direction leads to West 9th Street (a dirt road).

3.48 Reach a fork. Stay on the left side of the fork.

4.29 Reach a fork. Head straight (east), back onto the fire road.

4.64 Reach another fork. Continue straight (east) on the right side of the fork.

4.77 Reach a junction. Continue straight (east) on the fire road. Head back the way you came on the fire road.

5.01 Arrive back at the trailhead.

31 FRANK TRAIL (COMBINED WITH WILSON TRAIL)

KEYSTONE ANCIENT FOREST PRESERVE

Featuring the same view that captivated Washington Irving, author of "The Legend of Sleepy Hollow," in the fall of 1832, the Frank Trail includes a number of switchbacks and takes you into the heart of the Keystone Ancient Forest. Adding the Wilson Trail to the route offers a seasonal waterfall, rocky bluffs, and different perspectives of the cross-timber forest.

Start: Main trailhead, west of the Keystone Ancient Forest Preserve visitor center
Elevation gain: 804 to 1,050 feet
Distance: 3.92-mile lollipop with an additional loop
Difficulty: Moderate to difficult due to uneven terrain
Hiking time: 2–3 hours
Seasons/schedule: Open Thurs 7 a.m.–2 p.m., Fri–Sun 7 a.m.–6 p.m.; hours subject to change. (Check the City of Sand Springs website and Keystone Ancient Forest's social media for official open hiking dates.)
Fees and permits: None
Trail contacts: (Main contact) Keystone Ancient Forest Visitor Center, (918) 246-7795; (secondary contact) City of Sand Springs Parks and Recreation, 1050 W. Wekiwa Rd., Sand Springs 74063; (918) 246-2500, ext. 2661 (*Note:* At time of publication, a visitor center has been constructed to the east of the main trailhead. Staff is available during hours mentioned above for any questions and/or assistance.)
Dog-friendly: Leashed dogs permitted only on designated "Hike with Your Dog Dates." Check the City of Sand Springs website and Keystone Ancient Forest's social media for official dog-friendly dates.
Trail surface: Dirt and rocky path
Land status: City of Sand Springs in partnership with The Nature Conservancy
Nearest town: Sand Springs
Other trail users: None
Maps: USGS Wekiwa; Keystone Ancient Forest Trail System map (available at the trailhead and online at www.sandspringsok.org and on Keystone Ancient Forest social media page)

FINDING THE TRAILHEAD

From North Wilson Avenue in Sand Springs, merge onto US 412 W/US 64 W. Continue for a little over 6 miles and take the exit for 209th West Avenue. Turn right (north) onto 209th West Avenue/New Prue Road and travel 2.1 miles. The road leading to the Keystone Ancient Forest main trailhead and visitor center is to your left (west). GPS: N36° 10.868' W96° 13.786'

Butterfly and bumblebee on coneflowers at the Frank Trail entrance

THE HIKE

The Keystone Ancient Forest is a cross-timber congregation of resilient post oak, eastern redcedar, blackjack oak, ash, and hawthorn trees. The eastern redcedar and oak trees that surround you on the Frank and Wilson Trails date back hundreds of years and are incredible testaments of fortitude. At times, waltzing butterflies and blooming coneflowers will greet you at the entrance to the Frank Trail before you head into the forest.

The trail surface is paved until the 0.16-mile mark. Before the path surface changes, you will continue north past the Childers Trail connection. Once you reach the fork at 0.16 mile, bear left (southwest) to start on the Frank Trail. You encounter a small switchback and a rock outcrop shortly after. At the fork at 0.36 mile, continue straight (west) toward the bench. Trail posts that state "Frank Trail" start to appear at this point. The trail enters a prairie area at 0.42 mile. You will see the "Dead Tree Dollar" sign before you reach the fork after 0.53 mile on the trail. Stay on the right side (west) and follow the trail posts. The trail heads north before you reach a fork at 0.75 mile on the trail. Head west at this fork and also at the fork at 0.82 mile. At 0.88 mile, bear right (north).

The Frank Trail connects with the Wilson Trail and the fire road at 0.99 mile. Bear right (northwest) to continue on the Frank Trail. (This guide will include the Wilson Trail at a later point on this route.) There is a fork in the trail at 1.3 miles. Continue toward the signage for Rock Slide Pass. The right side of the fork is a side trail. The loop entrance to the Ghost of Washington Irving Lookout begins at 1.32 miles. Take the loop in a counterclockwise direction. The overlook and informational signage are at the 1.45-mile mark. Enjoy the same scene that captivated Washington Irving, author of "The Legend of Sleepy Hollow." The loop ends at 1.64 miles. Bear right (south) and head toward the Wilson Trail.

For an additional workout and distinctive scenery, bear right (west) onto the Wilson Trail entrance at 1.97 miles. This is at the same fork you encountered at 0.99 mile. The Wilson Trail can be taken in a counterclockwise direction. There are various types of activity on this trail, including scrambling up rocks, winding along craggy bluffs, and traversing seasonal creek beds. The first prospect of rock scrambling begins at the 2.06-mile mark. Bear left (southeast) after exiting the rock outcrop. The trail heads west and then north before you start to wind east along the edge of the bluffs at 2.19 miles.

After crossing a seasonal creek bed, you encounter a series of small switchbacks at 2.23 miles. To your right (west), you might be able to see a waterfall after a decent rainfall. The seasonal creek bed you just crossed feeds that waterfall. Continue north and head across the seasonal waterfall bed at 2.28 miles. You start to head west up some rocks before bearing north and back along the edge of the bluffs at 2.34 miles. Partial views of Keystone Lake appear. Reach another series of switchbacks at the 2.35-mile mark before you head east toward a large rock. Views of the seasonal waterfall appear again, this time to the south at 2.41 miles. Head southeast up the rocks. The trail curves in a northeast direction shortly after, and the rock scrambling portion ends. Ascend east toward another cluster of rocks.

You head south along the bluffs for a final time. The trail then curves northwest up some rocks and stays in a northerly direction back to the Wilson Trail entrance. Be mindful of the large boulder at 2.62 miles and a couple of seasonal creek beds in between. The Wilson Trail concludes at the 2.84-mile mark. Continue straight (northeast) to head back to the Frank Trail. Reach the Frank Trail junction you were at previously at the 0.99- and 1.97-mile marks. Continue straight (east) to head back the way you came.

Ghost of Washington Irving Lookout

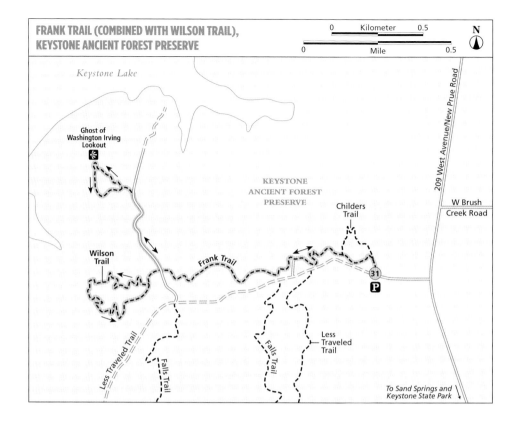

MILES AND DIRECTIONS

0.0   Start at the main trailhead.

0.02 Reach the Childers Trail connection. Stay straight (north).

0.16 Reach another fork. Bear left (southwest) to start on the Frank Trail.

0.2   Traverse a small switchback.

0.36 Reach a fork. Continue straight (west) toward a bench.

0.49 Come to the "Dead Tree Dollar" sign.

0.53 Reach a fork. Stay on the right side (west).

0.75 Reach a fork. Continue straight (west).

0.82 Reach a fork. Stay on the left side (west).

0.88 Bear right (north).

0.99 Reach a junction. Bear right (northwest) to continue on the Frank Trail. Straight (west) is the Wilson Trail. The other side leads to the fire road.

1.3   Reach a fork. Take the left side that leads to Rock Slide Pass. The right side leads to a dead end.

1.32 Enter the loop to an overlook. Take the loop in a counterclockwise direction.

1.45 Reach the Ghost of Washington Irving Lookout.

1.64 Complete the overlook loop. Bear right (south).

1.97 Reach the Wilson Trail connection. Bear right (west) to start on the Wilson Trail.

2.03 Reach a fork. Take the right side (northwest) to start the loop in a counterclockwise direction.

2.19 The trail starts to wind along the edge of bluffs.

2.21 Cross a small seasonal creek bed that feeds into a waterfall after decent rainfall.

2.23 Traverse a series of small switchbacks. Pass over a seasonal waterfall bed.

2.3 Head west up the rocks.

2.34 Bear north and the edge of the bluffs. Partial views of Keystone Lake emerge.

2.35 Traverse a small switchback down some rocks.

2.37 Head east toward a large rock.

2.44 The rock scrambling portion ends.

2.46 Bear right (south) along the bluffs.

2.53 Bear northwest up some rocks.

2.66 Cross a small seasonal creek bed.

2.8 Cross a small seasonal creek bed.

2.84 Reach the end of the Wilson Trail loop. Continue straight (northeast) to head back to the Frank Trail.

View from the Wilson Trail

2.91 Reach the Frank Trail junction from the 1.97-mile mark. Continue straight (east) to head back the way you came.

3.92 Arrive back at the trailhead.

32 REDBUD VALLEY OXLEY NATURE TRAIL

REDBUD VALLEY NATURE PRESERVE

A natural oasis in the Tulsa metro area that features six different habitats, the Redbud Valley Nature Preserve provides an abundance of prairie respites, desert blooms, forest foliage, cliff wandering, and bird-watching.

Start: Main Trailhead to the left of the Harriet Barclay Visitor Center
Elevation gain: 568 to 676 feet
Distance: 1.24-mile loop
Difficulty: Easy, if taking the Main Trail route; moderate if taking the Bluff Trail route, due to slippery large rocks and less-well-marked paths
Hiking time: 30–45 minutes, depending on choices along the way
Seasons/schedule: Open Fri–Sun, 8 a.m.–5 p.m.; closed most city holidays
Fees and permits: None
Trail contacts: Oxley Nature Center, 6700 Mohawk Blvd., Tulsa 74115; (918) 596-9054
Dog-friendly: No dogs allowed
Trail surface: For the most part, a dirt path, compacted with rocks in portions; turns rocky in the ravine portion.

Land status: Tulsa Parks Department in partnership with The Nature Conservancy
Nearest town: Catoosa
Other trail users: None
Maps: USGS Mingo; Oxley Nature Center map (available at the Redbud Valley Nature Preserve's Harriet Barclay Visitor Center and online at www.oxleynaturecenter.org/redbudtrails)
Special considerations: The Main Trail covered in this chapter starts at the trailhead, connects with the Prairie Fork Trail instead of the Woodland Fork Trail, and then continues onto the Main Trail instead of the Bluff Trail to the end of the trail. Hikers have the option to shorten the hike by taking the Woodland Fork Trail and bypassing the Prairie Fork Trail or continuing on the Bluff Trail instead of using the Main Trail.

FINDING THE TRAILHEAD

Take the 161st East Avenue exit off I-44 E. After making two lefts, head north on 161st East Avenue. In 4.4 miles you will see a sign for the Redbud Valley Nature Preserve to your left (west). Head toward the Harriet Barclay Visitor Center and then turn right (north) into the parking lot. There appears to be two entrances to the Main Trail from the parking lot. Start your hike at the first entrance (closer to the visitor center) that has actual signage indicating that it is the Main Trail. The second entrance from the parking lot is where the trail exits. GPS: N36° 13.208′ W95° 47.873′

Prairie in Redbud Valley

THE HIKE

Redbud Valley is a treasure trove of various environments. The Main Trail takes you on a short but rewarding journey through forests, arid grassland, and ancient coral reef caverns. From the trailhead, you start to ascend some log steps and then the path surface turns rocky. At about 325 feet, the path levels out. Bear left (south) and wind through a floodplain oak forest. In fall and winter, the rock–laden trail can be blanketed with oak and maple leaves.

PRAIRIE TAKEOVER

Lespedeza, an invasive plant in the pea family, has overtaken the prairie areas of Redbud Valley in the past few years. Unfortunately, this takeover has prevented the colorful natural wildflowers from flourishing. The Nature Conservancy has been brainstorming less-disruptive ways to remove lespedeza. In the meantime, this plant continues to be a growing problem. Do not let this incursion deter you from taking the Prairie Fork Trail portion of the Main Trail. The prairies are still wondrous, serene landscapes abundant with various greenery, painting-like trees, and bird-watching opportunities. If you are a bird-watching enthusiast, the bird feeders in the prairie areas are a real treat. Redbud Valley tends to draw various species of birds, including blue jays, sparrows, goldfinches, and woodpeckers.

Footbridge and stream in the ravine

Less than 0.25 mile into the trail, you reach a prairie. A couple trees and bird feeders greet you as you enter this open, picturesque landscape. You eventually leave the prairie and head back into a wooded area. When you come to the Woodland Fork connection, bear left (initially south, but then west) to follow the "Main Trail" sign. Going this way takes you on the Prairie Fork portion of the Main Trail. A little after 0.4 mile you reach another prairie. There is a bench to your right (north) for viewing the scenery. As you leave the second prairie, clusters of trees, yucca, and prickly pear are your companions during this portion of the trail.

Reach the ridgeline of Redbud Valley at the 0.63-mile mark. Two outlooks are offered at this point. Visibility is best in late fall and winter, when tree coverage is minimal. As you venture back into the forest, the path includes unearthed tree roots. Prior to reaching the ravine, there will be a "Main Trail" sign. (This is where the Prairie Fork Trail portion ends.) If you follow the "Main Trail" sign, you will head back to the trailhead. Instead, go left (east) and descend into the ravine. Use extra caution, as the path narrows and you are traversing slippery, moss-covered rocks. Once you reach the bottom of the ravine, you come to a large boulder. Go left around the boulder to stay on the trail, which has you winding along the cliffs. You will cross two footbridges in the ravine area. Within the cliffs that were once an ancient coral reef. There are several caverns to your right (south). In the fall and winter months, you will be able to see a small pond to your far left (north). After a decent rainfall, you might be able to see a waterfall flowing into the pond. The flow of the waterfall originates under the second footbridge. Be cautious of muddy surfaces and dripping water from the cliffs above you.

At the 0.82-mile mark, you will see the "Bluff Trail" sign. Adventurous hikers can take the rougher Bluff Trail. However, taking the Main Trail will lead you within a sugar maple forest and provide you with views of Bird Creek. You reach a wooden boardwalk and the sugar maple forest at 0.89 mile and then a bench on your left (north). A little after the 1.0-mile mark, bear left (initially south, then east) on the log-lined dirt path. Do not continue on the wooden boardwalk, which is in disrepair. Until you reach the "Bluff Trail" sign at 1.18 miles, you will encounter an overlook for Bird Creek to your left (north), a fallen tree trunk, and a large boulder to your left (north). Continue straight (south) from the "Bluff Trail" sign to reach the parking lot at 1.24 miles.

MILES AND DIRECTIONS

0.0   Start at the Main Trail trailhead.

0.1   Bear left (south) and walk through the floodplain oak forest.

0.21 Reach an open prairie.

0.35 Reach the Woodland Fork connection. Bear left (south and then immediately west) to stay on the Main Trail. This portion of the trail is known as the Prairie Fork.

0.4   Reach another prairie.

0.47 A bench is to your right (north).

0.63 Reach the ridgeline of Redbud Valley. There are two outlooks to the left (west).

0.73 Reach the "Main Trail" sign (also where the Prairie Fork ends) shortly after. Take a left (east) into the limestone ravine. At the large boulder, go to the left to stay on the path.

0.77 Cross two small footbridges, with caverns visible to the right (south).

0.82 At the "Bluff Trail" sign, bear left along the log-lined path to take the Main Trail route instead of the Bluff Trail.

0.9 Bear right (east) toward the wooden boardwalk and sugar maple forest.

1.02 Do not continue on the wooden boardwalk. (The bridge is in disrepair.) Bear left (south then east) on a log-lined dirt path.

1.06 Reach where the original wooden boardwalk intersects. An overlook of Bird Creek is to your left (north). Continue straight (east) on the dirt path.

1.18 A "Bluff Trail" sign is to your right (west) where the Bluff Trail meets back with the Main Trail. Continue straight (south).

1.24 Arrive back at the trailhead.

33 SKULL HOLLOW NATURE TRAIL

OOLOGAH LAKE

A quick jaunt from the Tulsa area, the Skull Hollow Nature Trail offers spectacular views of Oologah Lake and sights of blooming trees and wildflowers in the spring. It is a natural respite close to the metro area yet feels far away with its peaceful forests and rugged path along the bluffs.

Start: Skull Hollow Nature Trailhead, northeast of the Hawthorn Bluff Campground gate house
Elevation gain: 593 to 728 feet
Distance: 1.22-mile loop (not included in this hike description are the 0.3-mile Short Loop and the 0.75-mile Long Loop; including those would make the total hike about 3 miles)
Difficulty: Easy to moderate due to narrow paths along the bluffs
Hiking time: About 1 hour
Seasons/schedule: Open year-round, sunrise to sunset; best during spring and fall
Fees and permits: Day-use fee (self-pay)
Trail contacts: Oologah Lake Project Office, 8400 E. Hwy. 88, Oologah 74053; (918) 443-2250
Dog-friendly: Leashed dogs permitted

Trail surface: Dirt and rocky path
Land status: US Army Corps of Engineers
Nearest town: Oologah
Other trail users: Anglers
Maps: USGS Oologah; US Army Corps of Engineers Tulsa District map (available online at www.swt .usace.army.mil/Locations/Tulsa-District-Lakes/Oklahoma/Oologah-Lake/Oologah-Lake-Recreation)
Special considerations: The Skull Hollow Nature Trail can be done in three segments or all together—the Hiking Trail (1.3 miles), Short Loop (0.3 mile), and Long Loop (0.75 mile). This trail description does not include the Short Loop and the Long Loop.
  The road from the Hawthorn Bluff Campground gate house is closed during the winter season.

FINDING THE TRAILHEAD

From the US 169 and OK 88 intersection, turn right (east) onto OK 88 S/E400 Road. You will reach the Hawthorn Bluff Campground, on your left (east), after 1.9 miles. From the gate house, located in the Hawthorn Bluff Campground parking lot, head left (northeast) and onto the paved road. After 0.2 mile on the paved road, come to a path on your left. Turn left and proceed 0.1 mile to a round-about; both the trailhead and trail exit are to your right (east). Use the path to the right with the large sign overhead reading "Skull Hollow Nature Trail" to begin the hike. GPS: N36° 26.050' W95° 40.570'

THE HIKE

For residents of the Tulsa metro area seeking a quick getaway to nature, the Skull Hollow Nature Trail is about a 30-minute drive. Legends say the trail is named Skull Hollow for the skull found of a cowman who owed a blacksmith money. The beauty of the trail is quite the opposite of the feel of its name. Featuring oak-hickory forests, towering bluffs,

lake views, access to a sandy beach, and an old wagon road, this rewarding trail is great for families as well as avid hikers.

From the trailhead, the dirt path is relatively wide, and you venture through a wooded area until you reach a grove of red oak trees at 0.05 mile. There will be a series of log steps and possibly a fallen tree trunk prior to reaching a fork at 0.1 mile. An overlook entrance is to the east, where you can step up close on the bluffs and view Oologah Lake. Bear left (north) to continue on the nature trail. At the 0.14-mile mark, you reach the second overlook entrance, to your right (east). At this same junction, to your left (west), is the Short Loop entrance. Continue straight (north) on the nature trail.

At 0.17 mile, turn right to cross the wooden bridge. Shortly after crossing the bridge, the trail winds in a southeast direction and you reach a grove of mockernut hickory trees. Views of the inlet from Oologah Lake start to open up to your right (south). At 0.25 mile into the trail, bear away from the inlet and start to traverse the bluffs. The path surface turns rocky and contains an occasional unearthed tree root. The entrance to the Long Loop is to your left (north) at 0.29 mile. Continue straight (southeast) on the nature trail.

You cross over large slabs of rock at 0.32 mile, and then the trail heads northeast. Vantage points of Oologah Lake are more visible to your right (east) during fall and winter. At 0.4 mile, bear left (north). The trail narrows and can get overgrown during spring and summer—this portion of the route was once an old wagon road. There is a slight ascent of about 40 feet and then a slight descent of about 25 feet before the path levels out close to the 0.7-mile mark.

At 0.73 mile come to an overlook of the beach, to your right (northeast). Continue from this point and encounter a large stump on the left side of the trail at 0.75 mile. A path to your right (north) leads down to the sandy cove and grants access to Oologah

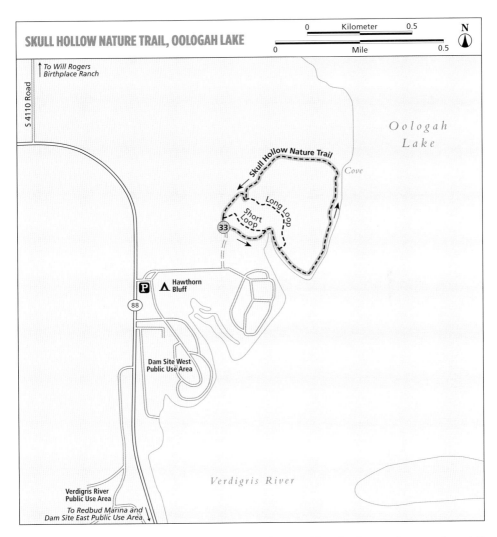

Lake when the water level is low. The pathway widens back up when you bear left (northwest) to continue on the nature trail.

At around 0.9 mile you approach a fork. Bear left (west) to stay on the nature trail; to the right is a private access road. Reach a grove of black walnut trees and the point where the Long Loop ends at 1.11 miles. The Short Loop exits onto the nature trail at the 1.18-mile mark. Continue straight (south) to return to the trailhead, completing the loop at 1.22 miles.

MILES AND DIRECTIONS

0.0   Start at the trailhead on the east side of the roundabout.

0.1   Reach an overlook to the east. Bear left (north) to continue on the nature trail.

0.14 Reach another overlook to your right (east). The entrance to the Short Loop is on your left (west). Continue straight (north) on the nature trail.

Blossoming eastern redbud tree

0.17 Bear right (east) and cross the wooden footbridge.

0.29 Reach the Long Loop entrance to your left (north). Continue straight (southeast) on the nature trail.

0.75 The path to your right (north) leads down to a cove. Bear left (northwest) to continue on the nature trail.

0.9 Reach a fork. Bear left (west). The right side (east) of the fork is a private access road.

1.11 The Long Loop reconnects to your left (south). Continue straight (west).

1.18 The Short Loop connects to your left (east). Continue straight (south).

1.22 Arrive back at the trailhead.

34 PRYOR CREEK NATURE TRAIL (VIA ELLIOTT TRAILHEAD)

PRYOR CREEK

Forests with a mythical aura, bridges and ecoregions with fairy tale–themed titles, wild berries alongside blooming wildflowers during spring and summer—Pryor Creek can be quite a charming area to hike.

Start: Elliott Trailhead, to the west of South Elliott Street/N4320 Road
Elevation gain: 558 to 600 feet
Distance: 6.05 miles out and back, with an additional spur and lollipop
Difficulty: Easy
Hiking time: 2–3 hours
Seasons/schedule: Open year-round, sunrise to sunset
Fees and permits: None
Trail contacts: The Leaf Collectors Foundation in Pryor; e-mail: bozo@pryorcreeknaturetrail.org (no one physically stationed at the park). Questions and comments can also be sent through http://pryorcreeknaturetrail.org/suggestionbox.aspx.
Dog-friendly: Leashed dogs permitted
Trail surface: Dirt and rocky path with intermittent, unearthed tree roots and mowed-grass sections
Land status: Managed by The Leaf Collectors Foundation on land overseen by the US Army Corps of Engineers
Nearest town: Pryor
Other trail users: Cyclists, equestrians, hunters
Maps: USGS Pryor; Pryor Creek Nature Trail map (available online at http://pryorcreeknaturetrail.org/trailmap.htm)
Special considerations: This trail description begins at the Elliott Trailhead and includes the spur through Troll Creek Falls to the Troll Creek Trailhead and the lollipop route through "The Deadwoods" to the Cable Trailhead.
  Bridges on these trails may not be capable of supporting horses and their riders. Cyclists must walk their bicycles across the bridges.
  This trail is in a floodplain area. Do not access the trail on days of excessive precipitation or inclement weather.

FINDING THE TRAILHEAD

From the OK 66 and 2nd Street intersection in Claremore, head east on 2nd Street for 1.2 miles; 2nd Street eventually becomes OK 20 E/E490 Road/Will Rogers Boulevard. Continue on OK 20 E for 16.2 miles. Turn right (south) on South Elliott Street/N4320 Road. The Elliott Trailhead with a small parking area is to your right (west) in 2.7 miles. GPS: N36° 15.985' W95° 18.616'

THE HIKE

Venturing on the Pryor Creek Nature Trail right after sunrise is an experience—the golden sunlight streams mystically between the trees. There is a storybook feel and a captivating quietness throughout this trail system, even though it is not too far from town. If you are lucky, you might even catch sight of a great egret nesting in the trees or a beaver swimming in Pryor Creek.

Enchanting greenery at Pryor Creek

The route for this hike begins at the Elliott Trailhead, west of the parking area. The trail heads north shortly after the trailhead, with a few side trails to your right (east and northeast). At 0.26 mile you reach Isaac's Bridge (formerly known as Beaver Crossing). The trail winds east soon after, and then back to a northerly direction. There are a couple more side trails before you reach a bench overlooking Pryor Creek a little after the 0.5-mile mark. There is a red diamond metal marker on a tree at this point. After a slight descent, cross the small footbridge at 0.61 mile and soon come to another bench. At 0.76 mile you may need to venture around a large fallen tree trunk.

You encounter another fork at 0.88 mile. Troll Bridge is to your right (east). This route includes the additional spur to the Troll Creek Trailhead before heading back to the Troll Bridge fork and going toward the Cable Trailhead. By including the spur to the Troll Creek Trailhead, you get to pass by Troll Creek Falls. This portion has green diamond plastic trail markers on trees. Come to a series of forks—one each at 1.27, 1.35, and 1.37 miles. Make sure to take the right side of each fork to continue toward Troll Creek Falls. You will cross a small creek bed and a footbridge on the way there. Troll Creek Falls appears at 1.43 miles. There is a bench and a rope tied to a tree branch with a handle to act as a swing. When the water level is low, the "swing" rope can be fun to hang from across the creek. (Use caution when using the "swing" rope; its level of durability is unknown.) Be sure to enjoy the view and the babbling of the creek water before heading west around the loop. Stay on the right side of the next two forks (1.52 miles and 1.58 miles) before reaching the Troll Creek Trailhead and N4310 Road at 1.85 miles. Unfortunately, due to its proximity to a vehicular road, there can be a lot of refuse at this trailhead. Turn around and head back to the Troll Bridge fork.

The mileage count once you reach Troll Bridge is 2.8 miles. Go across Troll Bridge and head north. Enter "The Deadwoods" area, where the withered trees resemble ones that might guard a wicked queen's castle. Red diamond markers on trees are your guide once again to the Cable Trailhead. After a possible fallen tree trunk in the path at 2.9 miles, the scenery interchanges between meadow and wooded area before settling back to a wooded area at 3.36 miles. During summer, wild strawberries and blackberries flourish in the meadows. At 3.39 miles you reach a fork. Continue straight (north) to start on the loop that connects to the Cable Trailhead. The trail winds west before you come to an informal BMX track at 3.98 miles. Go around this area along the creek to reconnect with the trail. Look ahead of you for the red diamond trail marker to ensure that you are on track.

Tree "swing" rope at Troll Creek Falls

After continuing straight (east) at the fork at 4.08 miles, the Cable Trailhead is 0.02 mile east of the second fork at 4.22 miles. Feel free to check it out and then head back to the fork. Bear right (east) to go back on the Cable Trail. From here, blue diamond trail markers lead the way to the end of the loop at 4.61 miles. Once the loop ends, bear right (southeast) to head back to Troll Bridge. Reach Troll Bridge at 5.17 miles. Bear left (southeast) from the bridge to head back to the Elliott Trailhead.

PRYOR CREEK NATURE TRAIL (VIA ELLIOTT TRAILHEAD), PRYOR CREEK

MILES AND DIRECTIONS

0.0 Start at the Elliott Trailhead, west of the parking area.

0.26 Reach Isaac's Bridge (aka Beaver Crossing).

0.51 A bench to your right (north) provides an overlook of Pryor Creek.

0.55 Watch for downed trees.

0.61 Cross a small footbridge. Come upon another bench shortly after.

0.76 Watch for downed trees.

0.88 Reach a fork. The route to Troll Bridge is to the right (east). Continue northwest to head toward Troll Creek Falls and the Troll Creek Trailhead.

0.96 Cross a seasonal creek bed.

1.27 Reach a fork. Take the right side (north) of the fork to continue toward Troll Creek Falls.

1.34 Cross a small footbridge.

1.35 Reach a fork. Head right (north) toward Troll Creek Falls.

1.37 Reach another fork. Head right (east) toward Troll Creek Falls.

1.43 Reach Troll Creek Falls. Head west to complete the loop.

1.52 Reach a fork. Bear right (west) to continue toward the Troll Creek Trailhead.

1.58 Reach a fork. Take the right side of the fork.

1.85 Reach the Troll Creek Trailhead and N4310 Road. Turn around and head back to the Troll Bridge fork.

2.8 Reach Troll Bridge. Cross Troll Bridge and head north. Enter "The Deadwoods" area.

2.9 Watch for downed trees.

3.39 Reach a fork. Continue straight (north) to start the loop (counterclockwise) that connects to the Cable Trail.

3.98 Reach an informal BMX track. Go along the creek to reconnect with the trail.

4.08 Reach a fork. Continue straight (east) on the trail.

4.22 Reach a fork. Bear right (west).

4.24 Reach the Cable Trailhead. Turn around and go back to the fork you encountered at the 4.22-mile mark.

4.26 Reach the aforementioned fork. Turn right (east) this time to continue on the Cable Trail loop.

4.61 Reach the end of the loop. Bear right (southeast) to head back to Troll Bridge.

5.17 Reach Troll Bridge. Bear left (southeast) to head back to the Elliott Trailhead and the parking area.

6.05 Arrive back at the trailhead.

35 RED (MOUNTAIN BIKE) TRAIL

OSAGE HILLS STATE PARK

Brimming with prairie verbena and fleabane daisies, this trail courses through oak forests, rocky bluffs, and prairieland. A checkered white butterfly or a northern cardinal may flutter along with you as you pass trickling streams and a small, snapshot-worthy waterfall.

Start: Red (Mountain Bike) Trailhead
Elevation gain: 650 to 945 feet
Distance: 3.3-mile loop
Difficulty: Moderate due to uneven terrain
Hiking time: 2–3 hours
Seasons/schedule: Open year-round, sunrise to sunset
Fees and permits: Parking pass required for day-use visitors
Trail contacts: Osage Hills State Park Office, 2131 Osage Hills Park Rd., Pawhuska 74056; (918) 336-4141
Dog-friendly: Leashed dogs permitted
Trail surface: Dirt and rocky path with intermittent, unearthed tree roots

Land status: Oklahoma State Parks
Nearest town: Pawhuska to the southwest, Bartlesville to the east
Other trail users: Mountain bikers
Maps: USGS Nelagoney; Osage Hills State Park map (available online at www.travelok.com/state-parks and via the Oklahoma State Parks mobile app)
Special considerations: This trail is also used by mountain bikers. Please be courteous to others while on the trail.

Red ties and red blazes serve as guides on this trail.

FINDING THE TRAILHEAD

From the Price Tower Arts Center in Bartlesville, head south on Southeast Dewey Avenue for 0.1 mile. Turn right (west) on Southeast Adams Boulevard/ US 60 W and travel for 1.3 miles. Turn right (north) on Western Street to reconnect with US 60 W (also known as Bartlesville Road) after 0.2 mile. Turn left (west), back onto US 60 W. After 10.4 miles on US 60 W, turn left (south) onto OK 35 S. Travel on OK 35 S for 1.7 miles. Make a left (southeast) on the gravel road and continue about 235 feet. The trailhead is east of the parking area and left (north) of an old structure. GPS: N36° 44.483′ W96° 10.832′

THE HIKE

The Red Trail is a gorgeous and underrated trail. While its backdrop, the Osage Hills, are enough to make the landscape wondrous, the riveting route contains many beautiful natural surprises. With an array of twists and turns that delight mountain bikers, the multiplicity in directions and changes in elevation engage hikers as well.

The trail is meant to be taken in a clockwise direction. It heads primarily in a northeast direction until the 0.44-mile mark. A creek follows along with you to your left (north). You cross this seasonal creek at about 235 feet from the trailhead and enter a varietal oak forest shortly after. At the fork at approximately 465 feet on the trail, bear left (northeast). Watch for downed trees. After crossing a couple more seasonal creek beds, you reach

Mixture of woodland and prairie

another fork at 0.32 mile. Continue straight (northeast) on the Red Trail. The Blue Trail is to the right (southeast). The creek continues to be on your left (north). Cross the large rocks in the stream at 0.42 mile, and then bear left (north) toward the red ties in trees and the red blazes. There is a mild ascent of 10 feet in elevation from here until 0.45 mile. The trail curves northwest at 0.44 mile, and then starts heading east at the 0.5-mile mark.

Once the trail heads east, it will mostly continue in this direction until 1.85 miles. As you ascend out of the valley at 0.56 mile, there is an elevation gain of 40 feet. A picturesque ravine is to your right (south) before you cross a seasonal creek at 0.64 mile. You soon reach a series of switchbacks. The last switchback on the north segment of the loop occurs around the 1.75-mile mark. Be aware of a few things during this segment. Portions of the trail can get overgrown at 0.77 mile, and there is a gain of more than 50 feet in elevation from 0.81 mile to 1.02 miles. After crossing a couple seasonal creek beds, you enter a prairie area. Grassy areas on this trail are flush with colorful wildflowers, including purple prairie verbena and white-petaled fleabane daisies. Reenter a wooded area from the prairie at 1.33 miles. You descend 15 feet in elevation from 1.57 miles to the 1.65-mile mark. At the fork at 1.66 miles, bear left (south). Several indicators—a red tie in a tree, a red blaze on a different tree, a yellow danger sign, and large slabs of rocks— let you know you are headed in the right direction.

After 1.85 miles the trail heads primarily south until the 2.54-mile mark. Another round of switchbacks, this time milder in nature, occurs until 2.06 miles. Portions of the trail at 1.95 miles can get muddy after some precipitation. Cross another seasonal creek at 2.06 miles and continue south toward the red tie in the tree. You gain 15 feet in elevation from the 2.13- to 2.15-mile mark. The last round of noticeable switchbacks occurs at 2.26 miles. You will wind along rocky bluffs during this segment. There is a descent

Small waterfall and pond in the Osage Hills

of 40 feet in elevation from 2.33 miles until you reach the small waterfall at 2.46 miles. At 2.34 miles cross the wooden plank walkway between the rock outcrops. Be careful as you tread across—there are multiple exposed screws in the plank. After crossing the same seasonal creek bed twice, you reach a small waterfall to your left (west) at 2.46 miles. This is a scene particularly worthy of a photograph, as a perfectly shaped cedar hovers over the small waterfall descending into the creek. Layered rocks act as a natural staircase for the

Kilometer

Mile

N

To 60 / Bartlesville Road
and Pawhuska

To Bartlesville

Lookout Lake

Red Trail

35

35

P

OSAGE HILLS
STATE PARK

2425

Sand Creek

Red Trail

Pond with
small waterfall

waterfall. After capturing this beautiful wonder, bear left (west) across the rocky side of the creek. The trail heads south immediately after. Look for red blazes on the trees. The creek then parallels the trail on your left (east).

Shortly after heading south around the bend containing the small waterfall, the trail primarily heads west until 2.73 miles. Until 2.61 miles, this portion of the trail can get muddy after a decent rainfall. You cross a couple more seasonal creek beds before the trail opens back up into prairie landscape. From here the trail heads northwest all the way to the 3.15-mile mark. Portions of the trail can get muddy once again when you reenter the forested area at 2.92 miles. At 3.06 miles you come to a dead end and the path widens. Bear left (north) toward the red blazes. To your right (south) is the Blue Trail. In between a couple of creek beds, you reach a fork at 3.08 miles. Continue straight (north) on the Red Trail. The right side (northeast) of the fork is the Blue Trail. The path narrows before you reach the final fork at 3.19 miles. Stay on the left side (southwest) of the fork. At 3.23 miles you have one more scenic viewing opportunity. Before crossing the large seasonal creek, take in the sights of water flowing from each end. Exercise caution when crossing this creek—it can rise fairly high in some parts. Continue toward the red blaze on the tree across the creek. From here, it is about 0.1 mile to the trailhead.

MILES AND DIRECTIONS

0.0   Start at the trailhead, east of the parking area.

0.04 Cross the large creek.

0.09 Reach a fork. Take the left side of the fork (northeast). Watch for downed trees.

0.12 Cross a seasonal stream bed.

0.25 Cross a seasonal stream bed.

0.32 Reach a fork. Continue straight (northeast) on the Red Trail.

0.42 Cross some large rocks in the stream. Bear left (north) toward the red ties in the trees and red blazes.

0.64 Cross a seasonal creek.

0.73 Traverse a series of switchbacks from here until the 1.75-mile mark.

0.77 This portion of the trail can get overgrown.

0.96 Cross a seasonal stream bed.

1.08 Cross a seasonal stream bed.

1.66 Reach a fork. Bear left (south) toward the red tie, red blaze on a tree, yellow danger sign, and large slabs of rocks.

1.85 Traverse a series of mild switchbacks until 2.06 miles.

1.95 This portion of the trail can get muddy.

2.06 Cross a seasonal creek. Head toward the red tie in a tree. Continue south.

2.26 Traverse another series of switchbacks, this time along some rocky bluffs.

2.33 Descend 40 feet in elevation until you reach the small waterfall at 2.46 miles.

2.34 Cross the wooden plank walkway between rock outcrops. Be careful of exposed screws.

2.35 Cross a seasonal creek bed.

2.45 Cross the same creek bed from the 2.35-mile mark and then bear right (north).

2.46 Come to a small waterfall to your left (west).

2.48 Bear left (west) across the rocky side of the creek. Head south immediately after. Look for red blazes on the trees. The creek parallels the trail on your left (east).

2.54 This portion of the trail until 2.61 miles can get muddy after a decent rainfall.

2.61 Cross a seasonal creek bed.

2.73 Cross a seasonal creek bed.

2.92 This portion of the trail also can get muddy.

3.06 Reach a dead end. Bear left (north) toward the red blazes.

3.08 Cross a seasonal creek bed. Reach a fork shortly after. Continue straight (north) on the Red Trail.

3.11 Cross a seasonal creek bed.

3.19 Reach a fork. Stay on the left side (southwest) of the fork.

3.23 Cross a large seasonal creek that can rise high in some parts. Head toward the red blaze on a tree across the creek.

3.3   Arrive back at the trailhead.

36 STUDY TRAIL (COMBINED WITH PRAIRIE EARTH TRAIL)

JOSEPH H. WILLIAMS TALLGRASS PRAIRIE PRESERVE

The protected American bison at the 40,000-acre Joseph H. Williams Tallgrass Prairie Preserve are the main stars. However, the peaceful, conserved scenery of the preserve is just as enrapturing. On both the Prairie Earth Trail and the Study Trail, experience rolling hills with grass billowing in the wind, wide-open views that emulate a painting, and the undisturbed wildlife that finds shelter in this beautiful area.

Start: Study Trailhead, east of the parking lot and informational signage
Elevation gain: 963 to 1,102 feet
Distance: 2.81 miles for two loops
Difficulty: Easy
Hiking time: 1–1.5 hours
Seasons/schedule: Open year-round, sunrise to sunset; best during spring to see the bison calves
Fees and permits: None
Trail contacts: Joseph H. Williams Tallgrass Prairie Preserve Field Office, PO Box 458, Pawhuska 74056; (918) 287-4803
Dog-friendly: No animals permitted
Trail surface: Combination of dirt and rocky path and mowed grass
Land status: Owned and managed by The Nature Conservancy

Nearest town: Pawhuska
Other trail users: Hikers only
Maps: USGS Pearsonia; The Nature Conservancy map (available online at www.nature.org/content/dam/tnc/nature/en/documents/tallgrass-trails-brochure-1.pdf)
Special considerations: The Joseph H. Williams Tallgrass Prairie Preserve is privately owned and has visitation guidelines different from Oklahoma's state parks. These guidelines foster preservation of the landscape and native wildlife. Visitation guidelines are available at www.nature.org/tallgrass.

This trail description includes the Prairie Earth Trail loop for additional mileage and scenic opportunities.

FINDING THE TRAILHEAD

To access the preserve from Pawhuska, drive north on Kihekah Avenue from where it intersects US 60/Main Street in downtown Pawhuska (at the corner with the triangle-shaped building and The Pioneer Woman Mercantile). Head north on Kihekah Avenue, which becomes Grandview Avenue and then CR 4201 at the north end of town. Stay on CR 4201 for 15.6 miles. Follow signage to head toward the visitor center, especially where CR 4201 splits from CR 4650. GPS: N36° 50.673' W96° 25.642'

THE HIKE

Free-roaming American bison and infinite prairie skies make the Joseph H. Williams Tallgrass Prairie Preserve a crown jewel of Northeast Oklahoma. Along the route to the Study Trailhead, you will have opportunities to see the protected bison. The hiking

trails are in an ungrazed area of the preserve (no bison). If you visit the Tallgrass Prairie Preserve in spring and summer, you will also get to see the wildflowers in full bloom.

Most of the Study Trail is a mowed-grass surface. It first heads east for 0.09 mile before bearing north. A creek is to your right (east) when heading north. The trail then bears west at 0.11 mile, with the creek still to your right (now north). Short of 0.25 mile, you reach a fork. Continue straight (northwest) on the trail. Heading left (south) leads back to the parking lot. The path begins to narrow after this point and there are unearthed tree roots and rocks. There are three benches for sightseeing to your left (west) after the 0.29-mile mark. The trail interchanges from south and west until you reach another fork at 0.6 mile.

You have access to the Prairie Earth Trail at this fork. Bear right (west) of the bison statue to continue on the Prairie Earth Trail. If you need to head back to the parking lot, continue straight (southeast). Come to another fork at 0.64 mile. This fork is the entrance and exit to the Prairie Earth Trail, which is a loop. Continue straight (northwest) to start the loop in a clockwise direction. The variety of wildflowers is plentiful on the Prairie Earth Trail. Take the time to notice the colors surrounding you. Bear right (north) at 0.73 mile. There is a bench to your left (west) at 1.02 miles.

At 1.5 miles there is a cross-timber area to your right (east), perfect for bird watching. Enter the cross-timber area at 1.62 miles; there is a steady decline of 50 feet in elevation.

BISON OF THE TALLGRASS PRESERVE

In 1993, 300 bison were reestablished into the Joseph H. Williams Tallgrass Prairie Preserve. Today the herd has grown to more than 2,000, freely ranging across 38 square miles. Bison, no longer an endangered species due to safeguarded lands such as this preserve, are critical to sustaining the tallgrass landscape. Bison calves are born from April through June and can be seen when you are traveling through the preserve.

The path eventually heads south, narrows, and changes to a gravel surface. Cross a small creek bed before reaching a rock outcrop to your right (west). A view of Sand Creek is to your left (east). Ascend large slabs of rock and a series of log steps before the path widens and returns to a mowed-grass surface at the 1.72-mile mark. Bear left (east) shortly after. The trail winds south then west, back south, and then finally east before you reach the footbridge at 1.98 miles. The scene at the footbridge is quite beautiful, with the quiet rushing of the creek in the bottomland forest, the blossoming trees, and at times deer grazing in the open prairie.

Bear right (south) up the log steps after crossing the footbridge. The trail winds east and back south again, returning to a mowed-grass surface. You encounter a couple small seasonal creek beds before reaching the end of the Prairie Earth Trail loop at 2.53 miles. Bear left (northeast) to head back to the Study Trail. The Study Trail connection you previously encountered at the 0.6-mile mark will be at 2.57 miles. Bear right (southeast) to continue on the Study Trail. The trail starts to wind east at 2.64 miles. At 2.73 miles, the path changes to a gravel surface and heads north. Bear sharply right (south) at 2.78 miles and see the parking lot ahead of you.

MILES AND DIRECTIONS

0.0   Start at the Study Trailhead, east of the parking lot.

0.24 Reach a fork. Continue straight (northwest) on the trail.

Prairie skies

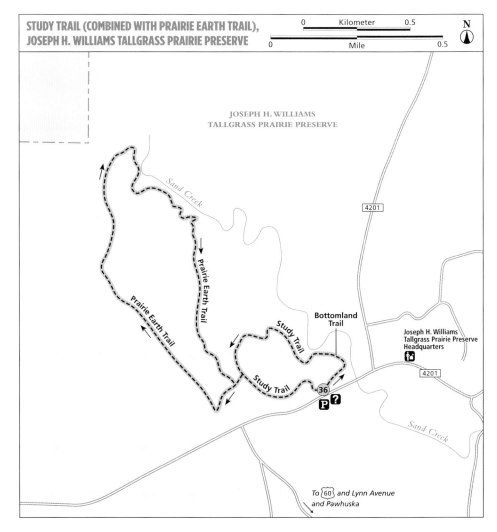

0   Kilometer   0.5

0   Mile   0.5

N

JOSEPH H. WILLIAMS
TALLGRASS PRAIRIE PRESERVE

Sand Creek

4201

Prairie Earth Trail

Prairie Earth Trail

Study Trail

Bottomland
Trail

Joseph H. Williams
Tallgrass Prairie Preserve
Headquarters

4201

Study Trail

36

P ?

Sand Creek

To 60 and Lynn Avenue
and Pawhuska

0.6   Reach a fork. Bear right (west) to access the Prairie Earth Trail loop.

0.64 Reach a fork. Continue straight to start the loop in a clockwise direction.

1.62 Head into a wooded area. Descend steadily for about 50 feet in elevation. Bear right (east).

1.72 Head up some large slabs of rock to a series of log steps.

1.98 Go up some log steps and then cross a footbridge.

2.53 Exit the Prairie Earth Trail loop. Bear left (northeast) to head back to the Study Trail.

2.57 Reach the Study Trail connection. Bear right (southeast) to take the Study Trail back to the trailhead.

2.81 Arrive back at the trailhead.

37 DEER RUN TRAIL (COMBINED WITH EAGLE ROOST TRAIL)

SEQUOYAH STATE PARK

Sequoyah State Park is known for its stately shortleaf pines and being surrounded by the recreational waters of Fort Gibson Lake. The Deer Run Trail and the Eagle Roost Trail take you through quiet evergreens, past a couple lily pad–adorned ponds, and to a Cherokee historical site.

Start: Deer Run Trailhead, about 410 feet south of the Sequoyah State Park Office
Elevation gain: 551 to 635 feet
Distance: 3.18 miles out and back with an additional loop
Difficulty: Easy
Hiking time: 1.5–2 hours
Seasons/schedule: Open year-round, sunrise to sunset
Fees and permits: Parking pass required for day-use visitors
Trail contacts: Sequoyah State Park Office, 17131 Park 10 Rd., Hulbert 74441; (918) 772-2046
Dog-friendly: Leashed dogs permitted
Trail surface: Dirt and rocky path

Land status: Oklahoma State Parks (US Army Corps of Engineers land leased in perpetuity to the state)
Nearest town: Wagoner to the west, Hulbert to the east
Other trail users: None
Maps: USGS Hulbert; Sequoyah State Park map (available online at www.travelok.com/state-parks and via the Oklahoma State Parks mobile app)
Special considerations: This hike description includes the Eagle Roost Trail loop that connects with the Deer Run Trail.

The trailhead for Deer Run Trail is located about 410 feet south of the park office parking lot. For your safety, walk in the grassy area next to the side of the road.

FINDING THE TRAILHEAD

Start from the Main Street/East Cherokee Street intersection in downtown Wagoner, and head east on East Cherokee Street for 0.6 mile. Turn right (south) onto OK 51 E (South McQuarrie Avenue) and continue, following the signs for OK 51 E, for 8.1 miles. Turn right (south) onto Park 10 at the Sequoyah State Park sign. The Sequoyah State Park Office is to your right (west) after 0.2 mile. Park in the lot and walk south about 410 feet to the Deer Run Trailhead. GPS: N35° 55.607′ W95° 14.991′

THE HIKE

The Deer Run Trail combined with the Eagle Roost Trail offers a peaceful trek through towering pines that are signature to this area of Oklahoma. Wildflowers, lichens, and moss are also prevalent on this trail. It winds parallel to Park 10 Road until the 0.19-mile mark. Prior to that, it intersects an old road (N4360 Road) at 0.14 mile. The trail then heads west and tends to get muddy after wet weather. A side trail may distract you at 0.22 mile, but continue straight (west). At 0.29 mile the trail changes, heading south, then east, and then south before reaching a series of clearings in the forest with power

lines at 0.46 mile. You wind though forest and back into the clearings with power lines three more times. Brown painted metal trail markers lead the way. Take note of the majestic pine forest you enter at 0.59 mile. Also be aware of unearthed tree roots, rocky surfaces, and small seasonal creek beds along the way.

After 0.9 mile there are no more power lines, and the trail heads west from here on out. You cross a small creek bed before reaching the end of the Deer Run Trail at 1.24 miles. At this point, you can either head back the way you came or cross the road east of you, head north, and take the Whispering Pines Trail back up to the park office. This guide continues on the Eagle Roost Trail. You will need to cross Park 30 Road to reach the Eagle Roost Trailhead, and will see signs for the Eagle Roost Trail across the way. Use caution; look both ways for vehicles before crossing the road.

Come to a stone slab at the Eagle Roost Trailhead at 1.27 miles. The loop can be taken in either direction. For this description, take the trail in a counterclockwise direction. Bear right (west). There is a bench to your right (north) at 1.29 miles. Stone slabs appear in the path shortly after. The trail starts to head northwest and has a slight descent of 36 feet to the 1.42-mile mark. You start to head west at 1.43 miles and then cross a small creek bed shortly after at the 1.45-mile mark. Bear left (south) to continue the loop. Do not go straight (west), heeding the "Not Designated Trail Beyond This Point" sign. Once you head south, the path widens and can get muddy. A seasonal creek follows along to your left (north). Both the creek and the muddy portion of the trail end around the 1.55-mile mark.

At 1.57 miles, a couple small ponds can be viewed to your right (south). The farther pond is brimming with lily pads, and both are picturesque. You encounter an old, small shelter at 1.6 miles. The path surface becomes rocky shortly after and there is a slight descent of 22 feet.

Top: Flowering trees along the Deer Run Trail
Bottom: Towering pines in Sequoyah State Park

Bear left (east) at 1.67 miles to continue on the Eagle Roost Trail loop (there is another "Not Designated Trail Beyond This Point" sign to your right). Reach a fork at 1.79 miles. Bear left (north) to continue the loop.

Come to the original burial site of a Cherokee woman, Ka-Tee Cockrum, at 1.88 miles. The initial site was established there in 1884, but after years of deterioration, her family retrieved her gravestone for safekeeping until it was returned to this spot in May 2000. The gravestone for Ka-Tee's son, Charles, was relocated next to hers the same year. The Eagle Roost Trail loop comes full circle at 1.93 miles. At this point, head toward Park 30 Road to go back the way you came on the Deer Run Trail.

DEER RUN TRAIL (COMBINED WITH EAGLE ROOST TRAIL), SEQUOYAH STATE PARK

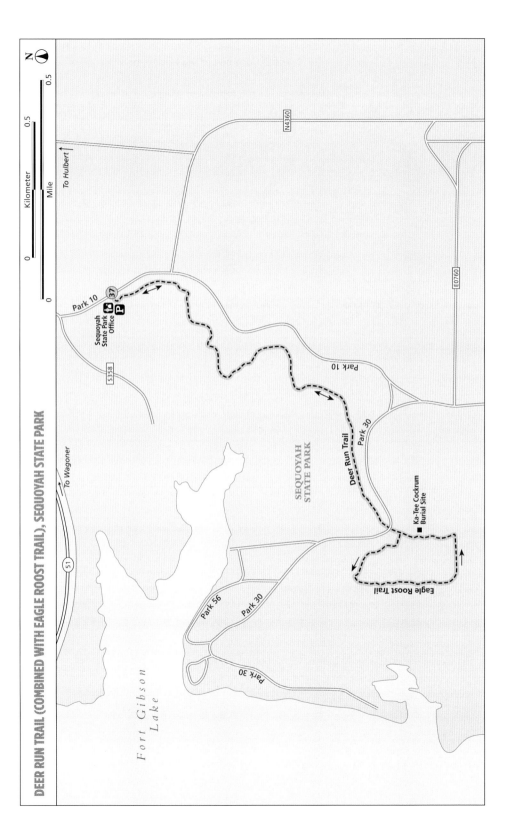

Burial site of Ka-Tee Cockrum and Charles Cockrum

MILES AND DIRECTIONS

0.0   Start at the trailhead, 410 feet south of the park office parking lot.

0.14 The trail intersects an old road (N4360 Road). Continue straight (south).

0.19 Bear right (west). The trail starts to head away from the Park 10 Road.

0.46 Reach a clearing with power lines. Continue straight (west).

0.59 Bear left (east). Reach the same clearing of power lines.

0.71 Reach power lines once again.

0.82 Reach power lines once again.

0.92 Cross a small seasonal creek bed.

1.24 The Deer Run Trail ends at Park 30 Road. Continue straight across the road (use caution) to continue on the Eagle Roost Trail.

1.27 Reach the Eagle Roost Trailhead. Bear right (west).

1.45 Cross a small seasonal creek bed. Bear left (south) to continue the Eagle Roost Trail loop.

1.57 See a couple small ponds to your right (south).

1.6   Pass a small shelter to your right (south).

1.67 Bear left (east) to continue the Eagle Roost Trail loop.

1.79 Reach a fork. Bear left (north) to continue.

1.88 Reach the Ka-Tee Cockrum grave site.

1.93 Reach the end of the Eagle Roost Trail loop. Head toward Park 30 Road to go back the way you came on the Deer Run Trail.

3.18 Arrive back at the trailhead.

38 PINE RIDGE TRAIL (COMBINED WITH SAVANNA TRAIL)

J. T. NICKEL FAMILY NATURE & WILDLIFE PRESERVE

Combining the Pine Ridge Trail with the Savanna Trail makes for a tranquil hike through forests and prairie land. On this path, hikers can also enjoy an abundance of wildflowers during spring and summer and panoramic views of the Cookson Hills.

Start: Pine Ridge Trailhead, about 0.1 mile northwest from the nature center parking lot
Elevation gain: 932 to 1,093 feet
Distance: 2.17-mile loop with an optional spur to an overlook
Difficulty: Easy to moderate due to a couple narrow declines
Hiking time: 1–1.5 hours
Seasons/schedule: Open year-round, sunrise to sunset; best during spring and fall
Fees and permits: None
Trail contacts: J. T. Nickel Family Nature and Wildlife Preserve Field Office, Tahlequah 74464; (918) 207-0671
Dog-friendly: No animals permitted
Trail surface: Combination of dirt and rocky path and mowed grass
Land status: The Nature Conservancy of Oklahoma

Nearest town: Tahlequah
Other trail users: Hikers only
Maps: USGS Chewey; The Nature Conservancy map (available online at www.nature.org/content/dam/tnc/nature/en/documents/nickel-preserve-map.pdf)
Special considerations: J. T. Nickel Family Nature and Wildlife Preserve is privately owned and has visitation guidelines different from Oklahoma's state parks. These guidelines foster preservation of the landscape and native wildlife. The visitation guidelines are available at www.nature.org/jtnickel.
Instead of returning to the parking lot at the end of the Pine Ridge Trail, this hike description continues on the Savanna Trail to head back to the parking lot.

FINDING THE TRAILHEAD

From the US 62 and Bertha Parker Bypass intersection in Tahlequah, head east on US 62 E for 5.9 miles. Turn left on North Oakdale Drive and travel another 3.2 miles before heading north on North Pumpkin Hollow. Travel 6.1 miles on North Pumpkin Hollow before turning left (east) on E685 Road/Pumpkin Flat. The parking lot for the nature center and the Pine Ridge Trailhead is on your right after 0.1 mile. GPS: N36° 02.130′ W94° 48.561′

THE HIKE

The J. T. Nickel Family Nature and Wildlife Preserve is a peaceful sanctuary for various wildlife and flora. Protected by the lush Cookson Hills, the preserve boasts vibrant wildflowers during warmer seasons, many opportunities for bird-watching, and plenty of greenery. The Pine Ridge Trail in combination with the Savanna Trail takes you

Flowering dogwoods along the Pine Ridge Trail

Dwarf crested iris along the Savanna Trail

through halcyon forests and sprawling prairies and ridgelines.

The trail starts at a grassy knoll about 0.1 mile northwest of the nature center. You reach the top of the hill at 0.18 mile, with a gain of about 92 feet in elevation. From here, proceed into the forest, a mixture of pine, oak, and hickory. Be careful of the fallen tree trunk a little after 0.25 mile on the trail. At 0.32 mile you will see a tree with a circular green metal marker; the path begins to narrow. A descent of 53 feet in elevation starts at the 0.55-mile mark. The descent continues and becomes very rocky at 0.6 mile.

The path levels out, and you cross a couple seasonal creek beds as the trail winds east at 0.62 mile. This portion can get a little overgrown, so look for the green metal marker on a tree as your guide. At 0.68 mile bear right (south). The trail surface widens and returns to mowed grass. You encounter a gravel road that goes north and south at 0.92 mile. Here the scenery changes to open grassland and signs indicate the Pine Ridge Trail and Savanna Trail. Heading right (south) on the gravel road leads back to the nature center parking lot. To continue on the Savanna Trail, which also leads to the parking lot, head straight (east). The trail curves to the right (south) soon after.

The Savanna Trail interchanges between going north and west up to the 1.18-mile mark. The topography returns to a wooded area at 0.98 mile, and the trail becomes rocky. Numerous wildflowers bloom in this area in spring and summer. Be sure to hit the trail during those seasons to enjoy the beautiful colors. There is a small switchback at 1.04 miles, and then the path widens and returns to mowed grass at 1.07 miles. The trail starts to head east at 1.18 miles, winding along a ravine shortly after. At 1.23 miles, the trail curves to the right (south). An optional spur to an overlook is available to your right (south) at 1.53 miles. However, the overlook with the best view of the valley, and without having to go off the trail, is at 1.68 miles. Visibility of the valley and Cookson Hills from this overlook is optimal during fall and winter, when there is less tree cover. There is another overlook to your right (east) at 1.92 miles after the trail begins to wind south. The path surface becomes rocky for a bit before the area opens up to a savanna at 2.09 miles. Pass a small marsh to your right (west). From here the trail winds west toward the parking lot.

MILES AND DIRECTIONS

0.0 Start at the Pine Ridge Trailhead, northwest of the nature center.

0.18 After ascending the hill, enter a pine-oak forest.

0.6 The trail starts to wind down a very rocky pathway.

Overlook view of Cookson Hills

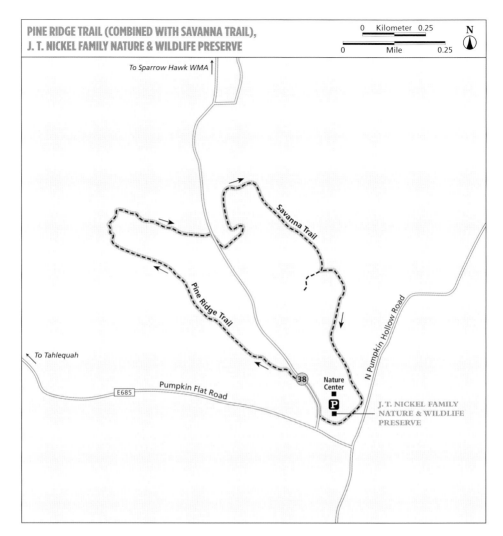

PINE RIDGE TRAIL (COMBINED WITH SAVANNA TRAIL), J. T. NICKEL FAMILY NATURE & WILDLIFE PRESERVE

0   Kilometer   0.25

0   Mile   0.25

N

To Sparrow Hawk WMA

Savanna Trail

Pine Ridge Trail

To Tahlequah

N Pumpkin Hollow Road

Pumpkin Flat Road

E685

38

Nature Center

J. T. NICKEL FAMILY NATURE & WILDLIFE PRESERVE

0.92 Reach a gravel road that goes north and south. Continue straight (east) on the Savanna Trail.

1.2 Wind along a ravine. A valley is to your right (south).

1.53 Bypass an optional spur to an overlook of the valley to your right (south). Continue east on the trail.

1.68 Reach an overlook with the best view of the valley.

1.92 There is another overlook to your right (east). Start a descent of 125 feet.

2.11 Pass a small marsh to your right (west).

2.17 Arrive back at the trailhead.

39 SPARROW HAWK WMA TRAIL

SPARROW HAWK WILDLIFE MANAGEMENT AREA

Sweeping views of the Illinois River winding through tree-studded bluffs are one of the highlights of this trail. With a good number of ascents and descents out and back, the Sparrow Hawk WMA Trail functions as a great workout as well as a scenic hike.

Start: Far left trailhead, north of the Sparrow Hawk WMA parking lot
Elevation gain: 852 to 1,138 feet
Distance: 3.38-mile lollipop
Difficulty: Moderate due to constant ascents and descents on the trail
Hiking time: 1.5–2 hours
Seasons/schedule: Open year-round, sunrise to sunset
Fees and permits: Oklahoma Wildlife Conservation Passport, Oklahoma hunting license, or Oklahoma fishing license required
Trail contacts: Oklahoma Department of Wildlife Conservation; (405) 521-3851 (no one physically stationed at the park)

Dog-friendly: Leashed dogs permitted
Trail surface: Dirt and rocky path
Land status: Oklahoma Department of Wildlife Conservation
Nearest town: Tahlequah
Other trail users: Mountain bikers, hunters, anglers
Maps: USGS Tahlequah; Sparrow Hawk WMA map (available online at www.wildlifedepartment.com)
Special considerations: Areas surrounding the latter part of the trail are private property. Consult WMA maps online and at the trailhead to be aware of the boundary lines.

FINDING THE TRAILHEAD

From the US 62 and Bertha Parker Bypass intersection in Tahlequah, head east on US 62 E for 1.9 miles. Turn left on OK 10 N and travel another 3.1 miles, where you will make a sharp right (almost a U-turn) onto E730 Road. The parking lot to the Sparrow Hawk Wildlife Management Area trailhead is to your left after 0.3 mile. GPS: N35° 57.556' W94° 54.155'

THE HIKE

The northeastern region of Oklahoma is known as Green Country, and rightfully so. Lush, emerald-hued timbers carpet towering bluffs, and rivers carve through endless grassy meadows and forests. The views from the Sparrow Hawk WMA Trail encapsulate this type of imagery, and the trail offers several changes in elevation.

North of where the parking lot meets the WMA signage, you will encounter three trailheads. The main trailhead is on the far left. The trail starts at about 850 feet above sea level and then ascends to a little above 980 feet at 0.14 mile. Between these two points are a fallen tree trunk and a trail connection to the right (east); the trail then narrows. At the 0.14-mile mark, the path widens as a grassy surface. There are a few more unearthed tree roots and then another trail that connects to the right (east). Reach a memorial to

a fallen hiker at 0.54 mile. Bear right (east) afterward. The trail surface turns rocky and starts to descend for about 65 feet in elevation until the 0.6-mile mark. There will be several scenic points to your left (north and west) from this point. Prior to reaching the rocky hill at 0.77 mile, the trail ascends one more time for about 50 feet in elevation.

When you reach the rocky hill, several side trails to the west lead to breathtaking vistas of the Illinois River and the Cedar Hollow area. Two branch off at the 0.77-mile mark. There is another at the fork at 0.8 mile. These paths are very narrow and steep, so use caution when heading down to the vistas. At this point, some hikers prefer to turn around and head back to the trailhead.

Sunset at vista on Sparrow Hawk WMA Trail

Those wanting more exercise as well as more nature will head back on the main trail at the 0.8-mile mark and continue northeast. The trail begins to ascend once again for about 110 feet in elevation until it levels out at 1.1 miles and returns to a dirt surface. The trail then winds away from the bluffs.

You may encounter several downed trees and rocky surfaces as the trail winds from northeast to an easterly direction and then back to a route due north. One fallen tree trunk is distinctive—the one you cross over at 1.52 miles. This is the reconnecting point after you complete the loop portion of the lollipop that begins here. At 1.63 miles signage indicates that the trail heads toward private properties (Sparrow Hawk Village) and

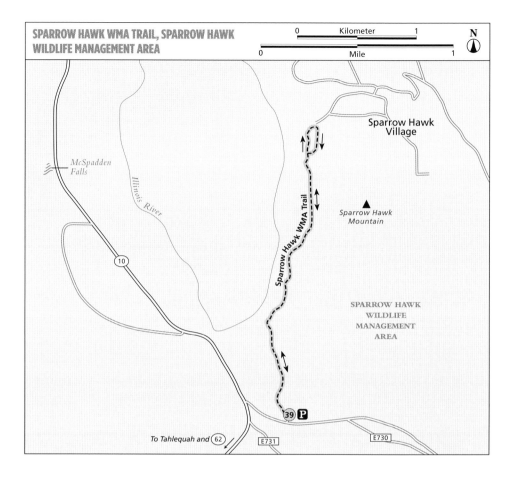

that hikers need to be aware of the boundary lines. You reach the private properties of Sparrow Hawk Village at 1.66 miles. Bear right (east) at this point and then bear right (south) again at 1.7 miles to head back into the woods. This portion of the trail can get a bit overgrown in spring and summer, but it is manageable to pass through. The trail starts to wind southwest at 1.78 miles, and you then bear right (west) at 1.85 miles. At 1.87 miles you return to the tree trunk you had to cross over earlier. Bear left (south) at this point and head back the way you came from the parking lot.

MILES AND DIRECTIONS

0.0 Start at the main (far-left) trailhead, north of the parking lot.

0.54 Bear right (east). A memorial for a fallen hiker is to your left (west).

0.77 Reach a rock outcrop and some side trails to several outlooks. (**Option:** Turn around at this point for a shorter, less-strenuous hike.)

0.8 Reach a fork. Stay on the right side of the fork (northeast).

1.52 Begin the loop portion of the lollipop.

1.66 Private property is to your left (north). Bear right (east).

Rocky hill on Sparrow Hawk WMA Trail

1.7   Bear right (south), back into the woods.

1.87 Finish the loop portion of the trail. Bear left (south) and head back.

3.38 Arrive back at the trailhead.

40 CHINKAPIN HIKING TRAIL

LAKE EUFAULA STATE PARK

The Chinkapin Trail, named for the golden chestnut-adorned tree, winds through various oak forests and tallgrass prairies before leading you to the shoreline of Oklahoma's largest lake.

Start: Chinkapin Hiking Trailhead, across from the Lake Eufaula State Park Office
Elevation gain: 551 to 623 feet
Distance: 3.92 miles out and back (includes a segment of the Savannah Trail)
Difficulty: Easy
Hiking time: 1.5–2 hours
Seasons/schedule: Open year-round, sunrise to sunset
Fees and permits: Parking pass required for day-use visitors
Trail contacts: Lake Eufaula State Park Office, 111563 Hwy. 150, Checotah 74426; (918) 689-5311

Dog-friendly: Leashed dogs permitted
Trail surface: Dirt and rocky path
Land status: Oklahoma State Parks
Nearest town: Eufaula to the south, Checotah to the north
Other trail users: Cyclists
Maps: USGS Checotah; Lake Eufaula State Park map (available online at www.travelok.com/state-parks and via the Oklahoma State Parks mobile app)
Special considerations: This hike description includes hiking a segment of the Savannah Loop to continue on the Chinkapin Hiking Trail.

FINDING THE TRAILHEAD

Head south on Old Highway 69 from Checotah for a little over 7 miles. Turn right on OK 150 and travel 3.6 miles to the Lake Eufaula State Park Office. The trail is on the other side of OK 150; park at the park office and carefully cross the road to the trailhead. GPS: N35° 23.973' W95° 36.331'

THE HIKE

Known as the "Gentle Giant," Lake Eufaula is Oklahoma's largest lake. It has more than 600 miles of shoreline, and the Chinkapin Hiking Trail brings you to its very banks. The chinkapin oak tree, for which the trail is named, is not the only oak species you'll see on this trail. While traveling toward Lake Eufaula, you will encounter wooded areas of serene post oak and blackjack oak.

The Chinkapin Hiking Trail starts off in a forested area before reaching the Savannah Loop junction at 0.28 mile. Continue straight (south) on this segment of the Savannah Loop. (The Savannah Loop becomes part of the Chinkapin Trail at 0.8 mile.) Short of 0.4 mile, the scenery opens up into a tallgrass prairie. The trail then splits in two. Make sure to take the path to the left that winds through the forest, not the path to the right that appears to be auto tracks. You are greeted by partial views of Lake Eufaula at 0.57 mile, and the trail starts to wind east before winding south again at 0.67 mile. Views of the lake continue on your right (southwest) after you cross a bridge at 0.72 mile. Portions of this trail may include fallen tree branches, and it can get very muddy after a rainfall; use caution. At 0.8 mile, you reach the end of the Savannah Loop at the Longhorn Loop connection. A sign directs you to bear right (east) to continue on the Chinkapin Hiking Trail.

Reach an overlook to a small pond on your left (north). Enjoy the view and bask in its tranquility when there are lighter winds. At 0.94 mile, signage to your left (north) indicates that you bear right (south). After 1.0 mile, another sign directs you to head left (east). Do not continue straight—that path leads into a ditch. Cross a footbridge and the ditch is visible to your right (west). This portion of the trail, all the way to the 1.14-mile mark, becomes rather muddy after a decent rainfall. Reach a junction at 1.09 miles. Continue straight (south). Do not turn left (east). There is a dead end at 1.21 miles. At this point, turn right (west) and head toward Lake Eufaula.

A little after 1.25 miles, you need to bear left (south) and cross a small seasonal creek bed. The trail winds in a southerly direction again before bearing right (west) toward the lake at 1.32 miles. There is another diversion to the left (east) of the trail shortly after. Make sure you continue straight (south). At about

Beginning of Chinkapin Hiking Trail

1.41 miles you head away from the lake and may encounter a downed tree where the wooded area opens up beautifully. Go around the fallen tree trunk with caution. After hiking on the trail for 1.5 miles, cross a rocky seasonal creek that features a small waterfall. A yellow trail marker on a tree indicates the direction to go. From here, bear right (west) until you reach another dead end. Another yellow trail marker on a tree guides you left (south) down the gully, which appears to be a spectacular tunnel of tall trees. During fall and winter, the gully up to the 1.7-mile mark can be deep with fallen leaves, so watch your step.

One of the several yurts at Lake Eufaula State Park is to your left (east) at 1.75 miles. Continue straight toward Lake Eufaula. Cross a stone slab, with a partial view of the bay to your right (west), at 1.82 miles. Unfortunately, this portion of the trail accumulates refuse from nearby campers. (This is a good reminder for all of us to pack out our trash and leave no trace.) At 1.93 miles there is another yurt to your left (east). There is also a sign stating, "Trail not maintained beyond this point." Make sure the conditions of the trail are safe before continuing straight (south) to the lake. The path to the shoreline is quite accessible—it is obvious that hikers travel it frequently to get a rewarding view of the lake. Reach the sandy shore of Lake Eufaula at 1.97 miles, after a few large slabs of

Lake Eufaula shoreline at sunset

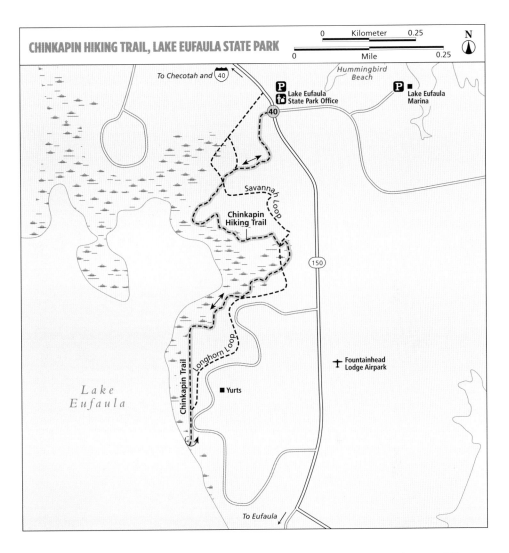

rock and a fallen tree trunk. The vastness of Lake Eufaula is quite a sight, especially near sunset. Once you have had a decent respite and enjoyed the panoramic scenery, turn around and head back the way you came.

MILES AND DIRECTIONS

0.0 Start at the Chinkapin Hiking Trailhead. The trail winds through a forest.

0.28 Reach the Savannah Loop connection. Continue straight (south) onto the Savannah Loop.

0.39 The view opens up into a tallgrass prairie. The path splits. Take the left path that winds through the forest.

0.72 Cross a bridge and a small seasonal creek bed.

0.8 Reach the end of the Savannah Loop at the Longhorn Loop connection. Bear right (east) to continue on the Chinkapin Hiking Trail.

0.87 Come to an outlook to a small pond, on your left (north).

1.0 Bear left (east).

1.03 Cross a bridge and a small seasonal creek bed.

1.09 Reach a fork. Continue straight (south). Do not turn left (east).

1.21 Turn right (west). Reach a dead end and head toward the lake.

1.26 Bear left (south) and cross a small seasonal creek bed.

Small pond on Chinkapin Hiking Trail

1.35 Bypass the diversion to your left (east). Continue straight (south).

1.5 Cross a seasonal rocky creek and bear right (west).

1.58 Turn left (south) and head down a gully.

1.75 Reach an intersection. Continue straight (south).

1.93 Reach a sign stating, "Trail not maintained beyond this point." Continue straight (south) to the lake if the trail conditions are safe.

1.97 Reach the Lake Eufaula shoreline. Turn around and head back the way you came.

3.92 Arrive back at the trailhead.

HONORABLE MENTIONS

(GREEN COUNTRY, NORTHEAST OKLAHOMA)

H. YELLOW TRAIL

TURKEY MOUNTAIN URBAN WILDERNESS

Although only about 800 feet in stature, Turkey Mountain is one of the tallest natural points in Tulsa. A favorite base for both mountain bikers and hikers, the Turkey Mountain Urban Wilderness Area offers myriad greenery, views of the Arkansas River, rocky outcrops, and sundry terrain. For history buffs, sandstone carvings at Turkey Mountain hail back to the oil exploration days of the 1920s.

Start: Yellow Trailhead, northeast of the parking lot
Elevation gain: 673 to 892 feet
Distance: 4.11-mile lollipop
Difficulty: Moderate to strenuous due to uneven, rocky trail with steep ascents and descents and multiple side trails
Hiking time: About 3 hours
Seasons/schedule: Open year-round; park hours 5 a.m.–11 p.m.
Fees and permits: None
Trail contacts: River Parks Authority, 2121 S. Columbia Ave., Ste. 205, Tulsa 74114; (918) 596-2001
Dog-friendly: Leashed dogs permitted

Trail surface: Dirt and rocky terrain
Land status: Managed by the River Parks Authority
Nearest town: Tulsa
Other trail users: Mountain bikers, equestrians
Maps: USGS Jenks; Turkey Mountain map (available online at www .riverparks.org/experience/turkey-mountain)
Special considerations: The Turkey Mountain area is widely used by mountain bikers and offers a lot of side trails. Be alert for mountain bikers heading your way or coming from behind you, especially on narrow portions of the trail.

FINDING THE TRAILHEAD

From downtown Tulsa, take I-244 W to US 75 S. After 5 miles on US 75 S, take the 61st Street exit. Turn left (east) on 61st Street, which eventually changes to South Elwood Avenue. Continue 1.3 miles on South Elwood Avenue to the Turkey Mountain Urban Wilderness Area parking lot, on your left (east). GPS: N36° 03.913′ W95° 59.561′

Fall colors at their peak
on the Yellow Trail

Lake Tenkiller from the Overlook view

I. OVERLOOK NATURE TRAIL

LAKE TENKILLER

While the scene of Lake Tenkiller at the trailhead is the paramount view, the Overlook Nature Trail is a lovely hike including dogwood trees, seasonal creek beds, footbridges, and a forest ablaze in fiery foliage during autumn.

Start: North side of the Tenkiller Lake Overlook parking lot
Elevation gain: 640 to 794 feet
Distance: 2.36 miles out and back
Difficulty: Easy to moderate due to uneven terrain
Hiking time: 1–2 hours
Seasons/schedule: Open year-round, sunrise to sunset
Fees and permits: None
Trail contacts: Tenkiller Lake Project Office, 446977 E980 Rd., Gore 74435; (918) 487-5252
Dog-friendly: Leashed dogs permitted
Trail surface: Dirt and rocky path with dirt steps

Land status: US Army Corps of Engineers
Nearest town: Gore to the southwest, Vian to the southeast
Other trail users: None
Maps: USGS Gore
Special considerations: There is another entrance to the Overlook Nature Trail across from the United Methodist Boys Ranch. The trail runs from the Overlook area to the United Methodist Boys Ranch area. Both areas have places to park.
   Note: At time of publication, the former route to Strayhorn Landing is in disrepair.

FINDING THE TRAILHEAD

From the US 62 and West Okmulgee Avenue intersection in Muskogee, head southeast on West Okmulgee Avenue for 3.4 miles. West Okmulgee Avenue eventually changes to Chandler Road. Merge south onto OK 165 S/OK 351 and continue for 19 miles. Use exit 55 to merge onto US 64 E. After 2 miles, turn left (northeast) to stay on US 64 E. After 2.3 miles, continue straight (northeast) onto Main Street/OK 100 E for 6.6 miles. Turn right (southeast) onto OK 100 W. Short of 1 mile, turn left (north) onto Corps of Engineers Road. The trailhead is at the fence north of the Overlook parking lot. GPS: N35° 35.891' W95° 03.126'

J. **DRIPPING SPRINGS TRAIL**

NATURAL FALLS STATE PARK

The two tallest waterfalls in Oklahoma are both 77 feet tall, and one of them is at the heart of this trail. The waterfall, which cascades into turquoise-hued waters, is not only a calming beauty to behold; it is also famous. The Dripping Springs Waterfall and its surrounding Ozark Highland scenery within Natural Falls State Park were featured in the film *Where the Red Fern Grows*. The trail is short but offers a good variety in trail surfaces, views, and memories from the film.

Start: Dripping Springs Trailhead, from the parking lot south of the Natural Falls State Park Office and east of campgrounds
Elevation gain: 915 to 1,071 feet
Distance: 0.5-mile lollipop
Difficulty: Moderate due to uneven, rocky trail that steeply descends 95 feet
Hiking time: 30–45 minutes, depending on how long you enjoy the waterfall view
Seasons/schedule: Open year-round, sunrise to sunset
Fees and permits: Parking pass required for day-use visitors

Trail contacts: Natural Falls State Park Office, 19225 E. 578 Rd., Colcord 74338; (918) 422-5802
Dog-friendly: Leashed dogs permitted
Trail surface: Paved trail to first observation deck and last bridge before exiting the trail; all other trail segments are either gravel or rocky terrain
Land status: Oklahoma State Parks
Nearest town: West Siloam Springs
Other trail users: None
Maps: USGS Siloam Springs NW; Natural Falls State Park map (available online at www.travelok .com/state-parks and via the Oklahoma State Parks mobile app)

FINDING THE TRAILHEAD

From West Siloam Springs, head west on US 412 E/US 59 for 5.5 miles. Turn left (south) on N4680 Road. Turn left (east) on E578 Road after 0.2 mile. After 0.1 mile on E578 Road, turn right (south) toward the Natural Falls State Park visitor center. From the visitor center, turn left (east) and head toward the parking lot after 300 feet. You will see the trailhead (signage and a bridge) to the south. GPS: N36° 10.475' W94° 40.037'

77-foot waterfall along the
Dripping Springs Trail

CHOCTAW COUNTRY (SOUTHEAST OKLAHOMA)

Possibly one of the areas most visited by out-of-staters, southeast Oklahoma's **CHOCTAW COUNTRY** hosts some of the most scenic areas in the state. This region is particularly popular in autumn. Visitors travel down the highly publicized Talimena National Scenic Byway, camp within the pine trees of the Ouachita National Forest, or head to Beavers Bend State Park's bald cypress–lined Lower Mountain Fork River area. Why? This portion of the state puts on one of the most spectacular and effervescent displays of fall leaf colors. Add gorgeous lakes such as Broken Bow Lake and Cedar Lake, and there is no shortage of what you can do in the outdoors in Choctaw Country.

Broken Bow Lake at sunrise (Hikes 46-48)

41 ROUGH CANYON TRAIL

ROBBERS CAVE STATE PARK

Looking for a Wild West hideout? Then the Rough Canyon Trail is for you. The trail descends along rushing Fourche Maline, winds through the bluffs of Rough Canyon, puts on stunning displays of Lost Lake, and continues to reward to the end by leading you right up to Robbers Cave. Legendary outlaws sought refuge in this Paleozoic sandstone cave.

Start: Rough Canyon Trailhead, west of the Robbers Cave parking lot
Elevation gain: 860 to 1,142 feet
Distance: 2.9-mile loop
Difficulty: Moderate due to uneven, rocky trail with unearthed tree roots and steep inclines
Hiking time: 1–2 hours
Seasons/schedule: Open year-round, sunrise to sunset; best during fall for scenery
Fees and permits: Parking pass required for day-use visitors
Trail contact: Robbers Cave State Park Office, 575 NW 1024th Ave., Wilburton 74578; (918) 465-2562
Dog-friendly: Leashed dogs permitted
Trail surface: Rocky dirt path occasionally laden with dried pine needles and intermittent, unearthed tree roots
Land status: Oklahoma State Parks
Nearest town: Wilburton
Other trail users: Equestrians
Maps: USGS Quinton South; Robbers Cave State Park map (available online at www.travelok.com/state-parks and via the Oklahoma State Parks mobile app)
Special considerations: Most of the trail consists of large rocks, unearthed tree roots, and seasonal creek beds. During rainy seasons and wet conditions, use extra caution—surfaces can be slippery and waterlogged.
  Blue trail markers with a hiker icon and blue blazes serve as guides on this trail.

FINDING THE TRAILHEAD

From Wilburton, head north on OK 2 for 6.5 miles. Turn left on Ash Creek Road, and then take the first right onto Robbers Cave Road. In 1.5 miles reach Group Camp #2 and Redbud Campground. Head toward the Robbers Cave parking lot by turning left (west) on Robbers Cave Road. After crossing the creek overpass, turn right (north) for the Robbers Cave parking lot. The Rough Canyon Trailhead is west of Robbers Cave. GPS: N35° 00.335′ W95° 20.267′

THE HIKE

Designated by both blue blazes and blue trail markers, the trail begins in a heavily forested area of southern yellow pine, oak, hickory, elm, and dogwood. Although the dirt path tends to be blanketed with dried pine needles, an occasional unearthed tree root or large rock will be on the surface. Watch your step. A little more than 0.1 mile from the trailhead, Fourche Maline, a tributary to Lake Wayne Wallace, becomes visible to the south. During the spring or after a decent rainfall, you may be welcomed by its roaring current. Continue to follow along the creek, and cross large clusters and slabs of rock.

Rough Canyon

About 0.3 mile on the trail, you start a steep ascent up large rocks to the ridge. Follow the blue trail markers as you ascend. The path flattens out and crosses a couple small seasonal creek beds after you reach the ridge.

At the Equestrian Trail junction, marked by a yellow blaze, head straight (west), following the blue trail marker to stay on the trail. The trail eventually intersects the Cave Trail. Bear left (west) to stay on the Rough Canyon Trail, which returns to a rocky surface. At the 1.0-mile mark, reach the Cattail Pond Trail junction, distinguished by its double blue dot marker. Bear slightly right (north) toward the blue trail marker and the path steers

Lost Lake from the shoreline

you into Rough Canyon. "Rough Canyon" is a misnomer for this area. In reality, it is a tranquil valley with bluffs short in stature. A winding creek to your left (north) joins you for a good portion of Rough Canyon, with a few small waterfalls along the way.

This hike through Rough Canyon leads you right to Lost Lake's shoreline. Several large logs are in the path before you reach Lost Lake, so be aware of what is in the path. In lieu of blue trail markers, blue blazes are the primary guides from the Cattail Pond Trail junction to Lost Lake. You will reach the point where the original Lost Lake sign once stood. It is still there, but in disrepair. Use the white sign attached to a tree to your left

ROUGH CANYON TRAIL, ROBBERS CAVE STATE PARK

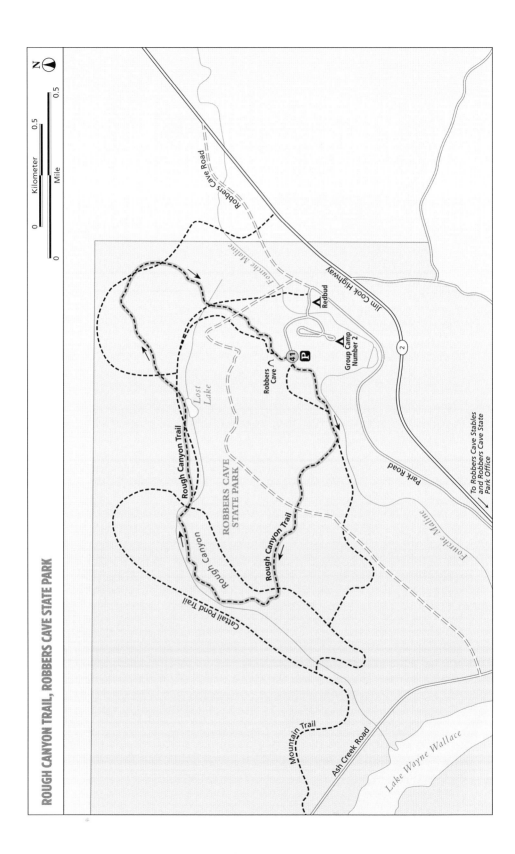

(west) for directions. It will direct you to bear right (east) toward Lost Lake to continue on the trail. The trail winds around a few times; look ahead for the blue blazes and trail markers on trees to stay on track.

Once you reach Lost Lake, you will be endowed with panoramic views to your right (south) all along the lily pad–adorned lake. You can bask in Lost Lake's serene beauty as its waters remain still. It is especially enchanting in the autumn season, when the fall foliage surrounding the lake reigns in all its glory.

Venturing on, single blue blazes will be your guide until a little after the 2.0-mile mark. There will be a couple seasonal creek beds and possible logs in the pathway before you reach the Multi-Use Trail connection. Following the blue blazes, continue straight on the trail. Cross several more seasonal creek beds before reaching an old dirt road. Bear left (west) toward the blue trail marker as you navigate across the dirt road to stay on the trail. The trail begins to descend as you advance toward the Robbers Cave outcrop. The infamous Robbers Cave, formed of Savanna Sandstone from the Pennsylvanian geological period, is to your right (west). Feel free to venture around Robbers Cave, but proceed with caution—there are many drop-offs without guardrails. You can hide out in the cave's crevices like infamous outlaws Belle Starr, Jesse James, and the Dalton Brothers supposedly once did. You can also ascend to the top of the cave to get spectacular aerial views of the San Bois Mountains. Otherwise, continue on the paved portion of the Cave Trail to the Robbers Cave parking lot. You will see the Rough Canyon Trailhead to your right (west).

MILES AND DIRECTIONS

0.0   Start at the Rough Canyon Trailhead. Follow the blue blazes and blue trail markers.

0.14   A clearing to the left (south) provides a view of Fourche Maline.

0.32   Bear right (north) where the trail starts to ascend a steep incline.

0.37   Continue straight up the large rocks to reach the ridge and then head into a wooded area.

0.6   Reach the Equestrian Trail connection. Continue straight (west) on the Rough Canyon Trail.

0.68   Reach the Cave Trail connection. Bear left (west) to stay on the Rough Canyon Trail.

0.93   Reach the Cattail Pond Trail connection. Bear slightly right (north) toward the blue trail marker to continue on the Rough Canyon Trail and wind along the east side of Rough Canyon. A creek to your left (north) travels along with you for a good portion of this segment.

1.4   Reach the old Lost Lake signage (in disrepair). A white sign attached to a tree on your left (west) provides directions. Bear right (east) to continue on the Rough Canyon Trail toward Lost Lake.

1.72   Reach Lost Lake.

2.0   Reach the Multi-Use Trail junction. Continue straight on the Rough Canyon Trail.

2.65   Cross the old dirt road. Bear left (west) to continue on the Rough Canyon Trail.

2.82   Reach the Robbers Cave outcrop to your right (west). Explore at will, then continue straight down to the paved Cave Trail walkway.

2.9   Arrive at the Robbers Cave parking lot. The Rough Canyon Trailhead is to your right (west).

42 TRAIL TO LAKE WAYNE WALLACE OVERLOOK

ROBBERS CAVE STATE PARK

Lake Wayne Wallace, the larger of the two lakes located in Robbers Cave State Park, boasts 4 miles of beautiful shoreline that captivates hikers, equestrians, campers, and anglers alike. This trail, with no shortage of interesting twists and turns, gives visitors the opportunity to see Lake Wayne Wallace in all its glory as it lies among the San Bois Mountains.

Start: Rough Canyon Trailhead, west of the Robbers Cave parking lot
Elevation gain: 781 to 1,017 feet
Distance: 6.7 miles out and back
Difficulty: Moderate to difficult due to uneven, rocky trail with unearthed tree roots and steep switchbacks
Hiking time: At least 4 hours
Seasons/schedule: Open year-round, sunrise to sunset; best during fall for scenery
Fees and permits: Parking pass required for day-use visitors
Trail contact: Robbers Cave State Park Office, 575 NW 1024th Ave., Wilburton 74578; (918) 465-2562
Dog-friendly: Leashed dogs permitted
Trail surface: Rocky dirt path occasionally covered in dried pine needles, log steps, intermittent, unearthed tree roots
Land status: Oklahoma State Parks

Nearest town: Wilburton
Other trail users: Equestrians
Maps: USGS Quinton South; Robbers Cave State Park map (available online at www.travelok.com/state-parks and via the Oklahoma State Parks mobile app)
Special considerations: Most of the trail consists of large rocks, unearthed tree roots, and seasonal creek beds. During rainy seasons and wet conditions, use extra caution—surfaces can be slippery and waterlogged.
  This trail comprises a few other interweaving trails. From the trailhead to the final Cattail Pond Loop Trail connection, follow the blue and double blue trail markers. Follow the yellow diamond trail markers to the Mountain Trail. For the Big John 2 switchbacks and Rim Rock Trail, use the posted signage as guides.

FINDING THE TRAILHEAD

From Wilburton, head north on OK 2 for 6.5 miles. Turn left on Ash Creek Road and take the first right onto Robbers Cave Road. In 1.5 miles you reach Group Camp #2 and Redbud Campground. Head toward the Robbers Cave parking lot by turning left (west) on Robbers Cave Road. After crossing the creek overpass, turn right (north) for the Robbers Cave parking lot. The Rough Canyon Trailhead is west of Robbers Cave. GPS: N35° 00.335' W95° 20.267'

THE HIKE

The extraordinarily scenic trail to Lake Wayne Wallace begins at the same trailhead as the Rough Canyon Trail. It also follows the same route until the 0.93-mile mark. Instead of bearing right (north) at the Cattail Pond Trail junction, bear left (south) to head toward

the connection to the Mountain Trail. Double blue trail markers (half light blue and half dark blue) will be your guide until 1.16 miles. From this point, the route can get tricky. There are quite a few intersecting trails, including equestrian trails, side trails, and other trails. Pay attention to the trail markers noted in this trail description.

After crossing a seasonal creek bed, you reach a fork at 1.11 miles. Take the right side of the fork (west) to continue toward the Cattail Pond Trail. The left side of the loop (southwest) is an equestrian trail. At 1.15 miles you reach another fork. Stay right to follow the double blue trail markers. The Cattail Pond Trail connection is to your right (north) at 1.16 miles. Continue straight (southwest), following the yellow blazes and yellow diamonds with black arrows. Proceed through a small rocky ditch. The creek parallels the trail to the right (north). (***Note:*** There are different options to connect with the Mountain Trail. This is just one of them. Another option is to take the Cattail Pond Trail for a short distance. That route reconnects with the route provided in this guide at the 1.38-mile mark.) A side trail coming from the southeast merges with the trail at 1.26 miles. Continue straight (south), following the yellow trail markers.

Reach a fork at 1.3 miles. Bear to your right (west). Follow the yellow diamonds with black arrows. Head down the rocks. When you reach the creek, you will know you are on the right path. Cross the creek and the trail begins to head north. The trail you are on begins to merge with the Mountain Trail at 1.38 miles. (The right side of the fork is the route that connects with the Mountain Trail via the Cattail Pond Trail.) Take the left side of the fork (west). Follow the yellow trail markers. The trail winds northwest and you come across a few downed trees and a seasonal creek bed. Dark blue trail markers

Fourche Maline

for the Mountain Trail begin to appear at 1.81 miles. Reach a gravel vehicle road at 1.91 miles after crossing another seasonal creek bed. Continue northwest toward the dark blue trail marker. Reach a fork shortly after. Bear left toward the dark blue trail marker as the trail heads south. Before reaching Ash Creek Road, you will encounter more fallen tree branches and large rocks in the path. You will need to cross another seasonal creek bed; this one is much wider than the others. You reach Ash Creek Road at the 2.29-mile mark; proceed across the road with caution and continue heading south.

Bypass a trail leading to the Eagles Nest Campground at 2.43 miles. Continue straight (south). A couple primitive campsites come into view to your right (west) at 2.45 miles and 2.52 miles. Rocky Top primitive campsite, the one at 2.52 miles, can be reached after crossing a seasonal creek bed. From the 2.54-mile mark to the Big John 2 Trail entrance, you will have to pass over several more seasonal creek beds, downed trees, and large rocks. The trail intersects an equestrian trail at 2.52 miles. Continue straight (south). Views of Lake Wayne Wallace show up to your left (east) at 2.62 miles.

At 2.7 miles you reach the Big John 2 Trail. This portion of the trail is particularly interesting and involves a series of several steep switchbacks. It begins with a mild ascent of 15 feet elevation before reaching a fork at 2.74 miles. Take the right side of the fork (southwest). Yellow diamonds with black arrows serve as trail markers. (**Note:** The left side of the fork [south]

View of trail to Lake Wayne Wallace Overlook

is the Mountain Trail. This is another viable route that reconnects with the Rim Rock Trail at 3.08 miles. The Big John 2 Trail is the more common connector with the Rim Rock Trail, and the more adventurous of the two.) From this point there is a steep ascent of about 300 feet in elevation in just over 0.2 mile. Be mindful of unearthed tree roots, downed trees, log steps, and large rocks in the path while traversing the Big John 2 Trail.

Once you have achieved the heart-pounding switchbacks of the Big John 2 Trail, take a breather at the fork at 2.91 miles. Then take the left side of the fork (southeast) to head onto the Rim Rock Trail. The right (southwest) side of the fork is the Big John Trail. As previously noted, the Rim Rock Trail intersects the Mountain Trail at 3.08 miles. Continue straight (southeast). The incredible overlook of Lake Wayne Wallace—one of the best panoramic vistas in Robbers Cave State Park—is to your left (east) at 3.33 miles. Be sure to immerse yourself in the spectacular view. From this point you can continue on the Rim Rock Trail to connect with the Governor, Dogwood, or Big John Trails. The route in this guide has you heading back the way you came from the Rough Canyon Trailhead.

TRAIL TO LAKE WAYNE WALLACE OVERLOOK, ROBBERS CAVE STATE PARK

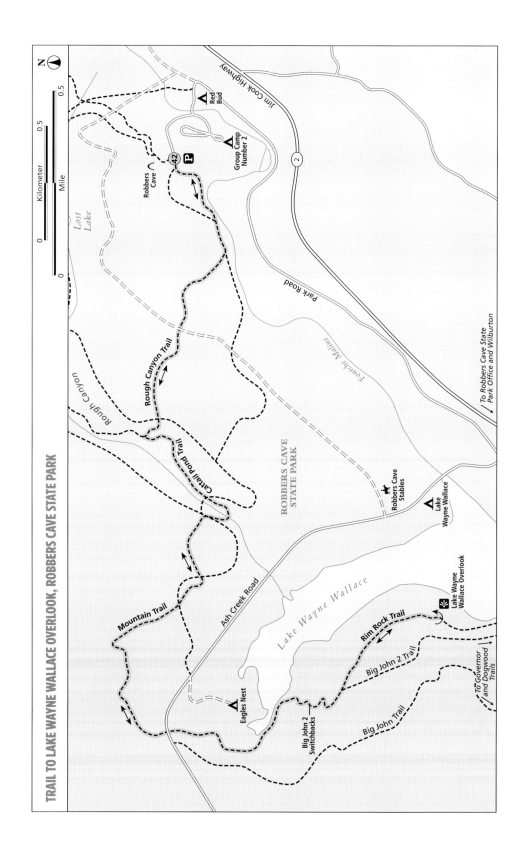

MILES AND DIRECTIONS

0.0 Start at the Rough Canyon Trailhead.

0.32 Bear right (north) where the trail starts to ascend.

0.37 Continue straight up some large rocks to reach the ridge.

0.6 Reach the Equestrian Trail connection. Follow the blue trail marker to continue straight (west) on the Rough Canyon Trail.

0.68 Reach the Cave Trail connection. Bear left (west) to stay on the Rough Canyon Trail.

0.93 Reach the Cattail Pond Trail connection. Bear left (south) to start the connector to the Mountain Trail.

1.01 Cross a seasonal creek bed.

1.11 Reach a fork. Take the right side of the fork (west) to continue on the Cattail Pond Trail to the right (north). Continue straight (southwest), following the yellow blazes and yellow diamonds with black arrows. Go through a rocky ditch. (*Option:* You also can connect with the Mountain Trail by taking the Cattail Pond Trail for a short distance.) The creek follows to your right (north).

1.26 A path merges with the trail from the southeast. Continue straight (south), following the yellow markers.

1.3 Reach a fork. Bear to your right (west). Go down the rocks and cross a seasonal creek.

1.38 Reach a fork. Take the left side of the fork (west).

1.63 Cross a seasonal creek bed.

1.81 Trail markers for the Mountain Trail begin to appear.

1.87 Cross a seasonal creek bed.

1.91 Cross a gravel vehicle road. Continue northwest. Reach a fork shortly after and bear left (south).

2.08 Cross a wide seasonal creek bed.

2.29 Cross Ash Creek Road. Continue straight (south).

2.43 The trail intersects a trail to Eagles Nest Campground. Continue straight (south).

2.45 A primitive campsite is to your right (west). Cross a wide seasonal creek bed after.

2.5 Cross a seasonal creek bed.

2.52 Pass the Rocky Top primitive campsite to your right (west).

2.54 Cross a seasonal creek bed. The trail intersects the Equestrian Trail shortly after. Continue straight (south).

2.62 Cross a seasonal creek bed. Views of Lake Wayne Wallace open up to your left (east).

2.66 Cross a seasonal creek bed.

2.7 Begin the Big John 2 switchbacks.

2.74 Reach a fork. Take the right side (southwest). There is a steep ascent of 300 feet until the 2.91-mile mark. (*Option:* Take the left side [south] for the easier Mountain Trail.)

2.91 Reach a fork. Take the left side of the fork (southeast) to head onto the Rim Rock Trail.

3.08 The trail intersects the Mountain Trail. Continue straight (southeast).

3.33 Reach an overlook of Lake Wayne Wallace to your left (east). Head back to the Rough Canyon Trailhead.

6.7 Arrive back at the trailhead.

43 CEDAR LAKE TRAIL

CEDAR LAKE NATIONAL RECREATION AREA (OUACHITA NATIONAL FOREST)

Cedar Lake, spanning more than 80 acres with its unflustered waters, is a sight to behold. This trail beneath a canopy of pines and hardwoods encircles the entire lake, offering hikers opportunities to see the lake from every awe-inspiring viewpoint.

Start: Cedar Lake Trailhead, north of North Shore Campground
Elevation gain: 666 to 774 feet
Distance: 2.93-mile loop
Difficulty: Easy
Hiking time: 1–2 hours
Seasons/schedule: Open year-round; best during spring through fall
Fees and permits: None
Trail contacts: Oklahoma Ranger District, 52175 US 59, Hodgen 74939; (918) 653-2991
Dog-friendly: Leashed dogs permitted
Trail surface: Dirt path with intermittent, unearthed tree roots

Land status: USDA Forest Service
Nearest town: Talihina to the west, Heavener to the north
Other trail users: Mountain bikers, anglers
Maps: USGS Hodgen; Ouachita National Forest maps (available online at www.fs.usda.gov/main/ouachita/maps-pubs)
Special considerations: Portions of this trail can get overgrown.
    White blazes on trees and white diamond metal markers serve as guides on this trail.

FINDING THE TRAILHEAD

From the US 59 S and Cavanal Scenic Expressway junction in Poteau, head south on the Cavanal Scenic Expressway for 4.5 miles. Merge onto US 59 S and continue south for another 20.3 miles. Turn right (west) onto Holson Valley Road. Continue 2.8 miles and turn right (north) onto Cedar Lake Road. After 1.2 miles, having already passed the North Shore Campground, reach the parking area for the Cedar Lake Trail and lake access. GPS: N34° 46.963' W94° 41.583'

THE HIKE

Popular for its trophy bass fishing opportunities, the relaxing Cedar Lake is just as popular for its astonishing landscape. The trail that encompasses the entire lake amazes with pristine views almost every step of the way. The paramount season to visit the lake is autumn, with its surrounding deciduous forests crowned in fiery colors.

The Cedar Lake Trail commences at the stone steps south of the Cedar Lake Dam. Go up the stone steps and head north across the dam, covered with mowed grass. At 0.13 mile, bear left (west) onto the narrow dirt path and head into the wooded area. Views of Cedar Lake will be to your left (south) and continue to be to your left throughout the trail. Note the white blazes on the trees as you traverse the wooded area; these will be your trail guides. The trail starts to head in a southwesterly direction at 0.35 mile before winding west shortly after. From this point until the 2.61-mile mark, you will cross several seasonal creek beds. At 0.56 mile you curve north around an inlet. You reach a footbridge at a little more than 0.75 mile. Views are exceptional and peaceful at this point as you catch a glimpse of the lake to your left as well as the silent trees hovering over the inlet to your right. Lake views become less visible as you reach 1.03 miles, and the trail returns heading southwest.

The trail curves south toward another footbridge at 1.44 miles. White diamond-shaped metal markers begin to appear, and they serve as trail guides along with the white blazes. After crossing the footbridge, you head northeast. From the 1.57-mile mark to almost the end of the trail, you may encounter several downed trees and branches. Be aware of them as you continue on the trail. The Sandy Beach Campground emerges to your right (east) at 1.73 miles. The trail starts to curve west around the Sandy Beach Campground, and views of Cedar Lake reappear to your left (north).

At 1.87 miles the trail changes to a paved surface. You wind between a pavilion and alongside the swimming area. At 1.92 miles, follow the dirt path that heads west through the woods toward the white blaze. The trail heads south shortly after. You cross another small footbridge at 2.14 miles before reaching a much longer footbridge at 2.19 miles. The trail heads north after the longer footbridge. Exercise caution—this portion of the trail up to the 2.26-mile mark can get overgrown in areas.

Cedar Lake

Inlet during the fall

From 2.26 miles to 2.48 miles on the trail, there are intermittent rock steps and educational signage describing flora and fauna. These engaging signs provide particularly fun learning for kids as they cover in the following order on the trail: toads, frogs, armadillos, roadrunners, red maples, the Ouachita National Forest itself, squirrels, and copperheads. At 2.48 miles, you come to the last sign, titled "Wildlife Sketchbook," and you will see a pavilion to your right (east). A couple benches as well as a dock to your left (west) welcome you at 2.53 miles. Take a break and head down to the dock for some additional, exceptional up-close views of the lake.

At 2.54 miles the path surface becomes smooth stone before returning to dirt after a short distance. You encounter a series of stone steps and seasonal creek beds between 2.56 and 2.68 miles. The North Shore Campground is to your right (east) at 2.68 miles. Head toward the fishing pier. Once you reach the fishing pier at 2.79 miles, the trail returns to a paved surface one last time. Take the left side of the fork at this point, which is the route closest to the fishing pier to your west. The trail heads south at 2.84 miles and then curves around toward the inlet. A pavilion is to your left (west) at 2.9 miles. After this point, you will recognize the stone steps you initially ascended from the trailhead.

MILES AND DIRECTIONS

0.0   Start at the trailhead. Go up the stone steps and head north across the dam (mowed grass).

0.13   Bear left (west) onto the narrow dirt path into the wooded area.

0.35   Cross a seasonal creek bed.

0.45   Cross a seasonal creek bed.

0.67   Cross a seasonal creek bed.

0.73   Cross a seasonal creek bed.

0.76   The trail heads west across a footbridge.

1.03   Cross a seasonal creek bed.

1.21   Cross a seasonal creek bed.

1.44   The trail curves south toward another footbridge.

1.85   Pass the Sandy Beach Campground to your right (south).

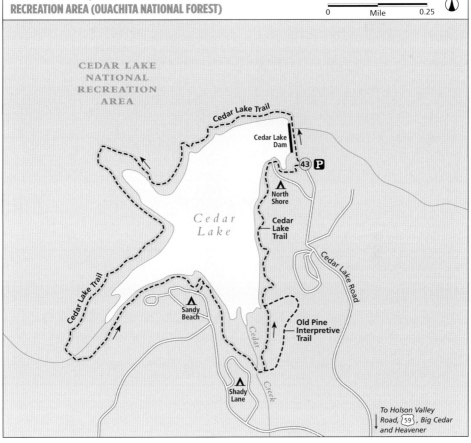

1.87 The trail becomes a paved surface for a short distance and winds between a pavilion and a swimming area.

1.92 Follow the dirt path through woods, heading west toward the white blaze.

2.14 Cross a small footbridge.

2.19 Head left (east) across the footbridge. The trail heads north after the footbridge. Follow the white diamond trail marker.

2.26–2.48 Traverse a series of rock steps and come to several interpretive signs.

2.53 Benches and a dock are to your left (west).

2.54 The path becomes a smooth stone surface.

2.55 Cross a seasonal creek bed. The path returns to a dirt surface.

2.56–2.68 Head up a series of stone steps.

2.68 Cross a seasonal creek bed. The North Shore Campground is to your right (east). Head toward the fishing pier.

2.79 Pass the fishing pier, to your left (west). The paved surface returns. Take the left side of the fork.

2.93 Arrive back at the trailhead.

44 MOUNTAIN TOP TRAIL

WINDING STAIR MOUNTAIN NATIONAL RECREATION AREA (OUACHITA NATIONAL FOREST)

For those with limited time and looking for a nice day hike, this trail overlaps the Ouachita National Recreation Trail (ONRT) and leads to the top of Winding Stair Mountain. You also will be provided with views similar to those seen from the Talimena Scenic Drive.

Start: Mountain Top Trailhead, in between Winding Stair Campground sites #16 and #17
Elevation gain: 1,750 to 1,988 feet
Distance: 2.06-mile lollipop
Difficulty: Easy
Hiking time: 1–2 hours
Seasons/schedule: Open year-round; best during fall for the foliage
Fees and permits: None
Trail contacts: Oklahoma Ranger District, 52175 US 59, Hodgen 74939; (918) 653-2991
Dog-friendly: Leashed dogs permitted
Trail surface: Dirt path
Land status: USDA Forest Service

Nearest town: Talihina to the west, Heavener to the north
Other trail users: Mountain bikers
Maps: USGS Big Cedar; Ouachita National Forest maps (available online at www.fs.usda.gov/main/ouachita/maps-pubs)
Special considerations: Portions of this trail involve crossing Talimena Scenic Drive. Use extra caution, and be aware of fast-moving vehicles when crossing the road.
   White trail markers serve as guides until the turnaround point at 0.98 mile. After heading southeast, use white blazes as guides.

FINDING THE TRAILHEAD

From Talihina, get onto US 271 N/2nd Street. At about 8 miles, turn right onto OK 1 E, also known as Talimena Scenic Drive. After going 18.6 miles, you will see a sign indicating the Emerald Vista and Winding Stair Campground to your left (north). Turn left into the campground and continue on the campground loop. The trailhead is between campsites #16 and #17. If you do not have a campsite reserved, please do not park in the parking spaces belonging to campsites. You can find parking at designated parking areas in the campground, Emerald Vista, and next to the backpacking camp. GPS: N34° 42.887' W94° 40.618'

THE HIKE

With the trailhead nestled within Winding Stair Campground and close to the Talimena Scenic Drive, both campers and tourists can enjoy the peaceful, forested Mountain Top Trail. This trail takes you to the peak of Winding Stair Mountain at above 2,000 feet in elevation, bestowing partial views of Holson Valley, Tram Ridge, and Cedar Lake.

   Access the trail in between campsites #16 and #17 in the Winding Stair Campground, and then cross a series of stream beds. About 380 feet into the trail, you reach a fork that connects the Mountain Top Trail with a path to the right (north) that leads to the backpacking camp. Continue straight (west) and reach a parking lot that connects with a gravel access road at 0.1 mile. Shortly after, and before the Talimena Scenic Drive, a dirt path heads back into the forest to your right (northwest). Go back onto the dirt path and wind through a diverse range of pine, blackjack oak, black gum, and dogwood.

White trail markers are your guides starting at 0.27 mile. You encounter several slabs of rocks and logs before reaching a junction short of 0.6 mile into the trail. This junction provides a shortcut to return to the trailhead. Continue straight, following the white trail marker. The trail narrows and switchbacks a little after 0.7 mile. Right before you reach the crest of Winding Stair Mountain, the trail opens back up again.

It gets a bit tricky when you have reached the top of the mountain. There is a rocky overlook straight up ahead of you (northwest). While you may not get unobstructed, panoramic views, it is still worth venturing just to get glimpses of the beautiful Holson Valley below you, glistening Cedar Lake, and several emerald-hued mountain ranges that define the Ouachita National Forest. The best views can be seen during fall and winter, when leaf abscission in trees occurs. After returning to the trail from the overlook, pay attention. Do not follow the white trail marker; instead make a U-turn and head

Left: The trees of the Ouachita National Forest
Bottom: View of Holson Valley and Cedar Lake from the Mountain Top Trail

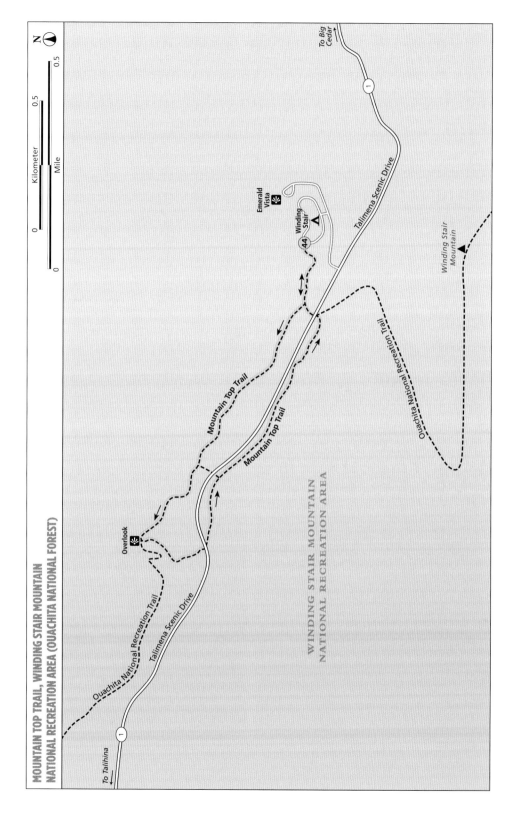

MOUNTAIN TOP TRAIL, WINDING STAIR MOUNTAIN
NATIONAL RECREATION AREA (OUACHITA NATIONAL FOREST)

N

Kilometer
0   0.5

Mile
0   0.5

To Talihina

Ouachita National Recreation Trail

Talimena Scenic Drive

Overlook

Mountain Top Trail

Mountain Top Trail

44

Emerald Vista

Winding Stair

Talimena Scenic Drive

1

To Big Cedar

Ouachita National Recreation Trail

Winding Stair Mountain

WINDING STAIR MOUNTAIN
NATIONAL RECREATION AREA

southeast, up the hill, where the dated "To Trailhead" sign directs you. Following the white trail markers will lead you west on the Ouachita National Recreation Trail.

As you head back east, you continue through the forested area. There will be several of the same breathtaking vistas that draw visitors to travel the Talimena Scenic Drive. Take in these views as you hike. At the 1.13-mile mark you reach the Talimena Scenic Drive. Before proceeding, look for the white marking on the tree across the road so you know where to connect back on the trail. This is a very popular road. Take your time and watch for vehicles before crossing.

Once you have safely crossed Talimena Scenic Drive, a small seasonal stream dances alongside of you to your right (south) at 1.32 miles into the trail. After 1.4 miles there are two side trails. Bypass both and continue straight (east), following the trail sign at the first side trail and the white blaze on the tree at the second. At 1.74 miles, you encounter the same stream that accompanied you earlier. Cross this small stream at 1.84 miles and bear left (north), meeting up with the Talimena Scenic Drive one more time. Again, please be mindful of vehicles before crossing the road.

After carefully crossing Talimena Scenic Drive for a second time, you will recognize the parking lot you navigated through at the beginning of the hike. Continue back the way you came, toward the trailhead at Winding Stair Campground. Take some time to check out the views at nearby Emerald Vista while you are still in the campground area.

MILES AND DIRECTIONS

0.0 Start at the trailhead between campsites #16 and #17 at the Winding Stair Campground.

0.07 Reach a fork. Continue straight (west) to stay on the Mountain Top Trail.

0.1 Reach an access road and a parking lot.

0.18 Turn right (northwest), back onto the dirt trail.

0.6 Reach a fork. Continue straight (northwest), following the white trail marker.

0.7 The trail narrows and you reach a switchback.

0.98 Reach a fork where there is an overlook facing northwest. Curve around to head southeast up the hill. Do not follow the white trail markers at this point.

1.13 Cross Talimena Scenic Drive. Look for a white marker on a tree across the road before crossing.

1.4 Continue straight on the path with the trail sign. Do not go left (north).

1.46 Continue straight toward the white blaze on a tree. Do not go left (north).

1.86 Bear left (north) to cross Talimena Scenic Drive once again.

1.9 Return to the access road and parking lot that leads back to the trailhead at Winding Stair Campground.

2.06 Arrive back at the trailhead.

45 WHISKEY FLATS TRAIL (VIA SOUTH RIM TRAIL, COMBINED WITH LITTLE BUGABOO TRAIL)

MCGEE CREEK NATURAL SCENIC RECREATION AREA

Abounding with the splendor of towering trees, babbling creeks, and views of a calm lake, this relatively leisurely route provides a decent amount of mileage and variation in natural surroundings.

Start: Main trailhead, north of the ranger office
Elevation gain: 591 to 976 feet
Distance: 7.2 miles out and back, with an alternate return route to the trailhead
Difficulty: Easy to moderate due to uneven, overgrown terrain
Hiking time: 5–6 hours
Seasons/schedule: Open year-round, sunrise to sunset
Fees and permits: For tracking purposes, a no-cost permit must be filled out and dropped off at the ranger office prior to hiking (subject to change).
Trail contacts: McGee Creek Natural Scenic Recreation Area Ranger Office, 2011 N. Centerpoint Rd., Atoka 74525; (580) 889-5822
Dog-friendly: Leashed dogs permitted
Trail surface: Dirt and rocky path, intermittently laden with dry pine needles

Land status: Managed by McGee Creek State Park on land owned by the US Bureau of Reclamation
Nearest town: Atoka and Lane to the west, Antlers to the east
Other trail users: Cyclists (all trails), equestrians (except for Whiskey Flats Trail)
Maps: USGS Lane NE; McGee Creek State Park and McGee Creek Natural Scenic Recreation Area maps (available online at www.travelok.com/state-parks and via the Oklahoma State Parks mobile app)
Special considerations: The waters within the McGee Creek Natural Scenic Recreation Area are a "quiet water" zone and no-wake area.
   Ticks are prevalent in this area during summer. Use bug repellent before embarking on the trails.
   Yellow metal signs act as guides throughout the trail.

FINDING THE TRAILHEAD

From the OK 3 and US 69 junction in Atoka, head east on OK 3 for 20 miles. Turn north onto Centerpoint Road. The ranger office and trailhead are to your right (east) after 10 miles. GPS: N34° 23.366' W95° 49.511'

THE HIKE

The trails within the McGee Creek Natural Scenic Recreation Area are a bit different from those located in McGee Creek State Park—they are on protected land. This allows diverse wildlife to be left undisturbed, as the area prohibits motorized vehicles

and watercraft. The Whiskey Flats and Little Bugaboo Trails encompass lofty, majestic pine and oak forests. Several quiet water sources can be seen from these trails, as well as designated places for backpack camping.

The main trailhead is located north of the ranger office. Be sure to fill out a free permit prior to hitting the trail. The permit is required, as it helps keep track of visitors on the trail system. All the trails in the McGee Creek Natural Scenic Recreation Area stem from this main trailhead, and there is a decent amount of yellow metal and wooden signs throughout the trail system to guide you.

Come to a fork in the trail at the 0.35-mile mark. Take the right side (northeast) of the fork to hike on the South Rim Trail. The left side (northwest) of the fork leads to the Little Bugaboo, West Branch, and Rocky Point Trails. This portion of the South Rim Trail connects with the Whiskey Flats Trail. You cross a creek bed at 0.7 mile, and large rocks are embedded in the path until the 1.0-mile mark. The trail begins to wind north at 1.26 miles and then northeast at 1.34 miles.

At 1.63 miles you reach another fork. The right side (east) of the fork is the very overgrown Bog Spring Trail. Take the left side of the fork (north) to continue on the South Rim Trail. Cross another creek bed at 1.72 miles; the trail heads west shortly after. An open grassland area greets you right before you encounter yellow metal signs for Box Spring Camp (backpacker's camp) and the Whiskey Flats Trail at 1.81 miles. Bear left (west) to start on the Whiskey Flats Trail. It is extremely overgrown from this point to the 1.85-mile mark during spring and summer. The signage might be hidden—look ahead for the rocky path and you will know you are heading in the right direction. Pay attention to the trail as you near 1.94 miles, because the path converges with a ditch.

The journey to the lakeshore includes rocky sections, small seasonal stream beds, and several fallen tree branches and tree trunks. You may have to go around a downed tree

a little after 2.7 miles. The trail begins to head northwest, and then the area turns into a grassland for a short time before the first Rocky Point Trail crossover at 3.01 miles. Continue straight (north) on the Whiskey Flats Trail. Bear left (west) at the backpacker camping area at 3.03 miles, following the wooden signage for Whiskey Flats. Heading straight (north) will take you to the Wildcat Canyon Trail. At 3.21 miles, you reach another Rocky Point Trail crossover. Continue straight (west), following the wooden "Whiskey Flats to Lake" sign. You are rewarded with panoramic views of the lake sourced from the McGee Creek Reservoir and surrounding Bugaboo Canyon at 3.5 miles. Feel free to take a break and enjoy the stillness before heading back to the Whiskey Flats and South Rim Trails intersection.

Reach the previously encountered Whiskey Flats and South Rim Trails intersection at 5.19 miles. Remember that this area is overgrown during spring and summer, so signage can be difficult to find. The entrance to the Little Bugaboo Trail is to your right (west) shortly after. You will have to venture through the thicket a little before reaching two yellow metal signs indicating you are on the Little Bugaboo Trail. Bugaboo Creek intermittently parallels the trail on your left (south) until 5.5 miles into the route. After opening into a small section of grassland and a backpacking camping area to your left (south), the trail resumes with a few slightly rocky descents. At 6.53 miles, you cross Bugaboo Creek, with views on both sides as you traverse the layers of rock.

The Little Bugaboo Trail intersects the West Branch Trail/Rocky Point Trail entrance at 6.65 miles. Continue straight on the Little Bugaboo Trail by taking the left side of the fork. After crossing a couple more seasonal creek beds, you reach the intersection with the South Rim Trail at the 6.87-mile mark. Bear right (south) to head back to the main trailhead.

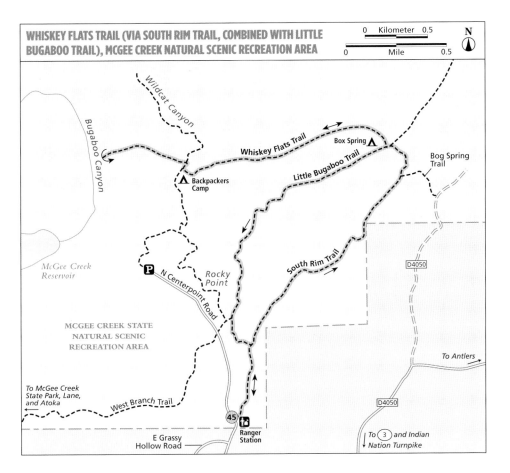

MILES AND DIRECTIONS

0.0 Start at the main trailhead, north of the ranger office.

0.35 Reach a fork. Take the right side (northeast) of the fork to hike the South Rim Trail.

1.63 Reach a fork. Take the left side of the fork (north) to continue on the South Rim Trail.

1.81 Bear left (west) to head toward the Whiskey Flats Trail connection.

1.94 The trail converges with a ditch. Stay on the trail.

2.71 Watch for downed trees.

3.01 Reach the Rocky Point Trail crossover. Continue straight (north) on the Whiskey Flats Trail.

3.03 Pass the backpacker camping area on the left (west) side of the fork. Head west on the Whiskey Flats Trail.

3.21 Reach another Rocky Point Trail crossover. Continue straight (west).

3.5 Come to an overlook of Bugaboo Canyon and the McGee Creek Reservoir. Head back to the Whiskey Flats and South Rim Trails intersection.

5.19 Reach the Whiskey Flats and South Rim Trails intersection.

Bugaboo Creek

5.2 Reach the entrance to the Little Bugaboo Trail.

6.53 Cross Bugaboo Creek.

6.65 Reach a fork. Take the left side of the fork to continue straight on the Little Bugaboo Trail.

6.87 Reach the intersection with the South Rim Trail. Bear right (south) to head back to the trailhead.

7.2 Arrive back at the trailhead.

46 FOREST HERITAGE TREE TRAIL

BEAVERS BEND STATE PARK

Trickling Beaver Creek carving into Stanley Shale (rock), fluttering dogwoods, and yaupon holly—these are all things you can look forward to seeing on the Forest Heritage Tree Trail. The trail was built next to the former homesite of John and Leuvina Beavers, for whom the park is named.

Start: Forest Heritage Tree Trailhead, west of the Beavers Bend State Park Office and Nature Center
Elevation gain: 394 to 512 feet
Distance: 1.18-mile lollipop
Difficulty: Easy
Hiking time: About 1 hour
Seasons/schedule: Open year-round, sunrise to sunset; best in fall for scenery
Fees and permits: Parking pass required for day-use visitors
Trail contacts: Beavers Bend State Park Office & Nature Center, 4350 S. Hwy. 259A, Broken Bow 74728; (580) 494-6300
Dog-friendly: Leashed dogs permitted
Trail surface: Dirt and rocky path
Land status: Oklahoma State Parks

Nearest town: Hochatown to the west, Broken Bow to the southwest
Other trail users: None
Maps: USGS Stephens Gap; Beavers Bend State Park map (available online at www.travelok.com/state-parks and via the Oklahoma State Parks mobile app)
Special considerations: After the 0.58-mile mark, make sure to bear right and head northeast. Do not continue on the side trail to the west. It is an unofficial and heavily eroded connector trail to the Lookout Mountain Trail.
   The Forest Heritage Tree Trail converges with the Beaver Creek Trail.
   Blue metal circles serve as your guides on this trail.

FINDING THE TRAILHEAD

From the OK 3/Old Highway 70 and US 259 N/North Park Drive junction in Broken Bow, head north on US 259 N/North Park Drive for 6.3 miles. Turn right (east) onto OK 259A W (south entrance to Beavers Bend State Park). Continue 4.4 miles until you reach the upper parking lot for the Beavers Bend State Park Office and Nature Center. The trailhead is west of the park office and nature center. GPS: N34° 07.956' W94° 40.816'

THE HIKE

The Forest Heritage Tree Trail is a great starter trail for visitors to the Beavers Bend area. It not only impeccably represents the state park's landscape but also includes informational signage along its path for an educational experience. The trail is meant to be taken in a "figure eight" direction, but if you take it as a lollipop (as this trail description does) and still end up at the trailhead, you will be fine. The trail is quite popular and family-friendly for its beauty and its ease. The dogwoods on the trail are deciduous, so their leaves burn bright in the fall. Yaupon holly is also a regular along this trail. Benches are stationed throughout the route for scenery viewing and repose.

Forest Heritage Tree Trail

The first interpretive sign, comparing poison ivy and Virginia creeper, stands within the arched entrance at the trailhead. Within 70 feet of heading south, the second interpretive sign, detailing the history and usage of yaupon holly, is to your right (west). Close to 170 feet from the trailhead, bear left (southeast) down the layered rock for about 30 feet in elevation before reaching the log steps at 310 feet into the trail. After the log steps, bear right (south) to continue on the Forest Heritage Tree Trail. Once you cross the seasonal creek bed, Beaver Creek parallels along the east side of your path. The lovely and tranquil creek continues on your left all the way to the Beaver Creek Trail connection at 0.55 mile.

At 0.13 mile the route gets a bit tricky. Take the left side of the fork to head toward the third interpretive sign and start the loop portion of the trail. The third interpretive sign describes the Stanley Shale formation. You are bound to be fascinated by the 250-million-year-old rocks that form the valley within Beavers Bend. There are several forks before you reach the fourth interpretive sign, at 0.38 mile. Make sure to head in a southeasterly direction at each of the forks to ensure that you are continuing on the Forest Heritage Tree Trail. The blue markers will indicate that you are going the correct way. The fourth interpretive sign is also about yaupon holly, this time describing the plant's physical characteristics.

A mild ascent of 10 feet occurs between 0.4 mile and 0.43 mile. The trail then starts to wind west at 0.53 mile. Come to the fifth interpretive sign shortly after. This one, about John Beavers and his full-blood Choctaw wife, Leuvina, and their home, is by far the most interesting. Behind the sign, you can walk around the perimeter of where their

THE STRENGTH OF YAUPON HOLLY

Yaupon holly is no stranger to southeastern Oklahoma. Used a long time ago by American Indians for medicinal and ceremonial practices, yaupon holly is an ornamental evergreen plant with glistening red berries. Its small but mighty leaves contain the most caffeine content of any native North American plant. Do not consume this or any other plant without positive identification of edibility. Exercise extreme caution.

Beaver Creek

home stood in the early 1900s. Beavers Bend State Park is named in their honor for providing the land they called home.

You reach the Beaver Creek Trail connection at 0.55 mile. Bear right (northwest) to stay on the Forest Heritage Tree Trail. The trail curves in a northeasterly direction at the 0.58-mile mark. (To your left [west] you will notice a side trail. It is highly recommended that you do not access this trail. It is an unofficial connector to the Lookout Mountain Trail. It is steep and very treacherous due to the large amount of erosion along the path. To access the Lookout Mountain Trail, use the designated Lookout Mountain Trailhead.) The final interpretive sign appears at 0.63 mile. This one expounds on the dogwood trees. On the way north to the covered bridge at 0.79 mile, you descend about 15 feet in elevation from 0.77 mile to get there. Immediately after exiting the bridge, a side trail will be to your right (east) and there will be a mild descent of 10 feet in elevation to the 0.82-mile mark. At 0.88 mile, the trail starts to wind northeast toward a footbridge. There will be a descent of 20 feet in elevation to the 0.92-mile mark. You cross the small footbridge at 0.89 mile and, after the descent, head back north. Once you cross a seasonal creek bed short of 1.0 mile on the trail, you reach the fork from the 0.13-mile mark, where you initially started the loop portion of the trail. Head back toward the log steps from the beginning of the trail to return to the park office and parking lot.

MILES AND DIRECTIONS

0.0   Start at the Forest Heritage Tree Trailhead. Interpretive sign #1 is to your left (west).

0.01 Interpretive sign #2 is to your right (west).

0.03 Head southeast. Descend layers of rock for about 30 feet.

0.06 Go down some log steps. Shortly after, reach a fork. Bear right (south).

0.08 Cross the seasonal creek bed. Beaver Creek parallels the trail on your left (east).

0.13 At the fork, take the left side toward interpretive sign #3 to start the loop portion of the trail. The right side of the fork is where you will exit the loop.

0.17 Interpretive sign #3 is to your right (west). Continue south along the creek.

0.24 Bypass the shortcut to your right (west) that leads back to the trailhead.

0.31 Continue straight (southeast). Bypass the side trail to your right (west).

0.34 Reach a bench. Bear right (south).

0.37 Reach another bench to your right (west).

0.38 Reach a fork. Take the right side (southwest), following the blue trail marker. Reach another fork shortly after. Take the left side (south) of the fork. Interpretive sign #4 is to the right (north) of the fork.

0.54 Interpretive sign #5 and John and Leuvina Beavers's homesite are to your right (north).

0.55 Reach the Beaver Creek Trail connection. Bear right (northwest) to stay on the Forest Heritage Tree Trail. There is a bench to your right (east) shortly after.

0.58 Reach another bench, this time to your left (south). The trail curves northeast; an unofficial, highly eroded connection to Lookout Mountain is to your left (west) shortly after. Do not use this shortcut. Access the trail from the official Lookout Mountain Trailhead.

0.63 Interpretive sign #6 is to your left (west).

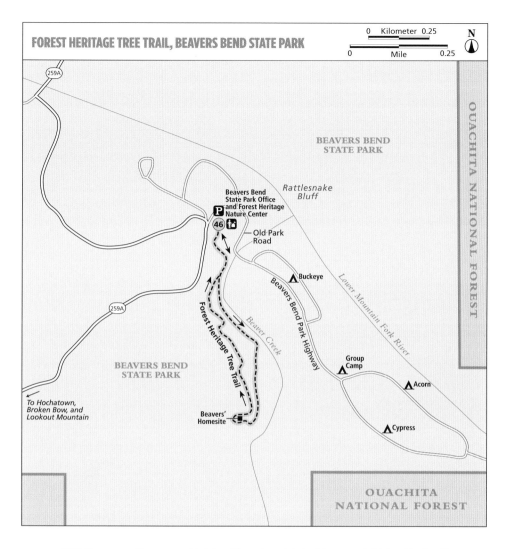

FOREST HERITAGE TREE TRAIL, BEAVERS BEND STATE PARK

0.79 Go across the covered bridge. There is a side trail to your right (east) after the bridge. Head straight (north).

0.89 Cross a small footbridge.

0.99 Cross a seasonal creek bed.

1.06 Reach the first shortcut, where you started the loop portion of the trail. Continue straight (north) to exit the loop.

1.11 Reach the log steps from the 310-foot mark. Bear left (west), back to the trailhead.

1.18 Arrive back at the trailhead.

47 DEER CROSSING TRAIL TO CEDAR BLUFF

BEAVERS BEND STATE PARK

This trail stays true to its name—it is highly likely that you will glimpse white-tailed deer scampering around the lofty trees bordering the trail. Although the iconic and mesmerizing Cedar Bluff can be accessed by its own trailhead, this route is popular with those looking to add extra adventure. It also provides some seclusion from the bustling crowds that tend to fill the immensely popular Beavers Bend area.

Start: Deer Crossing Trailhead, directly across the road from the Lookout Mountain Trailhead
Elevation gain: 410 to 743 feet
Distance: 4.14 miles out and back with an additional loop
Difficulty: Moderate to difficult due to uneven terrain and changes in elevation
Hiking time: 2–3 hours
Seasons/schedule: Open year-round, sunrise to sunset; best in fall for scenery
Fees and permits: Parking pass required for day-use visitors
Trail contacts: Beavers Bend State Park Office & Nature Center, 4350 S. Hwy. 259A, Broken Bow 74728; (580) 494-6300
Dog-friendly: Leashed dogs permitted
Trail surface: Dirt and rocky path with intermittent, unearthed tree roots
Land status: Oklahoma State Parks

Nearest town: Hochatown to the west, Broken Bow to the southwest
Other trail users: None
Maps: USGS Stephens Gap; Beavers Bend State Park map (available online at www.travelok.com/state-parks and via the Oklahoma State Parks mobile app)
Special considerations: For those who wish to take the Cedar Bluff Nature Trail only, the Cedar Bluff Nature Trailhead is on the south side of US 259A across from Dogwood Campground.
  At times this trail can contain several downed trees. The "Mile and Directions" section indicates where these downed trees were at the time of publication.
  Red metal circle trail markers serve as your guides for the Deer Crossing Trail. Blue metal circle trail markers are your guides on the Cedar Bluff Nature Trail.

FINDING THE TRAILHEAD

From the OK 3/Old Highway 70 and US 259 N/North Park Drive junction in Broken Bow, head north on US 259 N for 6.3 miles. Turn right (east) onto OK 259A W (south entrance to Beavers Bend State Park). Continue 3.9 miles. The trailhead is to your left (north), right across from the Lookout Mountain Trailhead. GPS: N34° 07.714' W94° 41.207'

THE HIKE

The Deer Crossing Trail entrances with its natural simplicity and idyllic ambience. This peaceful trail starts off by curving north across a seasonal creek bed. It heads back and

Cedar Bluff overlook of Lower Mountain Fork River

forth from west to north until the 0.97-mile mark. All along the route you wind through a valley with a variety of deciduous forests. You encounter an unpaved auto road at 0.53 mile. Continue straight (north). At the fork at 0.81 mile, bear right (north). Follow the red trail marker to stay on the path. Soon you descend about 30 feet in elevation over a 0.03-mile stretch to another seasonal creek bed. Go north across the creek; another path heads east and leads to a dead end.

Close to 1.0 mile on the trail, you start heading in a predominantly southerly direction. From 1.06 miles to 1.38 miles, the landscape changes to brush. This segment of the trail can get overgrown. Bypass the side trail coming from your right (west) at 1.25 miles. Once the brush has subsided, the trail heads west. At the fork at 1.39 miles, take the right side (west) to continue on the trail. Be aware of the overhanging tree branch at 1.44 miles, after which the trail starts to head northeast. Before reaching the Cedar Bluff Nature Trail and Skyline Trail connection, you make a steep descent of 120 feet in elevation from 1.55 miles to the 1.66-mile mark.

The trail heads north until the Cedar Bluff Nature Trail and Skyline Trail connection at 1.72 miles. Bear right (northeast) to take the Cedar Bluff Nature Trail in a counterclockwise direction. Blue metal circle trail markers lead the way from this point. You cross a seasonal creek bed before reaching a fork at 2.0 miles. Bear left (west) to continue the Cedar Bluff Nature Trail as a loop. The right side (east) of the fork leads to the Cedar Bluff Nature Trailhead and Dogwood Campground. You navigate a steep, rocky ascent of 86 feet in elevation until you reach the crest of Cedar Bluff at 2.15 miles.

Your reward appears at the main outlook at 2.17 miles. The view highlights one of the most recognizable scenes of Beavers Bend State Park. The impressive Lower Mountain Fork River carves through a congregation of bald cypress trees, with swells of forested mountains and hills as an all-encompassing mantle. As you continue south along the ridge of Cedar Bluff, you will have more opportunities to enjoy this photo-worthy view. Be careful as you head down this segment. Several edges do not have guardrails, and you have to descend about 50 feet in elevation until you reach the Skyline Trail connection at the 2.24-mile mark.

After immersing yourself in the sights, you reach the Skyline Trail connection. Bear left (northeast) to continue on the Cedar Bluff Nature Trail. Bypass the shortcut at 2.29 miles and continue straight (west). Once you reach the log barrier at the 2.32-mile mark, two other route options become clear. To head toward Dogwood Campground or the Cedar Bluff Nature Trailhead, continue north. To complete the Cedar Bluff Nature Trail in a full loop, curve around and head east. At 2.45 miles you reach the Deer Crossing, Cedar Bluff Nature, and Skyline Trails connection. Continue straight (south) on the Deer Crossing Trail to return to the trailhead.

MILES AND DIRECTIONS

0.0   Start at the Deer Crossing Trailhead.

0.06 Cross a seasonal creek bed.

0.16 Watch for downed trees.

0.49 Go down into a seasonal creek bed.

0.53 Continue straight (north) across the unpaved auto road.

0.81 Reach a fork. Bear right (north) again. Follow the red trail marker.

0.82 Watch for downed trees.

0.83 Make a 30-foot descent to the 0.86-mile mark. Watch for downed trees in between.

0.86 Cross a seasonal creek bed, then bear north again. At the creek, another route heads east and leads to a dead end.

0.97 Watch for downed trees.

1.06 Enter a brush area until the 1.38-mile mark. This section can get overgrown.

1.25 Bypass the trail to your right (west). Continue straight (south).

1.39 Reach a fork. Continue straight (west).

1.55 Make a steep descent of 120 feet until the 1.66-mile mark.

1.7   Watch for downed trees.

1.72 Reach the Cedar Bluff Nature Trail and Skyline Trail connection. Bear right (northeast) to take the Cedar Bluff Nature Trail in a counterclockwise direction. Blue metal circle trail markers lead the way.

1.95 Cross a seasonal creek bed. Watch for downed trees.

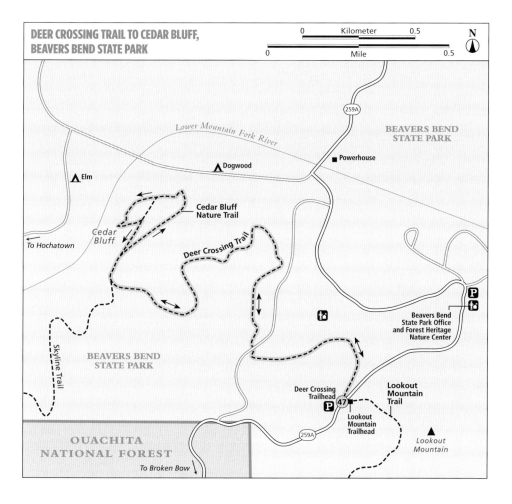

DEER CROSSING TRAIL TO CEDAR BLUFF, BEAVERS BEND STATE PARK

Kilometer 0 — 0.5
Mile 0 — 0.5

N

- Lower Mountain Fork River
- 259A
- BEAVERS BEND STATE PARK
- Powerhouse
- Dogwood
- Elm
- Cedar Bluff Nature Trail
- Cedar Bluff
- To Hochatown
- Deer Crossing Trail
- Skyline Trail
- BEAVERS BEND STATE PARK
- Beavers Bend State Park Office and Forest Heritage Nature Center
- Deer Crossing Trailhead
- Lookout Mountain Trail
- 47
- Lookout Mountain Trailhead
- 259A
- Lookout Mountain
- OUACHITA NATIONAL FOREST
- To Broken Bow

2.0 Reach a fork. Bear left (west) to head toward Cedar Bluff. Begin a steep ascent of 86 feet in elevation until you reach the crest of Cedar Bluff at 2.15 miles.

2.17 Reach an outlook. Head south. Several vistas are available to your left (west).

2.2 There is a rocky descent of 51 feet until you reach the Skyline Trail connection at the 2.24-mile mark.

2.24 Reach the Skyline Trail connection. Bear left (northeast) to continue on the Cedar Bluff Nature Trail.

2.29 Bypass the shortcut and head straight (west).

2.32 Reach a log barrier. Curve around and head east to complete the Cedar Bluff Nature Trail as a loop.

2.45 Reach the Deer Crossing, Cedar Bluff Nature, and Skyline Trails connection. Continue straight (south) on the Deer Crossing Trail to return to the trailhead.

4.14 Arrive back at the trailhead.

48 FRIENDS TRAIL

BEAVERS BEND STATE PARK

A strong newcomer to the Oklahoma hiking scene, this trail takes you on a breathtaking journey along the Lower Mountain Fork River. The iconic views of fairy-tale forests, sprawling valleys, and rushing water on this trail epitomize why so many outdoor enthusiasts come out to the Beavers Bend area.

Start: Friends Trailhead, northeast of the Lower Beaver Lodge parking lot
Elevation gain: 446 to 710 feet
Distance: 1.46-mile lollipop
Difficulty: Moderate due to steep ascent and narrow and rocky trail segments
Hiking time: 1–2 hours
Seasons/schedule: Open year-round, sunrise to sunset; best in fall for scenery
Fees and permits: Parking pass required for day-use visitors
Trail contacts: Beavers Bend State Park Office & Nature Center, 4350 S. Hwy. 259A, Broken Bow 74728; (580) 494-6300
Dog-friendly: Leashed dogs permitted
Trail surface: Dirt path that turns into a rocky surface along the Lower Mountain Fork River shoreline and then returns to a dirt path; numerous logs and severed tree trunks in pathway

Land status: US Army Corps of Engineers property leased to Oklahoma State Parks
Nearest town: Hochatown to the west, Broken Bow to the southwest
Other trail users: Anglers
Maps: USGS Stephens Gap; Beavers Bend State Park map (available online at www.travelok.com/state-parks and via the Oklahoma State Parks mobile app)
Special considerations: The trail narrows and turns rocky along the Lower Mountain Fork River shoreline. Several logs and severed tree trunks lie in the pathway intermittently throughout the trail. Exercise additional caution, especially while traversing the Lower Mountain Fork River shoreline.

Orange trail markers and orange ties in trees serve as guides on this trail.

FINDING THE TRAILHEAD

From the Beavers Bend State Park entrance on OK 259A, drive a little over 4 miles to the junction before Beavers Bend Dam. Turn right onto Beavers Bend Road. Just before you reach the Lower Mountain Fork River, you will see the Lower Beaver Lodge parking lot to your right. As you enter the parking lot, the Friends Trailhead is to your right (northeast). GPS: N34° 08.726' W94° 41.396'

THE HIKE

The Friends Trail was a highly anticipated addition to Beavers Bend State Park's trail system, and it was made possible by a joint effort of the nonprofit Friends of Beavers Bend, the US Army Corps of Engineers, Beavers Bend State Park, and private citizens. With Beavers Bend State Park already a scenic paradise, the Friends Trail offers glimpses of the natural treasures that draw visitors to Beavers Bend State Park. The trailhead is

marked by a beautiful, raven-hued arch. Orange trail markers and orange ties on trees will be your guides on this trail.

You encounter a small footbridge a little more than 500 feet from the trailhead. Once over the footbridge, you start a decent climb up a hill. Logs line your path as you ascend the hill. After reaching the top of the hill, bear to the left (west) to continue on the trail. Orange ties on trees lead the way starting after 0.3 mile, and the path starts to get rocky short of the 0.5-mile mark. Scenery of the valley and most of the Beavers Bend area opens up to your left (south). The view is more visible in autumn and winter, with the leaf abscission in trees. The path eventually begins to descend the hill as you head toward the Lower Mountain Fork River.

Orange trail markers pick up again at 0.7 mile. Shortly after, you have your first view of the Lower Mountain Fork River. There is a more advantageous outlook a few steps after the initial viewpoint. From the outlook, you can see the rushing Lower Mountain Fork River in all its glory, as well as a waterfall to your right (north). Take the time to be entranced by the mighty river's roar, and be careful if you choose to wander on the rocks to get a better glimpse of the waterfall.

THE FALLS OF THE LOWER MOUNTAIN FORK RIVER

The falls of the Lower Mountain Fork River that can be seen from the Friends Trail are a main attraction of the hike. A state park ranger and a US Army Corps of Engineers ranger laid out the trail together so that hikers would have the opportunity to enjoy the waterfall views. The falls are hydrogeomorphic features carved by a record flood release of water from Broken Bow Lake at 36,000 cubic feet per second.

View of Friends Trail path

Head back on the trail and bear left (south) from the outlook. Use caution as you traverse along the Lower Mountain Fork River. The path narrows, and there is obvious erosion near the shoreline toward the 1.0-mile mark. You may also encounter several downed trees and large severed tree trunks in the path all the way until 1.23 miles. Be sure to enjoy the views before you head east away from the river.

As you leave the river and continue to be aware of fallen trees, you cross a small seasonal creek bed. It gets a little tricky between 1.2 miles and 1.6 miles. As the path meanders around trees, you need to keep a lookout for both orange trail markers and orange ties on trees for guidance. You eventually reach the same small footbridge you crossed at the beginning of this hike. From here, retrace your steps to the Friends Trailhead arch.

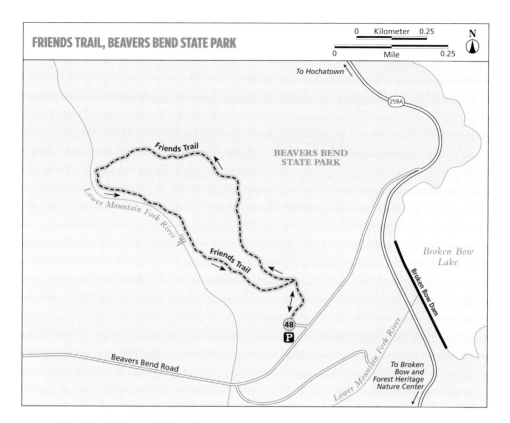

FRIENDS TRAIL, BEAVERS BEND STATE PARK

MILES AND DIRECTIONS

0.0   Start at the Friends Trailhead. Follow the orange trail markers and orange ties on trees.

0.1   Cross a small footbridge. Ascend the hill after you cross the footbridge.

0.2   Reach the top of the hill.

0.3   Bear right (north) toward the orange ties.

0.5   Views of the valley open up to your left (south).

0.6   The trail starts to wind down the hill.

0.8   Reach an overlook of the Lower Mountain Fork River and a waterfall. Bear left (south); views of the river continue to your right (west).

1.13   Head east away from the river. The trail winds along the riverbend.

1.19   Cross a small seasonal creek bed.

1.2   The route starts to get tricky. Follow the orange trail markers and orange ties to stay on track.

1.35   Reach the same footbridge you crossed at the 0.1-mile mark. Retrace your steps to the trailhead.

1.46   Arrive back at the trailhead.

HONORABLE MENTIONS

(CHOCTAW COUNTRY, SOUTHEAST OKLAHOMA)

K. LAKEVIEW LODGE TRAIL

BEAVERS BEND STATE PARK

With landscapes of reflective Broken Bow Lake and lofty storybook-like forests, this trail embedded with white quartz is a leisurely treat for those staying at the nearby Beavers Bend Lakeview Lodge or in the breathtaking Lower Mountain Fork River area.

Start: Lakeview Lodge Trailhead, north of the Beavers Bend Lakeview Lodge parking lot
Elevation gain: 574 to 774 feet
Distance: 3.72-mile loop
Difficulty: Easy
Hiking time: About 2 hours
Seasons/schedule: Open year-round, sunrise to sunset
Fees and permits: Parking pass required for day-use visitors
Trail contacts: Beavers Bend State Park Office & Nature Center, 4350 S. Hwy. 259A, Broken Bow 74728; (580) 494-6300
Dog-friendly: Leashed dogs permitted
Trail surface: Dirt and rocky path
Land status: Oklahoma State Parks

Nearest town: Hochatown to the west, Broken Bow to the southwest
Other trail users: Anglers
Maps: USGS Stephens Gap; Lakeview Lodge Trail map (available online at www.travelok.com/state-parks and via the Oklahoma State Parks mobile app)
Special considerations: This trail is intended to be taken clockwise, with views of Broken Bow Lake toward the end of the route.
   The area is open to hunters. Hikers need to be knowledgeable of hunting season dates when in the area.
   There are several fallen tree trunks and unearthed tree roots on this trail.

FINDING THE TRAILHEAD

Head north from Broken Bow on US 259 N/North Park Drive for 9.5 miles. Turn right (east) on Stevens Gap Road. After traveling on Stevens Gap Road for 1.7 miles, turn left (northeast) onto D1963. You reach the Beavers Bend Lakeview Lodge parking lot in a little over 0.5 mile. The trailhead will be to the left (north). GPS: N34° 10.456′ W94° 43.531′

View of Broken Bow Lake

Vista from the summit of Lookout Mountain

L. **LOOKOUT MOUNTAIN TRAIL**

BEAVERS BEND STATE PARK

Not for the faint of heart, the Lookout Mountain Trail has a consider-able amount of elevation changes compared to other trails in Beavers Bend State Park. The scenic outlook at the top of Lookout Mountain garners the best views during autumn.

Start: Lookout Mountain Trailhead, directly across the road from the Deer Crossing Trailhead
Elevation gain: 482 to 840 feet
Distance: 2.0 miles out and back
Difficulty: Moderate to difficult due to steep terrain and elevation changes
Hiking time: About 2 hours
Seasons/schedule: Open year-round, sunrise to sunset; best in fall for scenery
Fees and permits: Parking pass required for day-use visitors
Trail contacts: Beavers Bend State Park Office & Nature Center, 4350 S. Hwy. 259A, Broken Bow 74728; (580) 494-6300

Dog-friendly: Leashed dogs permitted
Trail surface: Dirt and rocky path
Land status: Oklahoma State Parks
Nearest town: Hochatown to the west, Broken Bow to the southwest
Other trail users: None
Maps: USGS Stephens Gap; Beavers Bend State Park map (available online at www.travelok.com/state-parks and via the Oklahoma State Parks mobile app)
Special considerations: Close to the 0.37-mile mark, make sure to veer right and head south. Do not continue east, which is an unofficial and heavily eroded connection to the Forest Heritage Tree Trail.

FINDING THE TRAILHEAD

From the OK 3/Old Highway 70 and US 259 N/North Park Drive junction in Broken Bow, head north on US 259 N for 6.3 miles. Turn right (east) onto OK 259A W (south entrance to Beavers Bend State Park). Continue 3.9 miles. The trailhead is to your right (south), across from the Deer Crossing Trailhead. GPS: N34° 07.710' W94° 41.192'

HIKE INDEX

THE TEN ESSENTIALS OF HIKING

American Hiking Society

American Hiking Society recommends you pack the "Ten Essentials" every time you head out for a hike. Whether you plan to be gone for a couple of hours or several months, make sure to pack these items. Become familiar with these items and know how to use them. Learn more at **AmericanHiking.org/hiking-resources**

1. Appropriate Footwear

6. Safety Items (light, fire, and a whistle)

2. Navigation

7. First Aid Kit

3. Water (and a way to purify it)

8. Knife or Multi-Tool

4. Food

9. Sun Protection

5. Rain Gear & Dry-Fast Layers

10. Shelter

PROTECT THE PLACES YOU LOVE TO HIKE

Become a member today and take $5 off an annual membership using the code **Falcon5**.

AmericanHiking.org/join

American Hiking Society is the only national nonprofit organization dedicated to empowering all to enjoy, share, and preserve the hiking experience.